Beyond Flesh

Beyond Flesh

Queer Masculinities and Nationalism in Israeli Cinema

RAZ YOSEF

RUTGERS UNIVERSITY PRESS
New Brunswick, New Jersey, and London

Library of Congress Cataloging-in-Publication Data

Yosef, Raz, 1967–
    Beyond flesh : queer masculinities and nationalism in Israeli cinema /
Raz Yosef.
        p.   cm.
Includes bibliographical references and index.
    ISBN 0–8135–3375–9 (hard. : alk. paper) — ISBN 0–8135–3376–7 (pbk. :
alk. paper)
    1. Motion pictures—Israel.   2. Masculinity in motion pictures.
    3. Homosexuality in motion pictures.   I. Title.
    PN1993.5.I86Y67 2004
    791.43′653—dc21

                                                            2003009390

British Cataloging-in-Publication information is available from the
British Library.

The publication program of Rutgers University Press is supported by the
Board of Governors of Rutgers, The State University of New Jersey.

Manufactured in the United States of America

*For my mother, Esther, and in memory
of my grandparents,
Garib and Sara Cohen, Jacko and
Sofia Yosef*

Contents

Acknowledgments

This book is based on my doctoral dissertation completed in 2001 at New York University. I would like to express my special appreciation to my dissertation adviser, Robert Stam, who has been a source of unmatched knowledge and brilliant inspiration for me. I would like to thank him for subsequent intellectual stimulus in the development of this project as well as for his personal generosity.

I would also like to thank the following people and institutions for various forms of help and support. My gratitude goes to the readers of my dissertation committee for their ongoing guidance and support: Chris Straayer for her insightful courses in queer theory and gender studies; William Simon for his careful and committed comments; Toby Miller for his wise insights; and Ella Shohat whose groundbreaking work on Israeli cinema and Zionism, in particular, and (neo)imperial culture, in general, greatly influenced this study. I am also grateful to the Department of Cinema Studies at New York University for its support in the form of scholarships; and to Tel Aviv University and ISEF for my dissertation fellowship. I also thank Annette Michelson, Richard Allen, Claudia Ribeiro, Alexandra Seibel, Jessica Scarlata, Karen Williams, Dan Arony, Sharrone Millo, Ayala and Daniel Hodak, David M. Halperin, Carol Bardnstein, Sam-Ishii Gonzales, and Elena Grofinkel.

At the Tel Aviv University, I would like to thank Judd Ne'eman, Regine-Mihal Friedman, Nurith Gertz, and Orly Lubin, my teachers, colleagues, and friends, for their warm encouragement and uncondi-

ACKNOWLEGMENTS

tional support that will be long remembered. To Michael Gluzman for convincing me to continue my graduate studies in the United States and to Alexandra Meiri for being a true friend and excellent co-scholar. Thanks to Tel Aviv Cinematheque for lending me stills. To my friends in Israel, Ronit Meshulam, Ronit Ben-Bassat, Yoval Ben-Atia, Allon Nahum, Alon Zinar, Galit Madar, Ayelet Nagar-Fariente, Dana Yekutieli, Miri Moav-Shaked, Sigal Yehouda, and Vered Zada for their love and for keeping Tel Aviv–New York phone lines constantly busy. I would like to thank my family, Esther, Reuven, and Kobi Yosef, for their love, their concern, and the pride they take in me.

Finally, I would like to thank to Oleg Shapiro, my companion and my love.

———

Throughout the book, all translations from the Hebrew are mine. Chapter Four and a portion of the material in Chapters One and Five appeared as "Homoland: Interracial Sex and the Israeli-Palestinian Conflict in Israeli Cinema," in *GLQ: A Journal of Gay and Lesbian Studies* 8, no. 4 (2002), 553–580. Used by permission of Duke University Press.

Beyond Flesh

Introduction

Beyond Flesh critically explores the complex and crucial role played by Israeli cinema in the construction of heterosexual masculinity, as well as its attempt to marginalize, sequester, discipline, and normalize queerness in Israeli national masculine identity. These issues are analyzed along the axes of cardinal historical and socio-political discourses of the Israeli society that have informed the representation of Israeli manhood: namely, the Zionist project, the military culture, the interethnic tension between Mizrahim (Sephardi/Oriental Jews) and Ashkenazim (Eastern European Jews) in Israel, the Jewish/Israeli-Arab/Palestinian conflict, and the emergence of Israeli lesbian and gay consciousness.

I shall argue that Israeli heterosexual masculinity and its seemingly unified collectivity cannot imagine itself apart from the conception of externalized, sexualized ethnic and racial "others" on whom it was founded and which it produced. Zionist phallic masculinity is constituted through the force of exclusion of the queer, the (homo)eroticized Mizrahi and the Palestinian male "others," a repudiation without which the national subject cannot emerge. The dominant subject is produced not by the refusal to identify with the sexualized "other," but rather through identification, a disavowed identification, with the abject "other." The process of incorporation through disavowal means that the "other" is structurally present within normative masculinity as a space of transgression and negation. In this sense, the "other" *internally* marks

1

the dominant national masculinity, opening an epistemological gap in maleness itself that threatens to undo the national, sexual, and racial authority on which Israeli male heterosexual identity is based.

Zionism was not only a political and ideological project, but also a sexual one, obsessed with Jewish masculinity and especially the Jewish male body. The political project of liberating the Jewish people and creating a nation like all other nations was intertwined with a longing for sexual redemption and normalization of the Jewish male body. In fin-de-siècle anti-Semitic scientific-medical discourse, the male Jew's body was associated with disease, madness, degeneracy, sexual perversity, and "femininity," as well as with homosexuality. This pathologization of Jewish male sexuality had also entered the writings of Jewish scientists and medical doctors, including Freud.

In this context, we should understand the desire of the Zionist movement to transform the very nature of European Jewish masculinity as it had existed in the diaspora. Thinkers such as Theodor Herzl and Max Nordau were convinced that the invention of a physically stronger, healthier heterosexual "Jewry of Muscles" would not only overcome the stereotype of the Jewish male as a homosexual, but also would solve the economic, political, and national problems of the Jewish people. Unlike the passive, ugly, femme diasporic Jewish male, the new Zionist man would engage in manual labor, athletics, and war, becoming the colonialist-explorer in touch with the land and with his body. This notion of a new Jewish masculinity became the model for the militarized masculine Sabra—the native-born Israeli in *Eretz Yisrael* (the land of Israel).

Documentary and narrative Zionist cinema, designed to attract potential pioneers from Europe, as well as financial and political support, was an important tool in the creation of Jewish male heterosexual subjectivity. However, in this book the history of the Israeli cinema will not be examined as a documentation of new Hebrew masculinity versus "feminine" diasporic Jewish manhood. This kind of analysis runs the risk of reinforcing and reproducing the dichotomized categories of the imaginary homogenous and coherent national Zionist narrative. Moreover, it does not theorize the place from which the queer Jew can speak *within* the framework of the dominant Zionist discourse. The relationships between the new Jew and the queer Jew is examined not in terms of dichotomies, but rather in terms of ambivalence, displacement, and disidentification. The overriding premise here is that the queer

Jew is not the "other" of the new Zionist "self," but rather a structural element of it.

At the same time, the "Zionist body Master Narrative" must be understood in terms of race and ethnicity. In her groundbreaking study on Israeli cinema, Ella Shohat critiqued the Orientalist and Eurocentric foundations of the Zionist movement that remained faithful to the ideological habits of the European colonial mind.[1] Shohat deconstructed the structural mechanisms of the Ashkenazi Zionist ideology that regarded Mizrahim and Palestinians through a prejudicial grid shaped by European culture. Examining the Zionist propaganda films, for example, she argued that the Ashkenazi pioneers embody the humanitarian and liberationist project of Zionism, carrying with them the same banner of a "universal," "civilizing mission" that European powers propagated during their surge into the "underdeveloped world." Shohat's insightful observations explain the relationships between the Zionist body politics and its colonial discourse of the Oriental body. A more complete analysis of the Zionist body Master Narrative, however, must consider the negative effects of Ashkenazi Zionist sexual politics, not only on the construction of Ashkenazi queers, but also on the (homo)sexual constructions of Palestinian and Mizrahi manliness.

Zionism's fantasy of a hypermasculine heterosexual Jewish male was intertwined with discourses on the breeding of children, body hygiene, and racial improvement. This fantasy was structured by Orientalist perspectives about the East, especially that of Eastern bodies, associated with lack of hygiene, plagues, disease, and sexual perversity. By assigning the Eastern population as objects of death and degeneration, Zionism created internal biologized enemies against which the Zionist society must defend itself. In the name of maintaining and securing life and the reproduction of the new Jewish "race," the Zionist society kept the right not only to discriminate and to oppress its enemies, the Palestinians, but also its citizens, the Mizrahim. Through the discourse of the new male Jew's sexuality, which was structurally linked to discourses on hygiene and racial/national survival, the Zionist society reinforced and legitimized its nationalism. Thus, Zionism produced a normalizing society through the discourse of sexuality and a kind of racism inscribed within it.

This book traces representations of masculinities from the first Zionist film pioneers' attempts to produce films in Palestine in the twenties and thirties, through the emergence of a national cinema after the establishment of the state of Israel in 1948. Its major focus is on the feature-film productions of the last five decades. Documentaries of the pre-state period, when feature filmmaking was limited, are also examined, as are those short films and television series that offer gay and lesbian cultural production. This book is not a chronological history of Israeli cinema, but rather an analysis of representations of the male body and sexuality in films that address major discourses on Israeli ideas of manhood: primarily, Zionist masculine ideology, as well as the Israeli military, tensions between Mizrahim and Ashkenazim, conflicts between Israelis and Palestinians, and the new queer culture. My approach to analysis of those texts is largely synchronic, namely, I move forward or backward to follow a comprehensive trajectory of an idea, to draw a trope, or to trace a discursive practice.

More specifically, the methodology of textual analysis used in this volume draws upon and reformulates recent developments in queer theory and postcolonial theory. Queer theory seems to lack any coherent methodology and its analysis draws upon a wide variety of theoretical positions (feminism, psychoanalysis, deconstruction, the work of Michel Foucault, or a mixture thereof) and their associated strategies and techniques. An attempt to summarize queer theory and to identify it as a homogeneous school of thought risks domesticating it and fixing it in ways that queer theory resists fixing itself. As Judith Butler puts it, "normalizing the queer would be after all, its sad finish."[2] As a theoretical model, it still encapsulates active and unresolved disputes among several scholars (such as Leo Bersani, Michael Warner, and David Halperin) and this book will not try to solve them, but rather attempt to add to the field's heterogeneity.[3]

As a working definition for this book, "queer theory" is understood as a form of analysis that systematically challenges any theoretical or political discursive practice of naturalness in sexuality. Historically in Western society, those practices naturalized heterosexuality and enforced heteronormativity. The term "queer" defines itself against the norm rather than against the heterosexual. Queer theory argues that the normative regimes inhabited and embodied by heterosexuals are ideological fictions rather than natural inevitabilities. Thus, in this context, heterosexuality is also queer.

This volume does not attempt to locate "positive" or "negative" images of queers in Israeli cinema, nor does it critique the fetishization, objectification, and stereotypical figuration of gays as a "misrepresentation" of preexisting queer experience. Neither will it critique the absence of queer subjects from cultural representation. Such an approach runs the risk of not only producing an essentialized queer subject and reinforcing a dichotomous codification of sexual differences that are inherent in the compulsory heterosexual Zionist culture, but also assumes that queer people and queerness are marginal or invisible. In fact, in most of the films that are explored, there are no ostensibly gay characters and, on the face of it, the films do not deal with homosexuality. In some of the films, the word "gay" is not even mentioned in any form or context—for example in Zionist propaganda films. Instead, this book traces complexities of queer desire and identification and tries to explain the positioning of "femininity" within the articulation of male homoeroticism, as well as the construction of male heterosexuality through and against the specter of homoeroticism.

The Israeli dominant cultural articulation seeks to conceal the artificial and historically motivated character of heterosexual masculinity it brings into effect by naturalizing the work of representation. The forming of the normative Israeli national subject requires identification with the Zionist fantasm of sexuality, identification that takes place through a disavowal of the threatening spectacle of "feminine" maleness. As Butler states, any "refusal to identify with a given position [suggests] that on some level an identification has already taken place."[4] Butler poses this as a question: "What is the economic premise operating in the assumption that one identification is purchased at the expense of another? If heterosexual identification takes place not through the refusal to identify as homosexual but through an identification with an abject homosexuality that must, as it were, never show, then can we extrapolate that normative subject-positions more generally depend on and are articulated through a region of abjected identification?"

Zionist male heterosexuality is a function of a disavowed identification with an imaged queerness, upon which Israeli straightness never ceases to depend. Zionist homophobia is not only a fear of queerness, but also a disavowal of this dependence on male queers, of the *structurating necessity* of this negation. That is, queerness is an essential structural element in the construction of Zionism—a structural element that must be disavowed. This abjected identification threatens to destabilize and unveil the self-establishing structural presumptions of the heterosexual male subject. This study exposes how the Israeli heterosexual subject's fear of and desire for queer masculinity undo the fixity of his identity, make him feel a sense of fluidity, estranged from himself, make him feel a painful need for "otherness." *Beyond Flesh* also investigates and historicizes the emergence of Israeli gay cultural products, such as the films of Amos Guttman and Eytan Fox. It analyzes how and in what ways these queer filmmakers in their cultural texts challenge and construct an alternative to the dominant Zionist body Master Narrative, or sometimes reconfirm and reinforce it.

While queer theory has questioned the seemingly "natural" status of epistemological assumptions of sex, it nevertheless has not been fully responsive to questions of race, ethnicity, and nationalism. Postcolonial theory in the last two decades has addressed questions of race, nation-state relations, class, and gender, among others, through analysis of texts of imperial cultures and has exposed structural contradictions in their colonialist ideologies and processes. Like queer theory, the field is strongly influenced by several methodologies (poststructuralism, Marxism, feminism, psychoanalysis, the works of Michel Foucault and Frantz Fanon), and even the term itself has been the subject of controversy ("post-colonial," "postcolonial," "postcoloniality," "anti-colonial-critique") by scholars such as Arif Dirlik, Anne McClintock, Robert Stam, Ella Shohat, and Aijaz Ahmad.[5] However, postcolonial theory is a method of analysis that investigates the construction of societies whose subjectivity has been constituted in part by the subordinating power of colonialism, as well as a set of discursive practices involving resistance to colonialism and colonialist ideologies and legacies. Edward Said's genealogical critique of Orientalism as a discursive practice, by which European culture was able to manage—and even to produce—the Orient during the post-Enlightenment period,[6] is crucial for the understanding of how ethnic and racial power relations operate within Israeli society, as Shohat had already eloquently discussed in her book on Israeli cinema.

In Orientalist discourse, the East is produced as aberrant, underdeveloped, and inferior in order to constitute the Occident's "self" as rational, modern, and superior, as well as to justify the West's privileges and aggressions. While Said discusses the differences and oppositions between colonizer and colonized, Homi Bhabha's work examines the complex mix of attraction and repulsion, fear and desire that characterize their relationship.[7] The colonial subject's attitude toward the "other" is not a simple rejection of difference but an acknowledgment and a disavowal of an "otherness" that holds an attraction and poses a threat. Hence, colonial identity is a problem arising in between colonizer and colonized, an ambivalent hybridized condition of fantasy and fear, far different from the clear-cut authority that the colonial domination wants to present. Therefore, ambivalence is a structural element of colonial discourse, undesired by the colonizer.

The colonizer seeks to constitute compliant subjects who mimic his assumptions and values. For example, Israeli cinema in the seventies expressed an anxiety about the emergence of a new Mizrahi macho masculinity and made an effort to domesticate Mizrahi men by disavowing ethnic differences, using practices of mimicry which were enforced through the military and interethnic marriage, compelling Mizrahim to reflect an image of Ashkenazi heteronormativity. Indeed, Bhabha describes mimicry as "one of the most elusive and effective strategies of colonial power and knowledge."[8] However, those practices of mimicry have the potential to constitute hybridized colonial subjects who threaten to disclose the ambivalence of the discourse of colonialism, which the use of stereotype tries to conceal. In his films, the Mizrahi filmmaker and actor Ze'ev Revach exploits strategies of mimicry and passing in order to transgress visible borders of sexuality and ethnicity and to present a version of Mizrahi manhood that deconstructs the heteronormative stereotype imposed on Mizrahi men by exposing masculinity as masquerade and spectacle.

In postcolonial scholarship, with a few notable exceptions,[9] there has been a general critical tendency to minimize the role of sexuality, and particularly homosexuality. This study insists on the importance of understanding the intersectionality of discourses on race and ethnicity and the discourse of (homo)sexuality within the particular national discourse of Israeli cinema. The terms "race" and "ethnicity" in this study refer to historical and ideological discourses rather than to ahistorical or biological categories. In Israeli cinema, the representation of Mizrahi and Palestinian men as savages, primitive and violent, reproduces certain Zionist ideological fictions and psychic fixations about the sexual nature of Oriental masculinity and the "otherness" that it is constructed to embody. Zionist colonial fantasy projected its own fears of and desires for homosexuality onto the male Mizrahi and Palestinian imagined sexuality and body. In the film *Paratroopers* (Judd Ne'eman, 1977), for example, the construction of the Mizrahi man as homophobic, that is, as repressed homosexual, enabled the Ashkenazi male protagonist to allay his own anxieties about homosexuality. In another film, *Hamsin* (Dan Wachsman, 1982), the Israeli man's fear of miscegenation between Arab men and Jewish women displaced his own homoerotic fantasies about interracial sex. The Oriental body was forced to stand in, to mimic, to be a mirror-image upon which the Israeli-Ashkenazi (sexual) ego props itself. However, other films, mainly produced by Mizrahi filmmakers, resisted these kinds of representations of the Oriental male body. They problematized the issue of self-representation and made the Zionist Ashkenazi fiction of identification visible, exposing it as a historically constructed identity dependent upon binaries of East/West, Arab/Jew, Palestinian/Israeli, Mizrahi/Ashkenazi, feminine/masculine, homo/hetero.

This study emphasizes that the categories of "race" and "ethnicity" are not exclusive properties of "truly" raced people, such as Palestinians and Mizrahim, but also constitute the identity of the Ashkenazim themselves. In Israeli cinema, Ashkenazi people have escaped and enjoyed the privilege of not being marked as part of an ethnic group. Instead, they imaged themselves as the norm. Zionist films articulate Ashkenazi pioneers as "whites," a construction that defines itself against the image of the "black" diasporic Jew and the Middle Eastern population. The "white" identity of the Zionist pioneer is founded on a paradoxical notion of being part of a race—the Jewish race—and, at the same time, of being an individual and universal subject who is not part of his racial genealogy. The figure of the Sabra, who is at once Jewish but born from nothingness—from the "elements"—embodies this paradoxical construction of Ashkenazi "whiteness." This book will try to embody the disembodied manifestation of "Ashkenaziness" in Israeli cinema.

―――――――

My work is indebted to the growing field of masculinity and the representation of the male body in film studies. Starting with mid-eighties articles by Paul Willemen about the films of Anthony Mann, Richard Dyer on the male pin-up, and Steve Neale about the spectacle of masculinity in popular cinema, and continuing with series of books in the early nineties such as Steven Choan and Ina Rae Hark's edited volume *Screening the Male*, Peter Lehman's *Running Scared*, Paul Smith's *Clint Eastwood*, and Dennis Bingham's *Acting Male*, these works contributed to the deconstruction of Western heteronormative masculinity and its institutions of power.[10]

Willemen describes two ways in which the male hero is displayed in Mann's Westerns. First the male body is represented as spectacle, producing an erotic visual pleasure for the (male) viewer. This erotic objectification of masculinity can be threatening for the normative subject; therefore it is always followed by the physical destruction of the male body through beating or mutilation. Those two representations are understood in terms of the sadistic/masochistic doublet. The objectification of the male body is linked to the sadistic gaze and the bodily destruction to masochistic pleasure. Following Willemen, Neale explores the implications of Laura Mulvey's observation about the sadistic nature of the cinematic gaze for issues of masculinity, arguing that the male body in popular imagery is "feminized" and objectified by the apparatus of the cinema and the viewer. However, as Smith eloquently states:

> Neale's contention, that in order for the male body to be thus objectified it has to be "feminised," is open to question, not least because it relies upon a sweeping generalization (increasingly often doubted in film studies) about the conventions and the apparatus of cinema—namely, upon the argument that they are oriented primarily and perhaps exclusively to the male spectator and his processes of identification. Neale's argument is in a sense self-fulfilling, or at least circular. If it is first assumed that the apparatus is male, geared to a male heterosexual gaze, then any instance of objectification will have to involve the "feminisation" of the object.[11]

Indeed, a generalization of the kind leads to theoretical deadlock that minimizes the complexities of desire and identification in representations of masculinity in cinema.

This book attempts to identify more liberating possibilities of masochism, based on the work of Leo Bersani, Gilles Deleuze, Gaylyn Studlar, and Kaja Silverman, for the production of "new" male sexualities.[12]

In *Running Scared,* Lehman offers a more flexible approach—informed by a variety of critical methods, including close textual analysis, feminism, psychoanalysis, auteurism, and cultural studies—for exploring the representation of the male body in film and culture. His book "confront[s] the silence surrounding the male body, particularly the male genitals."[13] Lehman focuses mainly on the (in)visibility of the male penis—its size, shape, color—unveiling and demystifying the taboo and awe surrounding its representation in popular and scientific discourses. The pivotal attention that Lehman gives to the male penis reinforces his frame of analysis: the construction of heteromasculinity. This is, in part, because identification of heterosexual masculinity demands prioritization of the penis as the only legitimized site of male eroticism.

This volume turns critical attention to another erogenous zone of the male body: the male anus. Even more than the penis, the male anus is surrounded by compulsive sexual fears, fantasies, and fundamental cultural taboos. As Eve Kosofsky Sedgwick and Michael Moon write: "On the conventional road map of the body that our culture handily provides us the anus gets represented as always below and behind, well out of sight under most circumstances, its unquestioned stigmatization a fundamental guarantor of one's individual privacy and one's privately privatized individuality."[14] Following the writings of D. A. Miller, Lee Edelman, and Leo Bersani, I would like to suggest that the anus is a structural element in both the construction of heterosexual and homosexual masculinity in Israeli national cinema.[15] The anus, as a site of penetration, operates for men as a phobic orifice that must be repudiated, if the male subject submits to the laws of castration and heterosexuality. In phallocentric culture, the anus is associated with "feminine" passivity and castration, something that must be disavowed and repressed in order for male phallic identification to succeed. Accordingly, the heterosexual national subjectivity emerges through a disavowed identification with anal penetration. In this sense, anality takes a repudiated constitutive part in heterosexual masculinity.

Gay men have a different relationship to the anus. Anality is an important zone for gay men in their deconstruction of phallic masculinity. In the act of anal sex, homosexuals embrace castration and passivity that is antithetical to fantasies of male phallic mastery and authority. Through anal passivity, the homosexual male subject summits the phallic male body to violation and transgression. In short, phallic masculinity is present in male homosexuality through the process of its repudiation. However, this presence is primarily conceived as a desired space of rejection, negation, and transgression.

An approach that only emphasizes the structural ambivalence of male subjectivity can be seen as part of the tendency of discourse analysis to de-historicize and de-locate masculinities from their temporal, spatial, geographical, and linguistic contexts. The emphasis on the plurality of masculinities suggests that dominant Israeli Ashkenazi masculinity is crisscrossed by its "others": queer, Mizrahi, and Palestinian masculinities.

Drawing on Mikhail Bakhtin's concept of "the dialogic imagination," this book examines the dialogic way in which images of male sexualities in Israeli cinema "work," as they circulate in the contingent and contradictory circumstances of historical, cultural, and artistic contexts. This approach does not aim to have the last word on the "value" of a given text, but rather recognizes the contextual character of relations among authors, texts, and audiences as they encounter each other in the worldly spaces of the social sphere.

For Bakthin, dialogism—defined by Robert Stam as "the necessary relation of any utterance to other utterances"[16]—is the process of generation of meanings and values, which are never finally fixed, but are constantly subject to coalescent and antagonistic efforts of articulation from one discourse to the next. The production of meanings is simultaneously determined from without (the referential status of the utterance, its context) and from within (the semantic and stylistic interaction between various utterances as they circulate endlessly throughout language itself). Any act of enunciation emerges in response to the relevant context, whether in response to the immediate social situation (what the speech performance is about and to whom it is being addressed) or to the wider socio-historical circumstances (the more inclusive economic, political, and cultural environment). In other words, for an utterance to have significance, it must be related to social existence. As Bakhtin states: *"Only that which has acquired social value can enter the world of ideology, take shape, and establish itself there."*[17]

Representations of masculinities in Israeli cinema is analyzed in relation to multiple contexts: political, historical, and cultural, as well as in relation to questions of the politics of positionality of cinematic authors and audiences. What kind of national, racial, ethnic, gender, sexual group do the filmmakers represent? What do they represent and how, and what remains silenced? To whom are those representations being addressed and how are audiences called to identify with them? The same representation could be read differently by opposed groups. The image is always the site of a struggle between multiple and intersecting meanings which, in turn, reflect wider social conflicts. For example, while representations of male-male desire between Palestinians and Israelis—produced by gay Israeli filmmakers and addressed to the Israeli audience—promote interracial sexual unions and subvert the heterocentric national hegemony, at the same time, they cannot be read outside the history of the Israeli occupation of the West Bank in 1967 that turned Palestinians into cheap labor, commodified bodies for sale not only for work but also for the sexual-visual pleasure of those gay Israeli directors and their audiences. In this analysis of images of male sexualities, text and context, cinema and politics are deeply and structurally intertwined.

However, contextual analysis does not exhaust the representations' significance. For Bakhtin, every utterance echoes not only its time and context, but also depends on a network of other utterances (past and present) for its significance. This kind of dialogic interaction accounts for the utterance's open-ended possibilities of meanings, its multiple and polysemic layers of semantic depth. Bakhtin argues that since a text can generate new meanings, which did not previously exist, it cannot be seen as a reflection of a prediscursive reality, but as part of a wider, infinite intertextual chain: "No one utterance can be either the first or the last. Each is only a link in a chain, and none can be studied outside this chain."[18] In short, for Bakhtin, there is no direct relation between the utterance and the external world, but only a mediated or interdiscursive one.

In this volume, images of manliness are analyzed in relation to other Israeli cinematic texts (past and present) and occasionally in relation to foreign cinemas that influenced Israeli cinema's representation of masculinities, such as Sergei Eisenstein's films, German Expressionism, Hollywood melodramas, and R. W. Fassbinder's cinema. Israeli films are explored in relation to noncinematic texts—such as literary texts, journalistic articles, medical-scientific reports, and political speeche—in order to view Israeli cinema's discourse of male sexualities as parallel to or structured by them. They are also a part of a larger discursive structure.

While Israel's unique nation formation has been subject to extensive intellectual inquiry in and outside Israel, only a few comprehensive scholarly works have been written about Israeli cinema. Most of the works outline production histories and plot synopses of Israeli films, for example, Nathan Gross and Ya'acov Gross's *The Hebrew Film: The History of Cinema in Israel*; Meir Schnitzer's *Israeli Cinema: Facts, Plots, Directors, Opinions*; Hillel Tryster's *Israel Before Israel: Silent Cinema in the Holy Land*; Amy Kronish's *World Cinema: Israel*.[19] Ella Shohat's book *Israeli Cinema: East/West and the Politics of Representation* was the first critical attempt in Israeli cinema studies to come to terms with the Zionist/Israeli national ideology, specifically with its objectification of the Mizrahi and Palestinian subjects, as well as with the absence or marginality of their experience, along axes of race, ethnicity, class, and gender. Following Shohat's work, Israeli cinema scholarship produced a body of critical literature on the history of Israeli cinema, using various theoretical models. For example, Igal Bursztyn's *Face as Battlefield* analyzes Israeli films through the representation of the cinematic close-up; Nurith Gertz's *Motion Fiction: Israeli Fiction in Film* explores the relationship between Hebrew literature and Israeli cinema; Nitzan S. Ben-Shaul's *Mythical Expressions of Siege in Israeli Films* traces metaphors of the "siege syndrome" in Israeli films; Ariel Schweitzer's *Le Cinema Israeli de la Modernite* investigates the modernist aesthetic and politics in Israeli cinema. The anthology *Fictive Looks: On Israeli Cinema,* edited by Nurith Gertz, Orly Lubin, and Judd Ne'eman, offers an interesting collection of essays on Israeli films from neo-Marxist, feminist, postcolonial, and historiographic perspectives.[20]

In this body of scholarship, there has been little attempt to explore questions of male sexuality. This elision is especially striking since one of the central forming elements of the Zionist ideology is the figure of the male Ashkenazi Sabra. Addressing Israeli cinema in the forties and fifties, Nurith Gertz examines the representation of the "new Jew" in relation to his "others": Holocaust survivors, Arabs, and women. She argues that the Israeli cinematic discourse elides the differences between those "others," who are "identified with each other and create hierarchy that supports the imagined homogeneity of the new [masculine] Hebrew identity."[21] By pointing out the identification between those "others," Gertz runs the risk of erasing the important distinctions between the different experiences of oppression of diasporic "queer" Jews, Arabs, and women, making homophobia, racism, and misogyny synonymous. Furthermore, this analogy obscures those who inhabit both identifications of "otherness," such as Mizrahi gay men who confront both racism and homophobia. Rather than suggesting that race, ethnicity, gender, and sexual orientation are "natural" analogies, this book seeks to explore the historical construction of intersections among different categories of identity at a particular cultural moment.

Israeli cinema scholarship as a whole is ensconced within a conspicuously heterocentric interpretative framework. Israeli film theorists remain silent when it comes to critical issues of homosexuality, queer desire, and queer identification. When scholars do address a queer imaginary, it is usually in reference to "openly" gay directors, who deal with "the subject," assuming that queerness can only express "local" concerns of a "special" sexually oriented group. This perspective, that governs Israeli film theory and culture as a whole, implicitly posits heterosexuality as the norm and refuses to see homosexuality as a constitutive part of Israeli cultural discourse. In other cases, discussions of homosexuality occur in a homophobic context, identifying gays as "anomalous" or "outcast" figures, even as "freaks." Referring to the films of the gay filmmaker Amos Guttman, Amy Kronish writes: "[Guttman] had a capacity for portraying homosexuality in a way which does not make the viewer uncomfortable. The film [*Amazing Grace*] includes no scenes of male love-making."[22] Homosexual sex frightens Kronish and makes her feel uncomfortable. Therefore she must disavow the specter of gay intercourse in Guttman's films, despite copious evidence to the contrary.

Jewish studies theorists, such as Sander Gilman, Daniel Boyarin, and David Biale, have been more attentive to representations of Jewish male (homo)sexuality in Western culture, using, like Boyarin, the Jewish male femme image as a critical practice.[23] I am indebted in many aspects to their insights on the nineteenth-century European discourse of masculinity and Zionist sexual politics. However, while concerned with questions of (Jewish) race within anti-Semitic discourse, those scholars have almost completely ignored the racial and racist politics of the Zionist project itself. When some of those scholars do address questions of Orientalism, they argue that racism is an effect of the Zionist sexual discourse and that the history of Zionist racial politics began only with the Euro-Jewish pioneers' arrival in Palestine.

On the contrary, Zionist racial and racist discourse is not a byproduct or an effect of Zionist sexual politics, but actually a constitutive element of it. Moreover, the racial thinking of the Zionist leaders, which informed their ideas of a new (hetero)sexuality, began long before the first pioneers reached the shores of Palestine. In addition, critical discussions of the Zionist heteronormatively referred, sometimes not directly, only to the Ashkenazi male body, thus eliding the specific body experience of Mizrahi (male) Jews and the role they played in the Zionist "white" male fantasies. Indeed, the Zionist discourse is structurally sexed, gendered, and raced, as Mizrahi feminism has already pointed out in its ongoing critical debate with Ashkenazi feminism.[24] The challenge of this study is to explore the historical and theoretical intersections between multiple categories of race, ethnicity, gender, sex, and nationalism and to expose them as ideological constructions produced by Zionist culture. Insistence on intersectionality of multiple categories of difference recognizes their instability and structural ambivalence and refuses to assume the fixity of one over the other.

   Beyond Flesh offers not only a theoretical and critical account of the construction of masculinities and queerness in Israeli cinema and culture, in particular, but also suggests a model for the investigation of the role of male sexualities within the constitution of national culture, in general. My aim in this book is to challenge the tendency within dominant critical discourses to treat race, sexuality, and nationalism separately. I hope that my insistence on the historical and theoretical intersectionality of race, ethnicity, gender, and sexual orientation within national culture will open up a space in between those multiple categories in which subjectivity is constituted.

1 | The Zionist Body Master Narrative

> The idealization of masculinity [is] the foundation of nation and society.
> —George L. Mosse, *Nationalism and Sexuality: Respectability and Abnormal Sexuality in Modern Europe*, 1985

In *The History of Sexuality: Volume I,* Michel Foucault argues that discourses on sexuality, not sexual acts and their histories, are important to an understanding of the workings of power in modern Western societies.[1] Foucault's work is not literally a history of sexuality, but a history of the discourses on sexuality and the different ways in which these discourses, and the pleasures and powers they have produced, have been deployed in the service of hierarchical relations in Western society over the past three hundred years. Foucault challenges Marx's and Freud's traditional notions of sex as an instinctual drive or force, intrinsically liberating for the individual when expressed and apparently disruptive of a necessarily repressive state. The central feature of such a notion of sexuality, Foucault argues, is that it understands the discourse of sexuality in terms of its repression. Foucault criticizes this "repressive hypothesis": the hypothesis that power relations bearing on sexuality always take the form of prohibition, censorship, or non-recognition. Foucault argues, in contrast, that Western culture, far from repressing sexuality, has actually produced it, multiplied it, and spread it out as a particularly privileged means of gaining access to the individual and social bodies, as a way of policing society through procedures and normalization rather than prohibition. As Leo Bersani summarizes, the main thesis of Foucault: "It is the original thesis of [*The History of Sexuality*] that power in our societies functions primarily not by repressing spontaneous sexual drives but by producing multiple sexualities, and that through the classification, distribution, and moral rating of those sexualities the individuals practicing them can be approved, treated, marginalized, sequestered, disciplined, or normalized."[2]

One expression of the discursive explosion of sex was the medicalization of the body and sexuality. The science of medicine and sex, Foucault writes:

> . . . set itself up as the supreme authority in matters of hygienic necessity, taking up the old fears of venereal affliction and combining them with the recent institutions of public health; it claimed to ensure the physical vigor and the moral cleanliness of the social body; it promised to eliminate defective individuals, degenerate and bastardized populations. In the name of a biological and historical urgency, it justified the racisms of the state, which at the same time were on the horizon. It grounded them in "truth."[3]

The medicalization of sex, served as a social tool to subordinate the "other." The pseudo-objective medical-scientific gaze measured skulls, noses, and sexual organs in order to construct differences between races and nations. The Jew was a central figure in this European medical discourse. Scholars such as Sander Gilman, Daniel Boyarin, and Michael Gluzman describe hundreds of years of European tradition that associated the male Jew with diseases, madness, degeneration, sexual perversity, and femininity.[4] Jewish men were believed to experience menstruation—a proof of their pathological difference, their bodily and moral inferiority. The psychoanalyst Carl Gustav Jung, for example, argued that Jewish men are "feminine": "[Jewish men] have this peculiarity in common with women; being physically weaker they have to aim at the chink in the armor of their adversary, and thanks to this technique which has been forced on them through the centuries, the Jews themselves are best protected where others are most vulnerable."[5] In fin-de-siècle Europe, along with the invention of the sexual categories of "homosexuality" and "heterosexuality," the male Jew was also identified as a homosexual. Both the Jewish male and the homosexual were represented as gender benders, as violating the natural gender order; they were both seen as hypersexual and as having a pathological "feminine" body.[6]

The categorization of the Jewish man as a sort of woman appeared not only in the anti-Semitic discourse and in Christian medical scholarship, but also entered the writings of Jewish scientists and medical doctors. Hans Gross, the famed Jewish criminologist, commented on the "little, feminine hand of the Jew." He claimed that it is the pathology of the Jew, the Jew's "feebleness" that "often gives him somewhat unmanly appearance."[7] The Jewish ethnologist Adolf Jelinek argued that "in the examination of various races it is clear that some are more masculine, others more feminine. Among the latter the Jews belong, as one of those tribes that are both more feminine and have come to represent the feminine among other peoples."[8] Freud himself tried to critique the anti-Semitic identification between the Jew and femininity. In the case history of Little Hans, he claimed that the European anti-Semitism results from marking of the male Jew as a woman:

> The castration complex is the deepest root of anti-Semitism; for even in the nursery little boys hear that a Jew has something cut off his penis—a piece of his penis, they think—and this gives them a right to despise Jews. And there is no stronger unconscious root for the sense of superiority over women. [Otto] Weininger . . . [in] . . . his remarkable book, . . . treated Jews and women with equal hostility and overwhelmed them with the same insults. Being neurotic, Weininger was completely under the sway of his infantile complexes; and from that standpoint what is common to Jews and women is their relation to the castration complex.[9]

Boyarin argues that more than just an anti-Semitic stereotype, the image of the femme male Jew was an historical product of premodern Jewish culture. The European Jewish culture needed an image—the image of the "feminine" male Jew—against which to define itself and produced the "goy"—the hypermale gentile—as a reverse of its social norm. He writes:

> Premodern Jewish culture . . . frequently represented ideal Jewish men as feminized through various discursive means. This is not, moreover, a representation that carries with it any hint of internalized contempt or self-hatred. Quite the opposite; it was through this mode of conscious alternative gendering that Jewish culture frequently asserted its identity over-against its surroundings.[10]

It was in the late nineteenth century, under the pressure of what Boyarin calls "the rise of heterosexuality," that the reconstruction of the Jewish gender by modern Jewish thought began. In this context we should understand Zionism's ideological longing for a new kind of strong, healthy, proud, and heterosexual Jewish masculinity that would contradict the image of the diaspora Jew as weak, queer, and "feminine." In their writings, Zionist leaders such as Theodor Herzl and Max Nordau believed that a creation of a new modern male Jew body would solve the physiological and psychological "complexes" of the Eastern European Jews that were imposed on them by anti-Semitism. Zionism was understood to be a cure for the Jewish gender illness, as well for the economic, political, and national problems of the Jewish people. The fact the Herzl was discharged form military service because of bodily deficiency did not prevent him from writing in 1894:

> I understand what anti-Semitism is about. We Jews have main-
> tained ourselves, even if through no fault of our own, as a foreign
> body of anti-social qualities. Our character has been corrupted by
> oppression, and it must be resorted through some other kind of
> pressure. . . . All these sufferings rendered us ugly and transformed
> our character which had in earlier times been proud and mag-
> nificent. After all, we once were men who knew how to defend
> the state in time of war.[11]

The case of Nordau is especially interesting because of his medical background that formed, in part at least, his understanding of the role of Zionism in the construction of a new Jew. In order to create what he called a "new muscular Jew," Nordau—in the spirit of Fredrick Ludwig Jahn, the father of German gymnastics—linked body culture and national heroism, emphasizing the need for Jewish men to exercise and to develop their bodies as a way to overcome "the horrible devastation that eighteen hundred years of exile caused us."[12] Contrasting the "coffeehouse Jews" with the "muscular Jews," Nordou believed that the new Jew was supposed to "expose as lies the fairy tale of the bent and crooked Jew, as our youth grows to maturity in good health and with straight bodies."[13] Unlike the degenerated feminine "ghetto Jew," the new Zionist manhood is composed of "men who rise early and are not weary before sunset, who have clear heads, solid stomachs, and hard muscles."[14] Hence the enthusiasm and fascination of Magnus Hirschfeld, the famous German-Jewish sexologist, for the new Zionist male body when he visited Palestine in 1932: "In their dress—hatless, bare-necked and with bare legs—in the ingenuousness of manner . . . [they] seem so full of joy, strength, and affirmation of life that they seem to have overcome all the repressions and unconscious feeling of erotic inferiority found at this age."[15]

Not only bodies needed to be reinvented, but also minds that had degenerated in the ghetto. Zionism demanded that the new muscular

Jew have a healthy body and healthy mind. This argument, as Gilman claims, "must be read within the inner circles of the Zionist movement, in which the Jewish opponents of Zionism were viewed as possessing all the qualities (including madness) ascribed to them by the anti-Semites."[16] Paradoxically, then, Zionism's (homo)phobia of the queer Jew and the Zionist movement's fantasy of a new heterosexual Hebrew male subject reinforced the same European anti-Semitic scientific-medical discourse that it tried to undo.

Although scholars have inquired into the Zionist longing to constitute an erotic revolution,[17] the important role played by Zionist cinema in the construction of a new butch Jewish male has not been fully explored. Moreover, it has become apparent that those discussions refer, sometimes not explicitly, only to Ashkenazi masculinity and elide the structural importance of race and ethnicity in the production of the new Zionist male Jew. By not including in their analytical scope the Eastern masculinity as a *constitutive element* in the construction of Zionist national manhood, those scholarly works not only establish the Ashkenazi manliness as a universal signifier, but also risk remaining enclosed within the Eurocentric borders of the official Zionist discourse.

This chapter examines the construction of the Zionist body Master Narrative in reference to the way Zionist films express, through various visual, narrative and formal tropes, the Zionist dream of a new masculinity. It also explores the role played by race in the construction of both Ashkenazi and Arab male subjectivities.

From Darkness to Light

The Zionist Movement used films for two main goals: to propagate Zionist ideology and to gather financial and political support to materialize it. But the relation between Zionism and cinema is much more complex. Jewish culture, in general, has a special relation toward vision. One can refer back to the Book of Genesis and to God's words "Let there be light" or to the Book of Exodus and its audiovisual spectacle of receiving the Ten Commandments at Mount Sinai as first steps for establishing the connection between Judaism and sight. Jewish people see themselves as "a light for the gentiles" [or *la'goyim*]; the yarmulke [skullcap], the mezuzah, and even the circumcision are visual signifiers for the affinity between the Jew and his God. At the same time, the second commandment forbids Jews from creating figurative representation of God and the Jew must cover his eyes at the beginning of the "Shma" prayer. And yet the Jews were always caught in the dialectic between the desire to see and what is not shown (for example, the biblical Golden Calf that expresses the desire to have a visible God and the story of Lot's wife who turn into a pillar of salt for being unable to resist seeing the wrath of God). Two hundred years of exile left the Jews literally "out of sight," unable to see their homeland. As long as the promised land remained outside their field of vision, the exile was often associated with darkness, as in the phrase "the darkness of the exile" [heshehat ha'galut].

Zionism's mission was to bring light to the Jews of the diaspora, to give rise to the Jewish desire to see the unseen. What was till then hidden, repressed, forever textualized, buried under years of literal representations, could be visualized by the power of the Zionist image. Hence Zionism was named "the Zionist vision" [ha'hazon ha'tziyoni] and Herzl was called "the envisioner of the state" [hoze ha'medina]. And what better way to conceive this task than through the visual medium of film. It is not coincidence that Zionism was born at almost exactly the same time as cinema. Back in 1899, A. Noyfeld, a Zionist from Warsaw, encouraged Zionist institutions to use the "latest invasions" of audio and visual media for propaganda purposes. Noyfeld asked to improve Zionist propaganda—then based on written media, lectures, and artistic performances—by using the "magic lantern," the kinematograph, and the phonograph that would "demonstrate and consolidate the word through image" and would "spread the Zionist word as widely as possible to larger audiences."[18] One Zionist report described the immense impact that the visual images left on the Jews of the diaspora:

> The images of light . . . produced a special desire in their spectators wherever they were shown. . . . We can use the images of light to show a larger audience the results of our fruitful work and to prove to them that it is possible to accomplish much in the land of Israel [Eretz Yisrael], if only the Jewish people would realize the important value of our institution, the institution of redemption. . . . The viewers were especially impressed with the image of Dr. Herzl who appeared as if he were alive against a white background.[19]

In this case, this visual image became a symbol for "nationalism," but it was not until 1911 when Murray Rosenberg, a British Jew, recorded the first moving images of Palestine in his travelogue The First Film of Palestine.

As an important part of the Zionist propaganda apparatus, cinema served as a crucial tool in the fantasy of a new pioneer masculinity. Documentary and narrative films such as *Sabra* (Alexander Ford, 1933), *Oded the Wanderer* (Natan Axelrod, 1933), *This Is the Land* (Baruch Agadati, 1935), *Avodah* (Helmer Lerski, 1935), *Over the Ruins* (Natan Axelrod, 1938), *Collective Adventure* (Alex Brais and Nigel Wingate, 1939), *Adama* (Helmer Lerski, 1947), *My Father's House* (Herbert Kline, 1947), among many others, were obsessed with the creation of a new ideal image of the male Jew: tall, handsome, muscular, tanned, strong, brave. Hard work was one of the major means to make the Zionist new body beautiful. Young pioneers coming from Europe in the second immigration wave believed in Zionist principles of "conquest of the work" [*kibush ha'avodah*] and "conquest of the land" [*kibush ha'adama*] that were drawn from Russian populism and Marxism, as a way to change the "unproductive labor" of the Jewish diaspora. Zionist thinkers like Itzhak Tabenkin and Yossef Berdichveski called for "a new attitude toward nature, work, culture, man, mind and matter, beauty and power."[20] Work became a moral category and was raised to the importance of religion, as in the phrase "religion of work" [*dat ha'avodah*] associated with the Aharon D. Gordon. Images of work in the fields (plowing, sowing, drilling wells) or in urban cities (working in construction or in factories) appear in many Zionist films, and the film *Avodah* [literally, "work"] is dedicated to the subject.

Work was not the only discourse that was used in the Zionist male gendering project. Gymnastics was also an important discursive means in the training of the new Jewish body to exercise the Zionist-pioneering mission. In the spirit of Nordau's call for a "muscular Jew," the film *This Is the Land,* for example, shows young pioneers exercising in different sports activities: swimming, running, thrusting an iron ball, boxing, and so on. The scene is narrated by an enthusiastic male voice-over that says: "We aspire not only for mental health, but also for physical health! A new generation has been raised that doesn't know the suffering of the diaspora, that marches towards a flourishing future! [*sic*]." A high-angled camera shows men and women marching upright in straight well-formed lines, demonstrating the ordered, disciplined, and unpenetrated Zionist body.

Zionist gymnastic groups adopted names of ancient Jewish warriors like Bar Kochba and Maccabee, models of strong masculinity that would repress and regulate the Jewish queerness. Linking the "Muscular Jew" to Bar Kochba, Nordau associated bodily regeneration with national revival. Bar Kochba was, Nordau claimed, an ideal "hero that didn't know defeats" and that embodied the notion of a "strong Judaism that is eager for arms in the war."[21] Films such as *Adama* and *Over the Ruins* refer to those heroic mythic figures in their narratives that describe the remasculinization trajectory that the "sissy" male Jew must undergo in order to become a new man.

The paradigmatic narrative structure of Jewish manhood reconstruction could be exemplified as follows: Coming from Europe preferably after the Holocaust, the diaspora Jew, usually a child who symbolizes the nation in its cradle, encounters difficulties in adjusting to the new "healthier" Zionist society, due to his pathological gender and mind. In the course of the film, with the help of the pioneers and the Zionist institution, the diasporic Jew sheds his historical traumas and gains bodily and spiritual-existential salvation. The trope of the infantile nation is represented clearly in *My Father's House*. The hero, a child who desperately seeks his father after losing him in the Holocaust, literally experiences an infantile mental regression and is committed to a mental hospital. Through this trauma, the child acknowledges his father's death and accepts Zionism as his new spiritual father. In these films, the body-building of the male Jew is allegorized as Zionist nation-building. Associating the male Jew's body with the nation's body, Zionism constructed a masculine national ideology that expelled from the national project all those subjects that did not have "legitimate" bodies. Further, the discourses of work and physical gymnastics served to construct not only the new Jewish male body, but more specifically the "whiteness" of the new Ashkenazi male body.

The Cutting Edge

Another means of tracing and theorizing the construction of Zionist male subjectivity is through the evolution of Zionist film form, or more specifically the evolution of the cinematic editing in the pioneers' films.[22] Igal Bursztyn observes that the early Zionist cinema of Murray Rosenberg, Ya'acov Ben Dov, and Natan Axelrod is characterized by long sequence shots, panning camera movements, documenting from a distance the landscape of Palestine and the achievements of the Zionist project. No close-ups of human faces appeared in these Zionist films. According to Bursztyn, "The pioneers are a collective. They are not separated from each other through singular shots that are joined together through the editing, but they are included in one shot unit by a camera movement that scans them."[23]

The montage, then, has no function in organizing subjectivity or sub-jective tension in these films. This was the naïve era of Zionist cinema, a "cinematographic Eden" with no conflicted desire and anxiety, in which the "natural" camera produced a homogeneous continuity of the action of Zionist "life."

When montage entered Zionist cinema, it slashed, cut up, and manipulated the action. The body of the new Zionist man lost its unity and homogeneity and became fragmented and dismembered. (In Zionist films, it is mostly the male body, not the female, that attracts the camera.) With the signifying revolution in editing, the close-up of the human face emerged along with its characteristic—the subjective gaze of the new Hebrew male pioneer. The subjective gaze linked images and shots, giving a new subjective meaning to Zionist cinema. Once the camera became focused upon the face or the gaze, desire made its entrance into this cinema: the desire within the film of the male char-acters who gaze at the land or at each other, as well as the desire of the spectator who links in his mind the different and fragmented sequen-tial images and determines their meaning.

In the montage sequence of a well drilling in a later film, *Avodah,* close-ups of muscular half-naked male pioneers are linked, diegetically and extra-diegetically, with close-ups of a drilling machine. Fetishistic shots of active men's bodies, hard muscles, sweaty tanned skins, and proud faces, seen from a low camera angle, intertwine with shots of machine gears and transmissions. Man and machinery, flesh and iron, organic and mechanic are merged in a magnificent masculine work harmony.

Early Zionist cinema, which began as innocent and unconflicted, became obsessional and fetishistic. Neither desire nor suspense existed in the naïve, continuous, and homogeneous space and time of the early Zionist film. Parallel montage enabled alternation of two inter-connected courses of action, creating subjective tension and suspense between the two. The introduction of crosscutting editing to Zionist cinema in the film *Sabra* corresponded with the first cinematic rep-resentation of the Jewish-Arab conflict. Close-ups of threatening faces and menacing gazes of the charging Arabs contrasted with shots of the peaceful, soon to be attacked Zionist camp. The eruption of a violent Arab presence generates a dramatic climax in which the Zionists defeat the Arab destructive power and establish their sovereign sub-jectivity. The parallel montage combines heterogeneous elements and produces new metaphorical meaning having nothing to do with the denotative value of it component parts. It is the editing of the images, not the images themselves, that creates the national tension between Arabs and Jews within which the new Zionist heteromasculinity emerges. Thus the entrance of parallel editing enabled the construction of the Zionist male subjectivity vis-à-vis the representation of the Jewish-Arab conflict.

While the parallel montage in *Sabra* offers tension between the idyllic interior of the Zionist camp and the threatening exterior of the Arab attack, the film *Adama* articulates a more complex form of suspense. It is not simply a menacing horror placed outside or next to the peaceable Zionist space, but one that comes from within. In *Adama,* the ambivalent relations between the Zionist Jew and the diasporic Jew generate a tension in which "old" and "new" male subjectivities are endlessly reflected in a double mirror play. This makes the viewer rethink the relations between the two, not in terms of binary oppositions, but in terms of ambivalence, displacement, and disidentification processes. The queer Jew is not the "other" of the Zionist "self," but rather a structural condition of it.

The Uncanny Zionist Body: Adama

Slavoj Žižek points to the paradox of the sacrifice of the Jew by the Nazis. Žižek argues that the Nazi had to sacrifice the Jew in order to maintain the illusion that it is the degenerate race of the Jew that prevents the establishment of the harmonious and homogenous German Nazi society. In fact, Nazi society was never harmonious and homogenous. The representation of the Jews as a degenerate race enabled the Nazis to construct the imaginary image of themselves as a whole and coherent society. Žižek writes: "[W]hat appears as the hindrance to society's full identity-with-itself is actually its positive condition: by transposing onto the Jew the role of the foreign body that introduces disintegration and antagonism to the social organism, the fantasy image of society qua consistent, harmonious whole is rendered possible."[24]

Within the Zionist national discourse the "feminine" male served a function similar to that of the Jew within the Nazi anti-Semitic discourse. The "sacrifice" of the "feminine" male Jew established for the Zionist heterosexual masculine society its fantasmatic consistency. The "feminine" male Jew is the positive condition that is crucial to the construction of Zionism as a utopic social organism, and therefore he is also the one that undermines its imaginary coherency. In this fashion, he deconstructs completely the binaries between "self" and "other." The ontological instability that the queer male Jew body produced provokes anxiety in the compulsory heterosexual Zionist discourse. Although the "feminine" Jew is represented as alien and external to the Zionist order, he is nevertheless closer to home than one expects. He evokes an uncanny anxiety precisely because he is at the same time familiar and unfamiliar. He makes the new Jew feel estranged and queer from himself, unfamiliar with his own reflected image.

For Freud, "The uncanny [*unheimlich*] is that class of frightening which leads back to what is known of old and long familiar."[25] In German, the word "heimlich" means familiar, intimate, hidden, homey. The added prefix "*un*" changes the meaning from something familiar, homey, and friendly into something unfamiliar and frightening. Thus, it is not the pure fantasy that evokes anxiety, but rather the uncertainty and the doubt about the familiar that produce the effect of the uncanny. In other words, the uncanny is produced in the sutured relations between knowledge and the doubting of that knowledge. Freud notes a few situations that can cause the effect of the uncanny: uncertainty whether an object is dead or alive uncertainty whether something is mechanic or organic, or uncertainty of the shadow or the double (someone who is exactly like me—familiar—yet evokes fear because he may take my place). At stake in the uncanny is the instability of the boundaries between human/automaton or live/dead, and the fragility of the limits of identity.

Although Freud argues that the effect of the uncanny is provoked because of uncertainty on the unconscious level, Malden Dolar adds that the effect of the uncanny could be also arise from too much certainty on the conscious level: the desire not to believe something frightening that one knows is going to happen. In this case, escape from uncertainty is not possible because the subject is too conscious of the dangerous closeness of the object that evokes in him the uncanny feeling or, as Dolar puts it, "when escape through hesitation is no longer possible, when the object comes too close."[26]

This is exactly how uncanny feelings are evoked in Binyamin, the hero of the film *Adama*. The film is narrated by Binyamin's voice-over that tells, in a flashback, the story of his arrival and reception in Ben Shaemen's children's village, after losing his family in the Holocaust. Binyamin identifies the Zionist village as a Nazi camp: "For me it is another concentration camp." Looking at the wire fences, he experiences the historical trauma of the death camps. The Zionist instructors produce in him uncanny feelings because they remind him of SS soldiers. The boys and girls who obey them are seen through his eyes as sheep that march to slaughter, as if they are lifeless automatic dolls "that sit where they are being told." He refuses to take part in the pioneering work, because it reminds him of Nazi forced labor. Gazing horrified at the bent backs of the kids at work, he says, "I hate work. Didn't I work enough in the camps? I worked enough for Hitler!" Even the innocent, and friendly sight of children bathing their bare feet in the lake makes him feel uncanny, because he remembers that Nazis forcibly took children's shoes, as in Auschwitz. Moreover, the most distinguished Zionist ritual—the Hora dancing—is perceived by Binyamin as "crazy dancing," with terrible, loud music.

Freud describes how he felt an uncanny feeling when he lost his way in a foreign town and, when he tried to find his way back, he returned time after time to the same place. Similarly, although he tries to escape the places that evoke anxiety in him, Binyamin returns, obsessively again and again, to those same places. He escapes the play yard, yet a few minutes later he returns there and says: "I lost my way and have doubled back again." Binyamin returns to the same places that evoked anxiety in him in order to control the unpleasurable feelings that they express. He repeats his relation to his historical trauma and thus transforms a controlled passive position to an active one. Yet Freud argued that the compulsive character of repetition—the desire to repeat painful situations over and over again—is opposed to the notion of mastery. That is, repetition is not active. Uncontrolled reiteration is passive and Freud links it to the death instinct—the subject's instinct to reduce himself to nothing.[27] Binyamin's compulsive desire to repeat his relation to historical trauma prevents him from occupying the traditional subject position that constructs the Zionist fiction of masculinity.

Binyamin's labyrinthine and anxious feelings are also represented through Lerski's use of expressionist lighting and diagonal, distorted composition. (Before he was recruited to the Zionist propaganda project, Lerski was one of the leading cinematographers in the German UFA studios, the habitat of the horror Expressionist films of the twenties). Moreover, Lerski inscribes in his film classical motifs that evoke the effect of the uncanny, such as representations of doubles: the Italian twins, two boys named Binyamin; the local name that is given to the children that "now have," as Binyamin says, "two names." Looking at the shadows of two girls jumping rope, he asserts, "Their shadows hang in the air." This is a classical uncanny image—disembodied shadows that move of their own will.

Binyamin is controlled by a historical trauma that produces effects of the uncanny and, within it, he does not distinguish or refuses to distinguish between reality and fiction, friendly and unfamiliar, and thus fails to relate to the Zionist Law of the Father. Elements of the uncanny are structurally intertwined within the national discourse and thus subvert the imaginary coherency of the dominant Zionist narrative that tries to produce an illusion of social homogeneity. Homi Bhabha argues that the continuity and homogeneity of national discourse is an imaginary one. National discourse is, in fact, a heterogeneous, ambivalent, and duplicated discourse that is constructed by the same conflicted elements it tries to disavow. Through its uncanny imaginary, *Adama* dramatizes, unwittingly, the ambivalent structure of the civil Zionist nation and its figurative space, as it draws its rather paradoxical boundary between the private and the public spheres. The effect of the uncanny unveils the paradoxical borders of the nation that merge the familiar with the alien, the friendly with the hostile, the personal with the national. Binyamin experiences, to put it in Bhabha's terms, an "unhomely moment" that "relates the traumatic ambivalences of a personal, psychic history to the wider disjunctions of political existence."[28] The uncanny is also characterized by temporal discontinuity. It simultaneously, and in a conflicted manner, merges past, present, and future within its structure. In this way, the uncanny's disruptive temporality displaces the narrative of the Western nation, which Benedict Anderson describes as being written in homogenous and serial time.

The effects of the uncanny are also represented in the film in terms of the male body. Binyamin's body is represented as "feminine," weak, lean, with a pale skin color, contrary to the hard, muscular, tanned bodies of the other boys. He walks like a ghost on the paths of the village with arms held stiffly. Represented as passive and associated with closed and dark spaces, Binyamin suffers from paranoid hallucinations. (He tells his classmate, "Don't tell anybody that you are a Jew, not even to a Jew.") His body is marked as sick and as having a defective nature ("He is like a bird with a broken wing.") This makes the village instructors feel pity for him. Unwilling or unable to take part in the Zionist male gendering project, he feels alienated from the other boys who understand the new masculine codes. Zionist masculinity, as a code he must learn and adapt to, seems foreign and threatening to him. The only children that he dares approach are a girl, Miriam, who empathizes with his emotional distress and a younger "feminine" boy, also named Binyamin. These two characters underline his "feminine" representation in both gender and name.

Zionism perceives Binyamin's queer body as an uncanny body. It is familiar yet, at the same time, alien, because it undermines the Zionist fantasy of a new proud manhood. In order to exclude the uncannyness of the queer male body, Zionism produces it as an abject body; a body that is different from the masculine signifier; an abject being who is not yet a subject; an abject being who designates, as Judith Butler argues, "those 'unlivable' and 'uninhabitable' zones of social life."[29] Yet, as Butler asserts, the need of heterosexuality to construct the imaginary "natural" and "normal" subject by discursive means of abjection exposes the structural instability of the hegemonic body itself. As she states. "[T]he [heterosexual] subject is constituted through the force of exclusion and abjection, one which produces a constitutive outside the subject, and an abjected outside, which is, after all, 'inside' the subject as its own founding repudiation."[30] The uncanny body of the queer Jew unveils the performative structure of Zionist heterosexual masculinity, textualizes male sexuality itself, exposes it as only a signifying practice.

The stormy night in the village marks Binyamin's metamorphosis from "sissy" Jew to a new Zionist man. But his entry into the new national masculine order is accompanied by effects of the uncanny that underline the fluidity and performativity of the masculine signifiers. The name of the film, *Adama* [earth], represents the birth site of the new man. Binyamin says, "From earth came Adam—the first man." (In Hebrew, the biblical name "Adam" also mean "man," so the film plays on the Hebrew etymology *adama/Adam*). The earth is represented as a metaphor for a mother, a womb or a female vagina, from which the new Jew emerges. Yet this "female vagina" evokes in Binyamin uncanny feelings. Freud argued, "It often happens that neurotic men declare that they feel there is something uncanny about the female genital organs. This *unheimlich* place, however, is the entrance to the former "Heim" [home] of all human beings, to the place where each one of us lived once upon a time and in the beginning."[31] Earth, is depicted in the film as familiar and friendly, the Zionist homeland. Yet it produces anxiety and death memories, for Binyamin because it reminds him of the pits in which Jews were buried alive in the Holocaust. Through the uncanny imagery of the earth, the naturalness and authority of the homeland, the place of birth of the new man, is estranged from within. "I have needed the earth in order to become a man," Binyamin says. This ambivalent and conflicted structure of the homeland is represented as the apparatus that constructs Binyamin as a man. Therefore, the discursive production of Zionist male subjectivity and the Zionist home itself are revealed as a set of unfixed, unstable, changeable signifying practices, that evoke at the same time attraction and repulsion, identification and disavowal, fear and desire.

A more complex representation of the uncanny metaphor is expressed in the film through the relationships between Binyamin and a younger boy of the same name. Like Binyamin, the child Binyamin is also associated with femininity, since he has not yet passed the masculine training. He is identified with "feminine" music, and opposed to "masculine" pioneering work. Because of their resemblance in name and in physical status, we can see in Binyamin the child a mirror image or a double of the older Binyamin. The strong attraction between the two is marked as a narcissistic desire, desire for physical closeness that could also be understood in homoerotic terms. When he refers to his double, Binyamin remembers affectingly how little "Binyamin touched me and I touched him."

As Žižek observes, the double does not represent only the "other" through which the "self" is established. The double disturbs "normal" sexuality, representing an excess of "self." He is the "[t]hing that is me more than myself."[32] This excess is what the subject must sacrifice in order to construct a "normal" life in the community. But Binyamin is not experiencing in his double a fear of its radical "otherness," but rather a pleasure in being close to him. Gazing at his double, Binyamin does not see an object that is separate from him, but he sees himself as a subject that is "out there," looking back at him. Looking at his "feminine" double, Binyamin encounters and identifies with his own "feminine" gaze, a gaze materialized in the figure of the double. When Binyamin acknowledges and identifies himself as "feminine" through the double's gaze, he starts a long series of physical rituals, becoming masculine in his body to carry out the national missions. Only when he meets the double's gaze face-to-face—constructed as his own "feminine" gaze— can the older Binyamin establish himself as a normative subject. After gaining the power of the gaze through his double, Binyamin can enter the new Zionist masculine order. From this self-constituting moment on, he can also look at others, especially at women. And, indeed, in one scene in the film, Binyamin gazes through the window at a woman that puts the children's village to sleep—a woman that reminds him, as he says, of his own mother. In the course of the film, he will be able to look at and desire another woman, Miriam.

Binyamin needs his double in order to confirm, time after time, his masculine gaze. That is, in order to see himself, to see his own heterosexual masculine gaze, he needs to look at his queer double who looks back at him. He can never see what his own "other" sees. As Lacan puts it, "[Y]ou can never see me at the point from which I look at you."[33] This is why Binyamin is compelled to return, time after time, even after he completes his masculine training, to Binyamin the child, his own mirror image, his queer double. Through repetitive encounters with his double, Binyamin marks, over and over again, his masculinity. This gendering repetitive process exposes the structural instability of the constitutive apparatus of the Zionist subject that is based upon reiterated signifying practice in order to produce male heteronormativity.

Kaja Silverman distinguishes between the "gaze" and the "look." She argues that the gaze occupies much the same position in relation to the look, as the phallus does to the penis. The gaze, in other words, is the transcendental ideal—omniscient, omnipotent—which the look can never achieve, but to which it ceaselessly aspires. The best the look can hope for is to pose and pass itself off as the gaze.[34] Similarly, the only thing that Binyamin, the new Zionist subject, can hope for is to pass as a phallus, as a gaze, when, actually he needs the "other's" feminine gaze in order to constitute his authority. In other words, the structural need of the Zionist heterosexual gaze for the queer gaze forces heterosexuality to see queerness not as "essentially" different from heterosexual masculinity, but as that which signifies heterosexuality's own internal difference.

Binyamin narrates the film. As a new man, he tells with an authoritative voice the story of his rite of passage into manhood. The fact that his voice-over produces uncanny metaphors in order to tell the story of his masculine construction turns the viewer's attention to the ambivalent position of Binyamin's voice and body, as well as to the ambivalence of the "voice" and "body" of the film itself—to the performativity of apparatus of the cinema that produces a "true" story about the Zionist male subject.

Colonialism, Racism, and the Zionist Biopolitics

The Zionist body Master Narrative must also be understood in terms of race and racism.[35] In her pathbreaking work on Israeli cinema, Ella Shohat exposed the Orientalist colonialism of Zionist cinematic texts that represent pre-Zionist Palestine as a deserted, undeveloped, and unproductive land awaiting Western

penetration and fecundation.[36] The assumption is that the Zionist pioneers, with their enlightened mentality and advanced technology,
bring only beneficial effects on the primitive land and people. Shohat
writes:

> The "pioneer" films . . . claim to initiate the Western spectator into
> Arab culture. The spectator, along with the settlers, comes to
> master, in a remarkably telescoped period . . . the (presumed) codes
> of foreign culture, shown as simple, stable, unselfconscious, and
> susceptible to facile apprehension. Any possibility of dialectic
> interaction and of a dialectical representation of the East/West rela-
> tion is excluded from the outset. The films thus reproduce the colo-
> nialist mechanism by which the Orient, rendered as devoid of any
> active historical or narrative role, becomes the passive object of
> study and spectacle.[37]

Theoretical scholarship in and outside Israel on the question of
Jewish and Zionist gender politics has tended to avoid the question of
Zionist Eurocentrism. While the idea of the Jews as a race was central
to debates about the construction of the Jewish body in the anti-
Semitic European discourse, the racial and racist politics of the Zionist
project itself were almost completely ignored. David Biale is slightly
more attentive to the Orientalist dimension of the Zionist Ashkenazi
sexual culture when he claims:

> For the early Zionists, Oriental Palestine promised the liberation
> of senses from the suffocation of Europe, a suffocation at once tra-
> ditional and bourgeois. The image of the Arab as a sensual sav-
> age played a key role in this mythology: later, when the national
> struggle between Zionism and Palestinians became sharper, the
> Arab was frequently seen as effeminate in opposition to the vir-
> ile modernism of Jewish nationalism. The image of the impotent
> diaspora Jew was now projected onto the Palestinian, who, like
> the exilic Jew, refused to free himself from medieval traditions.[38]

For Biale, the history of the Zionist racial and sexual politics
began only with the Zionists' arrival in Palestine. However, the racial
thinking of the Zionist leaders, which informed their ideas of a new
sexuality, began long before the first Zionist pioneer set foot on
Palestine's land. Nordau's fantasy of a "Muscular Jew" was structured
by his Orientalist perspective of the East. He thought that Jews could
not change their bodies "within the Asiatic savageness, the culture's

enemy."[39] Nordau represents the East as a threat to the integrity and per-
fection of the Zionist male body and sexuality, and thus Zionism must
not "be a withdrawal to barbarism."[40]

Herzl was not different in his Orientalist understanding of the East.
His idea of a new Jewish masculinity was formed, in part at least, by
his Eurocentric dream to establish a European state for the Jews of
Europe in the Middle East. He linked the future Jewish state to the
European colonial world and did not consider the Jews of the Islam
world as partners for nation-building. When he reviews the world's
Jewish population in his book *The State of the Jews* [*Der Judenstaat*,
1896], he represents the Jews of Algeria as the only Arab-Jews, only
because of their "Euro-French" cultural orientation that fit his definition of the Jew as European. The East appears in Herzl's writings only
if it is Westernized, cultured, and civilized. In his utopian 1902 novel
Altneuland [*Old-Newland*], he refers to a "loyal and wise" pure
Sephardi Jew and to an Arab man who dresses in a European suit and
speaks fluent German with a Berlin accent. Otherwise, the East is
seen as premodern and a savage site. In *The State of the Jews,* he
writes: "For Europe, our presence there [in the Middle East] could be
part of a defense wall against Asia. We could be a vanguard of culture
against barbarism."[41]

Herzl's desire for a hypermasculine Jew must be read within this
context. As Boyarin brilliantly shows, Herzl's new Jew is informed by
Christian-European ideals of manhood—the ideal Aryan male. Herzl
thought that in order to solve the problems of anti-Semitism and
the Jews' gender pathology, Jews must convert their religion into
Christianity. Paradoxically, the re-masculinization of the Jewish male
body was involved in turning the Jew into a German-Christian man.
However, when he did not get the Christians' support for his strange
idea of Jewish conversion, Herzl found another solution to the Jews'
masculinity complex. He thought that Jewish men could become more
manly, if they imitated European colonialism. This explains why
Herzl insisted that the Jewish state must be established in Africa or
South America, which, as Boyarin claims, were ideal sites of colonialist
performance of male gendering: "Herzlian Zionism imagined itself as
colonialism because such a representation was pivotal to the entire project of becoming 'white men.' "[42]

Herzl's colonial mimicry was not, as Boyarin suggests, intended
to take a violent form, although it had, and still has, its violent and discriminatory consequences. Boyarin argues that this argument "should

not be read as a trivialization of the disastrous *effects of* this discourse, especially with respect to its primary victims, the Palestinians."[43] Boyarin understands racism as an effect of the Zionist colonial construction of the new Jewish male.

I would like to offer a more complex reading of the relation between the new Zionist body and the Zionist colonial discourse. Rather than understanding race and racism as byproducts or effects of the colonial Zionist new Jew, I shall argue that Zionist racial and racist politics is a constitutive element in the construction of the new male Jewish body and, more specifically, in the construction of the "whiteness" of the new Ashkenazi Zionist male.

Central for Foucault's account of proliferating sexualities and discourses about them is the emergence of "biopower," a political technology that "brought life and its mechanisms into the realm of explicit calculations and made knowledge/power an agent of transformation of human life."[44] In the nineteenth century, the state, through the discourse of sexuality, became occupied with the production, maintenance, and regulation of life and the species—biopolitics. But this does not mean that death was not the aim of the biopower state. Foucault argues that biopower replaces the power of the sovereign "ancient right to *take* life or *let* live" and instead becomes the "power to *foster* life or *disallow* it to the point of death."[45] When Foucault argues that "sex in worth dying for" he means that preserving the regime of sex is worth dying for and that political wars are waged so that populations and their reproduction can be secured. He writes:

> Wars are no longer waged in the name of sovereign who must be defended; they are waged on behalf of the existence of everyone; entire populations are mobilized for the purpose of wholesale slaughter in the name of life necessity: massacres have become vital. . . . The principle underlying the tactics of battle—that one has to be capable of killing in order to go on living—has become the principle that defines the strategy of the states. But the existence in question is no longer the juridical existence of sovereignty; at stake is the biological existence of population. If genocide is indeed the dream of modern powers, this is not because of the recent return of the ancient right to kill; it is because power is situated and exercised at the level of life, the *species,* the *race,* and the large-scale phenomena of population.[46]

However, for Foucault, race and racism are nineteenth-century *effects* of European technologies of sexuality that regulated the hygienic social body. In her postcolonial critique of Foucault's *History of Sexuality,* Ann Stoler argues that racism is the most revaluing effect of biopolitics that bore on the species and its reproduction.[47] She claims that Foucault understood racism as an effect of European sexuality, because colonialism was outside of his analytic scope. The emergence of Western sexuality in the nineteenth century is structurally linked to the imperial project and thus race and racism are constitutive elements of the European sexual social body. She shows how the surveillance of sexuality was manifested also in the colonial landscape. The imperial discourse linked its children's health program to racial survival, tied domestic hygiene to colonial expansion, made childrearing an imperial and class duty, and so on. In short, biopower that produces a normalizing society through the instrumentality of sex was part of the colonial regime.

In Zionist writings, the construction of a new male Jew was structurally intertwined with discourses on the breeding of children, body health, and racial improvement. Zionist thinkers and writers connected national revival with racial upgrading and body hygiene. For example, in his utopian manifesto *The Jewish People and Its Youth* [*Ha'am ha'yehodi ve'hanoar shelo,* 1920], Siegried Bernfeld wrote that "the breeding of small children is a eugenic problem and hygiene is most important."[48] Another Zionist, Shalom Ben-Averaham, in his essay *Sovereignty* [*Komemiyut,* 1922] linked directly, the new Zionist manhood and body health as a primary condition for racial improvement. He writes:

> Fundamental characteristics of the [Jewish] people, characteristics that seemed for hundred of years as basic and natural, like a second nature, suddenly began to change. . . . Many [Zionist] companies [that are concerned with] the upgrading of the race, body education, and the fight over hereditary illnesses . . . paid attention to this gladdening phenomena. . . . Soon we will be a people of Samsons.[49]

Ben-Averaham needs the anti-Semitic image of the diseased Jew in order to produce the notion of the purified and improved new Jewish "race," and thus paradoxically reinforces the same discourse he tries to deconstruct. Contrarily, Boris Schatz, in his novel *Built Up Jerusalem*

[*Yerushalayim ha'benoya,* 1924] displaces the stereotypes of the anti-Semitic discourse:

> Our blood was not so much poisoned . . . in syphilis and other ill-nesses, unlike all the enlightened nations that were struck by it after the world war. The fact that our public was composed of Jews that were gathered from all over the world, and who lived in all sorts of different climates, and even their skin colors were different, was useful to our blood's upgrading and to the improvement of our type in matter and spirit. . . . We brought the best of European culture, we did not take with us the "white slavery" that the cultured nations had suffered from.[50]

The term "white slavery" refers here to the European sexual diseases, and thus Schatz inverts the anti-Semitic association between the figure of the Jew and racial and sexual illnesses, projecting it onto the Europeans themselves. But here lies another paradox that emphasizes the ambivalence of the Zionist racial discourse. For Schatz, Europeans are associated, on the one hand, with "white slavery" and, on the other hand, the Europeans are "enlightened nations." As Shohat eloquently shows, this ambivalent approach toward Europe characterizes the Zionist movement as a whole: "On the one hand, then, Europe represents the locus of progroms, persecution, and anti-Semitism; a place a Jew must abandon in order to be free; on the other, it represents civilization, knowledge, and enlightenment."[51]

This ambivalence also structured the Zionist male body politics. On the one hand, the Nazi is the racist emasculator and, on the other hand, the Aryan male is the model for the Zionist hypermasculinity. These competing notions of masculinity evoke anxiety because the Zionist imitation of European manliness was also necessarily an internalization of the anti-Semitic image of the Jew as degenerated emasculated male. Thus, in order to disavow the anti-Semitism that is structurally embedded within the gentile virility, Zionism needed to project the anti-Semitic image on a closer, domestic, even intimate enemy against which its new Jewish "race" could be asserted.[52] The Zionist biopower society portrayed the Orient's people and land as diseased, plagued, and infected—in short produced them as objects structured by death—from which the purity of the new Jewish "race" must be protected.

In Zionist medical discourse, the East's geography, climate, natural resources, and people were invented, time after time, as objects of death, available for Zionist research and domination. Palestine's land was figured as a locus of unsanitary conditions, polluted water, swamps, and dangerous diseases such as malaria, smallpox, tuberculosis, meningitis to name a few. The poverty and diseases of the Arabs were perceived as an inherent condition of their culture, awaiting redemption by forces of Zionist-Western modernization. Missions of medical doctors, sponsored by Jewish-European philanthropists, were sent to deliver "the first fruits of European civilization [to] the East."[53] Malaria was declared as the number-one enemy of the Zionist project. In 1894, the Zionist doctor Hillel Yafe expressed his frustration at not finding a cure for malaria: "As my experience teaches me, the development of malaria is linked to the quality of the water the natives drink. . . . Everybody knows that a number of kinds of foods cause an intense fever. . . . There is no way we are going to find a vaccine for malaria. On the contrary, once you get ill, you might get it again. . . . What a cursed land!"[54] For the doctor, the East's land is not only a site of unhygienic deadly living conditions, but its people are responsible for spreading the disease. These associations of the land of Palestine and its people with lack of cleanliness and sickness made Zionist doctors feel self-pity for the cost at which they liked to think their dominance was acquired. Disease and its extermination reflected later in Israeli culture through slogans and songs written by leading Israeli poets, such as Averham Shlonski, inventing Zionism as the healer of the "sick" Orient. Similar to the Western literary and cinematic construction of colonialist doctors as cultural icons (for example, Dr. Dolittle), Israeli culture glorified the figure of Dr. Shalomon, the famed doctor who defeated malaria in Petach Tikve, reinforcing the notion of the East as a site of death in a song that goes: "I don't hear birds/ and this is a bad omen/ if birds are not seen/ then death rules here."

Imagery of the diseased land of the East served in Zionist films such as *This Is the Land, Sabra,* and *Collective Adventure* to construct the notion of Palestine as an empty, wild, uncultured land, waiting passively for the scientific enlightened penetration of the Zionist settlers. In the documentary film *Collective Adventure,* the camera pans over the blooming and fertile Jezreel Valley, while an authoritative male voice-over narrates the ideal images: "Two thousand years ago, this was a land of flowing milk and honey. Twenty years ago, this was covered with sands. . . . A generation ago, malaria swamps covered the valley . . . giving life only to mosquitoes." In this scene, not only had Zionism metamorphosed the so-called arid desert into a blooming land, but moreover

Zionism here sees itself as the creator of life itself, brings life to the lifeless Arab land and people. This representation is part of a larger Zionist discursive structure in which, as Edward Said has argued: "The main idea was to not only deny the Palestinians a historical presence as a collectivity but also to imply that they were not a people who had a long-standing peoplehood."[55] In the film *This Is the Land,* a close-up of a jar full of infected swamp water presents to the spectator the deadly hazards that the pioneers are facing as they conquer the wilderness. In another scene, one of the characters links malaria to the Arabs: "We suffer . . . to revive this desert, to defeat the snakes, to weaken this heat, the malaria and the attack of the enemies." The film *Collective Adventure* makes the same racist linkage when the narrator claims: "In the last few years Nazi propaganda in the Near East has been inflamed by hatred in Palestine. . . . In addition to the [fight against] diseases and the Eastern sun, they [the pioneers] have to stand on constant guard defending their home."

The stereotype of the Arab's diseased body is paradoxical and ambivalent. The Zionist medical discourse associated, on the one hand, the violent behavior of bacteria with the Arabs, arguing that Bedouins—as well as Yemeni-Jews—because of their nomadic "nature," carry the virus in their bodies.[56] On the other hand, the Arab body is perceived as being immune to the disease. In a conversation with Herzl, one of the Zionist doctors complained to the leader: "Fever! All the colonies suffer from malaria!"

And Herzl answered: "I will bring in masses of laborers to drain and eliminate the swamps."

"I am afraid they'll all die," the doctor rejoined.

"Nonsense," Herzl responded, "What about the Suez Canal?"

"The Suez Canal was built by African Negroes!" the doctor answered.

But Herzl was not discouraged: "It will cost billions, but will also create billions of new wealth! As workers we might employ such Arabs as are immune to the fever."[57]

Through this ambivalent construction of the diseased Oriental body, Zionism exercised its power and authority. This paradoxical discourse allowed Zionism to exploit Arabs and Arab-Jews as a central cheap labor force in the battle against malaria, and at the same time to blame them for the disease (they are hosting the virus) while not taking responsibility for their health (because they are immune).

This ambivalent view of Arabs' bodies justified and was part of the Zionist colonial project and nation-building. Oriental bodies were invented as having indiscreet anatomy and mysterious physiology, bodies that could be marginalized, sequestered, and disciplined. By inventing the East's population as objects of death, Zionism created internal biologized enemies against whom the Zionist society must defend itself. In the name of maintaining and securing life and the reproduction of the new Jewish "race," the Zionist biopower society kept the right not only to discriminate and to oppress its enemies within—the Palestinians—but also its citizens, the Arab-Jews. Through the discourse of the new male Jew's sexuality, structurally linked to the discourse of hygiene and racial survival, Zionist society reinforced and legitimized its nationalism. Zionist biopower produced a normalizing society through the discourse of sexuality and a form of racism inscribed within it. Through those discourses, Zionism also constructed the "whiteness" of the new Zionist Ashkenazi male.

"White" Sabras

Ashkenazi pioneers in Zionist cinema are articulated as white. However, Ashkenazim are not really white. Some of them are pink, while others are more brownish and have black hair. That is, there are degrees of whiteness/brownness among Ashkenazi Jews. At the same time, Sephardi Jews and Arabs are not all brown or black. Some Moroccan-Jews, for example, have white skin color and blond hair and some Druze have blue eyes and light skin color. Although Ashkenazim are everywhere in Israeli cultural representation, they are rarely identified as whites, contrary to Arab-Jews and Arabs who are always raced or ethnicized as non-white. Precisely because of this and because they are being pictured as the norm, Ashkenazim have enjoyed the privilege of not being part of the racial and ethnic image regime. In Israeli cinema, Ashkenazim constructed the notion that Ashkenazim are seen as a race or ethicity only in contrast to the presence of "truly" raced subjects like Sephardim and Arabs. Ashkenazim do not represent themselves as "whites," but as people who are gendered, sexualized, and classed. In other words, Ashkenazim are not of a certain race or ethnicity, they are just Jews or Israelis.

But this was not always the case for Eastern European Jews. As Sander Gilman describes, the long history of European science viewed Ashkenazi Jews as "blacks."[58] European eighteenth- and nineteenth-century medical discourse saw the "blackness" of the Jews as a sign not only of racial inferiority, but also of the diseased nature of the Jew who suffers from illnesses of the East. It was also claimed that the Jew's diseased Jewishness resulted from living in filth and poverty and from his unhygienic nature. Jews were unable to "pass" as non-Jewish and to escape anti-Semitic persecutions, because their "disease" was marked on their skin. However, a certain shift in the perception of the Jewish "blackness" occurred in the popular and medical imaginary of the nineteenth century. Along with Jewish acculturation, Jews were imagined as having whiter, paler skin color. But not acculturation, nor even baptism, could erase the "blackness" of the Jewish race. The German-Jewish revolutionary and political theorist Moshe Hess wrote:

> Even baptism will not redeem the German Jews from the nightmare of German Jew-hatred. The Germans hate less the religion of the Jews then their race, less their peculiar beliefs then their peculiar noses. . . . Jewish noses cannot be reformed nor black, curly Jewish hair be turned through baptism or coming into smooth hair. The Jewish race is a primal one, which had reproduced itself in its integrity despite climatic influences. . . . The Jewish type is indestructible.[59]

It is not surprising that Hess refers to the notion of Jewish baptism. As we have already seen, Herzl himself thought that by mimicking Christian masculinity Jews could change their feminized body. Gilman notes that Fritz Wittels, a Viennese-Jewish physician and Freud's first biographer, had a Jewish patient who was unhappy about his Jewishness and wanted to be baptized and pass as a Christian. Freud, who heard about the case, understood his patient's desire to pass as a rejection of his father, who was also a Zionist activist. In this case, however, Freud did not link the new strong Zionist male identity with the wish to be racially unmarked.

The Zionist vision of the "Muscular Jew" also expressed Zionism's desire for Jews to pass as white Christian-like male. By "curing" the Jewish "disease" which haunted the poverty and unhygienic conditions of the European diaspora, Zionism could constitute Jews as "white." Through Zionism, the "sickness" of Jewishness could no longer be seen on the skin and Jews could be men like all other (gentile) men: invisible, unmarked, unraced, passing as white people. Zionism allied itself to Western culture and to its ideals of white European male beauty. Thus, for Zionism, Ashkenazim were not just Jews, but more importantly they were part of the Western white race, that is to say, they were the human race.[60]

How can one locate and embody the non-located and disembodied position of Ashkenazi Jews within the particular experience of being white? In his study on whiteness, Richard Dyer argues that the embodiment of whiteness in Western culture involves "something that is in but not of the body."[61] Whiteness is founded on the paradoxical idea that somehow there is in the body something that is not of the body, which can be termed spirit or mind. From this notion, the concepts of white race and imperialism are derived. Dyer argues that to think that some bodies contain spiritual qualities and others do not is what produces white racism; and to think that bodies have inside something that controls them and extends beyond them to control others produces white imperialism. The notion of the white race emphasizes that white people, in contrast to non-white people, cannot be reduced to their bodies and thus to race, because they have more spirit, or soul, in their bodies. By spirit, Dyer means aspiration, awareness of the highest reaches of intellectual comprehension and aesthetic refinement. While white spirit can master the white body, the non-white soul is prey to the promptings and fallibilities of the body. White imperialism is an aspect of both spirit itself and its effect—discovery, science, and nation-building. Imperialism, as an aspect of spirit, is associated with the concept of will—the control of self and others. Dyer writes:

> White identity is founded on compelling paradoxes: a vividly corporeal cosmology that most values transcendence of the body; a notion of being at once a sort of race and the human race, an individual and a universal subject; a commitment to heterosexuality that, for whiteness to be affirmed, entails men fighting against sexual desires and woman having none; a stress on the display of spirit while maintaining a position of invisibility; in short, a need always to be everything and nothing, literally overwhelmingly present and yet apparently absent, both alive and dead.[62]

The Sabra, the native-born Jew in *Eretz Yisrael,* is the Zionist prototype for the "white" male pioneer. As a counter-image of the feminized and passive diasporic Jew, the Sabra was represented in Zionist national mythology as a healthy, strong, hard-working man, as well as being conceived out of pre-genital reproduction. The Sabra was born from nature itself, as in Moshe Shamir's canonic novel *Bemo yadav* [*In His Own Hands*], which opens with the famed sentence: "Elik was born from the sea." The spiritual birth of the new Ashkenazi masculinity constitutes the idea of the Zionist man as having and not having a body at the same time, as being "in" and "out" of the body simultaneously, and thus as being "white." The birth from water gives the Zionist male magical and even "white" Christian qualities (baptismal water, Genesis) and makes his body divine, a kind of superman who is free of movement—and thus possessing control—over time and space. He is both of humanity and above it.

In the opening sequence, the film *Avodah* represents the rebirth of the new Zionist male through the purifying power of water. The scene starts with a close-up of the worn-out shoes of the new pioneer, marching through arid land, approaching a water reservoir, where he washes his weary feet. The camera then tilts up over his body and exposes his smiling face, looking proudly and in a visionary manner at the new land, subjectifing the landscape through his sovereign gaze. Moving through a match-cut to the next shot, the camera tilts up over a palm tree, establishing the phallic image of the Zionist male. The Zionist Ashkenazi male body contains inner visionary, dreamy, and idealistic qualities, which are associated with the Zionist missions of nation-building and of the conquering of the wilderness. This representation of the Zionist body assumes the unproblematic availability of Palestine's land, a land outside history and culture, a site for the elaboration of "white" Ahskenazi power. The Sabra is established as a creator, blessed with divine prerogative over the "timeless" land, and thus elides the existence of another civilization in the "Promised Land." By constructing a spiritual and an ahistorical new Jewish male who was "born from nothingness," Zionism disavowed the materiality of the body and its own bodily legacy, as well as disavowing the materiality and the history of Palestine's "body," which like the Sabra's body, was conceived from the void.

The muscles of the Zionist pioneer articulate "white" masculinity. The body shape is draw from ancient Greek male visual culture. The Zionists often imagined themselves as figures from the Greek mythology, like Hercules and Prometheus.[63] In the gymnastic scene in *This Is the Land,* athletes are shot in postures that evoke the classic world's iconography. Zionist directors were influenced also by the twenties Soviet cinema's standards of beauty. Filmmakers such as Nathan Axelrod, Baruch Agadati, and Helmer Lerski were not only inspired by Sergei Eisenstein's use of montage, but also by his representation of the male body.[64] As in Eisenstein's films, male bodies in Zionist films are forever striving upward, always shot against the promised land's horizon—visual signifiers for the aspiration and aesthetic refinement of the Ashkenazi pioneers.

In films such as *Sabra* and *This Is the Land,* the Zionist male's capacity to withstand pain and torture due to the climate, disease and hard work in Palestine emphasizes his spiritual qualities and resourcefulness. The muscles symbolize of power, strength, and hardness, like the hard stones that the pioneers had to uproot while cultivating the land. In *Adama,* the hero, Binyamin, builds up his muscles by tearing out a massive stone from the ground that seems to him "like a great tooth." It is not only muscles that are "cut" into the body as into stone, but also the cinematic "cut" of the montage editing—as in the well-drilling scene in *Avodah*—that cuts the contours and the muscles of the Zionist male body. For Binyamin, as for other Zionist cinematic heroes, building bodies through hard work is a triumph of mind over matter, imagination over flesh. In Zionist films, the Zionist male body is half-naked, tanned, and hairless most of the time. The nakedness makes the power of the body visible. The tan comes to signify the pioneers' hard work under the bare sun. Body hair is "animal-like," and thus the hairless body of the Zionist male connotes striving over nature.

Arabs' muscles are rarely visible in Zionist cinematic imagery. The Arab male body is usually covered and dressed, which signifies his lack of power and strength. They are seen on the sides of the frame, shot from a distance, as part of the scenery that the pioneers' gaze controls. Contrary to the ordered and disciplined Zionist body, the Arab body is represented as fluid, amorphous, and out of control. In *Sabra,* crosscut editing contrasts the organized bodies of the pioneers dancing the circular Hora dance, symbolizing harmony and collectivity, with the possessed wild bodies of the Arabs practicing a kind of pagan ritual. One of them floats into ecstasy, tearing his clothes from his body and crying out: "O righteous Allah, curse those who caused our misfortune!" The others gather around him, twisting their bodies while praying: "Mohammed, his only prophet!" The Arab body is represented here as borderless, irrational—irrationality often associated with the Muslim religion itself—and as posing a threat to the integrity and survival of the Zionist "self." Only the hard, visible, bounded body can resist being submerged into the horror of non-whiteness.[65]

Hygiene and cleanliness also become central to the demarcation of the Zionist body's boundaries and the policing of social hierarchies. In another scene in *Sabra,* the camera pans over the disgusted facial expressions of the Zionists, who must, out of politeness, taste the inedible Arab food, served and eaten with the hands in a "barbaric," "unsanitary," non-European fashion. The Zionist body must protect itself from the fluidity of the Arab body, as it must from other Eastern habits and hazards, in order to secure its "white race" and "self."

The Zionist "white" body, as a body that is extended beyond itself, is a body that is guided by internal divine light, an enlightened awareness of higher meanings, hidden from non-whites who cannot see beyond their mortal bodies. As Ella Shohat and Robert Stam argue, the trope of light/darkness is explicit in the Enlightenment ideal of rational clarity: "Earlier religious Manicheisms of good and evil become transmuted into the philosophical binarism of rationality/light versus irrationality/darkness. Sight and vision are attributed to Europe, while the 'other' is seen as living in 'obscurity,' blind to moral knowledge. Color, complexion, and even climatic hierarchies emerge, privileging light/day over darkness/night and light skin over dark skin."[66]

In the film *This Is the Land,* images of the Zionist pioneers building a new power station are narrated by a male voice-over that says: "The river Jordan, whose water once flowed unused into the Dead Sea, now brings prosperity to the land." Those images are then cut by inter titles: "WATER—POWER—LIGHT—LIFE." As with the birth of the enlightened Sabra from water, here also the land is being "rebirthed" by water that produces power and light. The Sabra, as the creator of life, brings prosperity to a land that is structured by death. The difficulty of Palestine's terrain, its unfamiliarity and its dangers, provide the opportunity for the Zionist male subject to exercise his "white" spirit and power. He has adjusted to the East's climate and geography, like the Arabs, but his body is superior, because he possesses a spirit that non-whites lack. Further, his superior body and mind enable him to solve the problems of the Arabs who cannot sort things out for themselves.

In *Sabra,* the Zionists help the Arabs to discover that it is their own Arab sheik who is responsible for their shortage of water and not the Zionists, as the sheik has made them believe. The Askkenazi male subject is constructed as superior, yet also, what Dyer calls an "everyman"— a white subject that can intervene anywhere, capable of doing the job of colonial world improvement.[67]

To be white sometimes means to be dead. "What makes whites special," Dyer argues, "is the light within, though modern man must struggle to see, let alone regain this. This light, which is white, is dirtied ('stained') by blood, passion, movement, which is to say, isn't it, life . . . the very struggle of whiteness is a sign of whiteness, but . . . to recapture whiteness is also to shed life, which can mean nothing else than death."[68]

This paradoxical embodiment of "whiteness," as presence and absence of life and death simultaneously, has a structural analogy with the paradoxical embodiment of the perfect national body, which is also a dead body. The ideal Zionist body is the dead pioneer's soldier's body—a body sacrificed for national ideology. In order to justify the death of the individual in battle, the national discourse subordinates the death of the pioneer into the imagined community by blurring and eliding its materiality and by granting it a higher transcendental national metaphoric meaning. In other words, the private death is canceled and incorporated into the national revival process. Like religion, nationalism also, as Benedict Anderson argues, "concerns itself with the links between the dead and the yet unborn, the mystery of regeneration. . . . It is the magic of nationalism to turn chance into destiny."[69] In a certain sense, the dead soldier becomes some kind of living-dead figure, a zombie, who is physically dead, yet he is still alive in the collective memory of the nation.[70] The dead body is not only the ideal national body, but also embodies the essence of its own "whiteness" through a similar paradoxical concretization. Thus, the national myth of the "living-dead" must also be understood in racial terms. The myth of the Zionist national dead body is a "white" Ashkenazi myth.

The dead body of the Ashkenazi pioneer is never visualized in Zionist imagery. By eliding the representation of the materiality of death, Zionist cinema subjects the pioneer's dead body to the national collectivity and produces it as an oxymoronic metaphor of the "living-dead." In the film *This Is the Land,* a pioneer who collapses in the field due to hard work is merged into the national earth—and thus into the national discourse—by a cinematic dissolve. The dissolve suits perfectly the figure of the national "living-dead," because the dissolve itself, as Christian Metz observed, "is a dying figure, a figure which is dying right from the start . . . : two images go to meet one another, but they go backwards, turning their backs on each other."[71] The two figures have more in common: They both resist the divisions imposed by reality as they abolish the very duality of objects, thus their "magical" quality. But the dissolve can also unmask the fantasmatic consistency of life and death produced by national discourse. As Metz claimed, "by *hesitating* a little on the threshold of textual bifurcation, the text [that is, the dissolve] makes us attend more closely to the fact that it performs a weaving operation, to the fact that it is always adding something."[72] The dissolve makes us aware of the very process of the cinematic suturing, aware of the actual workings of nationalism.

If the spirit controls the Zionist "white" male body, it also masters its sexuality. Although the ideology of erotic liberation was a necessary part of Zionism's revolt against the bourgeois culture of the diaspora, it was never a means for individual fulfillment. Instead, one must sacrifice family life and erotic relations for the fulfillment of national goals. As David Biale argues, asceticism and the sublimation of sexual desire in the service of the nation were common themes in Zionist discourse.[73] In *Sabra,* one pioneer's girlfriend tries to seduce her lover with a provocative European dress and wastes precious water on a luxury bath. The pioneer condemns her inappropriate behavior: "You only know how to drink, while we go hungry. You would have danced all your life, but here dancing is death. Your desire: lust of the flesh. And me: action and work." Sexual impulses are present within the Zionist man, but he must see beyond them in order to be truly "white."

The rejection of the sexual "excess" of the Jewish woman in *Sabra* points to the Zionist gender politics according to which Ashkenazi women, unlike Ashkenazi men, do not have or should not have sexual impulses. Their sexuality is manifested only in their duty to serve Zionist men and the nation by bearing offspring. This construction of Ashkenazi male sexuality enables Zionism to regulate sexuality and to channel it to national goals. It also portrays the Zionist male subject as superior to other gendered and raced forms of (inferior) sexual subjects who fall easily into the temptations of the flesh.

One of the major fears of the Ashkenazi pioneer is the sexual excess and the reproduction of the Arabs. Because Arabs are perceived as having no control over their bodies and sexuality, they are represented not only as being better at sex, but also as being better in reproduction. The construction of the Arabs as raising large families expresses the Zionist anxiety of being swamped and engulfed by Arab multitudes. This Zionist "white" paranoia appears in *Sabra* in the representation of the Arabs as an enormous war machine, composed of numerous blood-lusting warriors who attack the outnumbered pioneers. Although the pioneer settlers have no weapons, they succeed in defeat-

ing the Arabs' mechanisms of war, while the Zionists own fighting apparatus is disavowed.

Early Zionist cinema constructed, through various visual and narrative tropes (pioneering, gymnastics, allegories of bodybuilding and
nation-building, references to ancient Hebrew mythic heroes), the
Zionist fantasy of making the Jewish male body beautiful. Zionist
films linked the new Zionist manhood and body hygiene as a condition for "racial" improvement and nation-building. Zionist racial and
racist politics was a constitutive element in the construction of the new
male Jew's body. This discourse also articulates the "whiteness" of the
Ashkenazi masculine national identity. The "whiteness" of the
Ashkenazi pioneers is based upon paradoxes: having a body and transcendence of the flesh; commitment to heterosexuality and straggle
against sexual passions, being a presence and absence, alive and dead
at the same time. These paradoxes produce the Ashkenazi Zionist
identity as "white," but also point to the internal ambivalence and structural fluidity of subjectivity that claims to be invisible and universal.

2 | Cannon Fodder
National Death, Homoeroticism, and Male Masochism in the Military Film

Death is to [male] friendship what marriage is to romance.

—David M. Halperin,
One Hundred Years of Homosexuality:
And Other Essays on Greek Love, 1990

Death on the battlefield as a fundamental concept of Israeli society played a crucial role in the heroic-nationalistic film genre.[1] This genre was related to the emergence of a generation of native-born Israelis who formed, in different military organizations, a worldview in which military force would provide a solution for national problems. The desire for power was integrated with a cult of heroism characterized by a high level of pathos and readiness to die for the homeland. The value of self-sacrifice was shaped by heroic myths of fierce Jewish warriors in the Bible and the story of Masada, as well as by modern myths such as that of Joseph Trumpeldor, the one-armed hero of Tel-Hai who, near death in combat, allegedly proclaimed: "It is good to die for our country."

This nationalistic mythology was represented in a long line of films from the fifties to the late sixties, among them *Hill Twenty-four Doesn't Answer* (Thorold Dickinson, 1954), *Pillar of Fire* (Larry Frish, 1959), *They Were Ten* (Baruch Dienar, 1960), *Clouds over Israel* (Ilan Eldad, 1962), *What a Gang!* (Ze'ev Havatzelet, 1962), *Rebels against the Light* (Alexander Ramati, 1964), *He Walked through the Fields* (Yoseph Millo, 1967), *Every Bastard a King* (Uri Zohar, 1968). According to the historian Anita Shapira, two historical events, the Arab rebellion (1936) and the Holocaust, caused the shift from a defensive ethos to an offensive ethos:

> Up until the world war, the dominant mythos had been that of the pioneer and the worker. That myth expected young people to be faithful workers on the soil of the homeland and to defend it if necessary. Now the message was communicated that the role of the worker continued to be important but was secondary to the role of the fighter. The message imparted by the heroic myths stated that youth was destined to carry to completion the Jewish struggle in Palestine—to fight a war of national liberation—and that this was the first national priority.[2]

The heroic-nationalistic genre propagated this new ethos that was shaped in the late thirties. In the film *He Walked through the Fields,* for example, the platoon commander of the Palmach (a pre-state Zionist underground organization) says to Uri, the hero of the film: "If not for the Palmach, there will be no kibbutz." The ethos of the new Jewish warrior was fully constituted in the War of Independence (1947–1949) and through the establishment of the Israel Defense Force (IDF) and the State of Israel in 1948. The national slogan of those days, "all the country a front and all the people an army," reflected the shift from the social status of the pioneer to that of the warrior. Instead of the pioneering group, it was now the nation-state that embodied the collective whole for which the warrior was supposed to sacrifice his life.

Israeli films, among other cultural products, were concerned with constructing a myth, which would mask death in war and emphasize the meaningfulness of fighting and sacrifice. As George Mosse has argued, "The Myth of the War Experience transcended death in the war, giving a happy ending to the war's drama: those who sacrificed their lives will be resurrected; indeed they are already among us."[3] In the context of the heroic-nationalistic genre, it was the new Israeli fighter who replaced the pioneer as the national figure of the "living-dead." As Ella Shohat has claimed, "The death of the protagonists . . . is allegorically compensated for by the rebirth of the country—the ultimate protagonist of the film[s]."[4] Or in terms of the body, the private death and the materiality of the male body were elided and incorporated into the national body's revival process. This myth, explained Mosse, "help[s] to overcome the fear of death and dying. The expectation of an eternal and meaningful life—the continuation of a patriotic mission—not only seemed to transcend death itself but also inspired life before death. . . . [I]ts true importance was apparent only after the war, when it could overcome the sense of loss many veterans felt for their fallen comrades and help fashion a new solidarity."[5] According to this nationalist logic, the more blurred the identity of the fallen soldier, the more powerful the collective national identity becomes. Death is decontextualized from the body of the soldier and thus shared by everyone. Therefore, as Benedict Anderson has argued, the empty Tomb of the Unknown Soldier becomes the "hallmark of modern nations":[6] "Void as these tombs are of identifiable mortal remains or immortal souls, they are nonetheless saturated with ghostly *national* imaginings."[7] According to Anderson, the production of the imagined national identity is based upon the simultaneous existence of subjects who do not know each other personally. Thus the lack of specificity of the body in the Tomb of the Unknown Soldier nourishes the communal imagination and serves as a powerful source for national identification.

In *He Walked through the Fields,* based on Moshe Shamir's 1947 famed nationalist novel by the same name, Uri's death in not shown.[8] Instead of an image of his dead body, the film freezes the frame of Uri's surprised face, a second before he was shot. The cinematic freeze-frame becomes a metonymic signifier of the threshold between life and death, establishing the national myth of the "living-dead." As I have already argued in the first chapter, the lap dissolve symbolizes the merger of the Zionist male body into the national discourse and it perfectly suits the figure of the "living-dead" as the lap dissolve itself is a "dying figure." As in the Zionist cinema, the frozen image of Uri's face dissolves into an image of the sea from which new immigrants arrive in Israel. Uri's life, sacrificed in a diversion operation of an explosion of a bridge, enabled the safe arrival of the immigrants, and therefore paved the way for the constitution of the Israeli imagined community. His body has not only transcended death, but has also dissolved and given meaning to other bodies, especially to the national body.

In this national myth, war was displayed as an education in masculinity. The ideal of manliness was represented as a symbol of personal and national regeneration. As Mosse suggests, "Manhood was cast in the warrior image, symbolizing youth grown to maturity without losing its attributes of youthfulness. . . . Youth and death were closely linked in that myth: youth as symbolic of manhood, virility, and energy, and death as not death at all but sacrifice and resurrection."[9]

During and after the War of Independence, the literary figure of Uri became an influential cultural icon of the beautiful, young male Sabra who died tragically on the nation's altar, inspiring Israeli youth to accept fighting and sacrifice as the special mission of the generation. The filmic adaptation of the novel was released after the smashing victory of the Israeli army in the Six Days War (1967). Uri's heroic deed, an expression of an ideal and courageous masculinity, suited the atmosphere of vigor and military superiority of those days. Uri also gave rise to the first Israeli male film star, Assi Dayan, playing the role of the handsome Sabra. Assi Dayan was the son of Moshe Dayan, the famed one-eyed Israeli commander of the Palmach and of the War of Independence, who later became IDF Chief of Staff and (during the production of the film) Israel's Minister of Defense. The worldwide military prestige of the father gave an additional masculine glamour to the son's stardom. (In a later career, Assi Dayan became a film director whose work has tried to demystify his and his father's male image.)

Mosse writes that in the myth of war "the obvious fact that soldiers were men was emphasized in order to project a moral posture exemplifying courage, strength, hardness, control over passions, and the ability to protect the moral fabric of society by living a so-called manly life. This life was lived outside the family structure, wholly within a camaraderie of males."[10] There is an important aspect of masochism at play here. Masochism plays a crucial role in the construction of the male soldier's body as a hard, strong, and perfect war machine. In his study of the Freikorps soldiers, Klaus Theweleit argues that only the hard, visible, bounded body can resist being submerged into menacing liquidity, associated with women and the enemy. What the soldier really fears and thus displaces onto the "other," is the eruption of floods pent up in himself, libidinal energies that have "hitherto been forbidden, buried beneath the surface."[11] The male soldier reacts to this threat by standing firm, asserting his discrete identity, his fixed boundaries, through "a kind of sustained erection of the whole body."[12] In effect, he transforms his corporeal boundaries into a dam to hold back the floods threatening him both from inside and outside.

Theweleit writes: "The most urgent task of the man of steel is to pursue, to dam in and to subdue any force that threatens to transform him back into the horribly disorganized jumble of flesh, hair, skin, bones, intestines, and feelings that calls itself human."[13] The strengthening of the soldier's body begins in training, where the penalty takes the form of an assault on the bodily periphery. "Every exercise," Theweleit observes, "reaches the 'ultimate limits,' the point where pain shifts to pleasure. . . . The body swallows attack after attack until it becomes addicted. Every exertion becomes a 'means of enhancing an already intoxicated conciseness, of adding strength to strength.'"[14] Rituals of pain and suffering are common in the heroic-nationalistic genre. The soldier was willing to sacrifice his body to tortures and humiliation—up to death—in order to serve the national ideals. Masochism was not a means of individual sexual gratification, but rather a means for the fulfillment of the national goals. Individual masochistic pleasures were disavowed and the erotic energies were channeled into the tasks of nation-building.

The critical Israeli military films of the eighties exposed and challenged the masochism that was embodied in the heroic-nationalistic genre.[15] In an important essay, Judd Ne'eman traces subversive trends in the eighties' Israeli cinema "exhibiting a dystopian view of Zionism along with a pronounced nihilistic temper,"[16] resulting from the drastic social and political changes following the Six Day War and the Yom Kippur War (1973). "While on the surface," Ne'eman argues, this "political cinema voiced the dissent ideology of the elite, in its inner structure it articulated a much more radical critique of Zionism. The critique . . . exceeded in its rigor and dissidence the protest discourse of the political left."[17] Discussing the military film corpus, he suggests that those films that challenged the ideal of self-sacrifice for the nation were structured by an existential philosophy in which the soldier faced a pointless and meaningless death—a death without nationalist significance. We can also read Ne'eman's claim in terms of the male body. In the military films of the eighties the warrior's body loses his metaphoric transcendental position—abandons his status as the mythical "living-dead"—and returns to its physical corporeality of being only flesh, blood, and bones. However, Ne'eman argues that in those films the body takes a higher transcendental meaning, although contradictory to the national ideal: a nihilistic existential meaning.

In a sense, Ne'eman's argument reinforces and reproduces the rhetoric of the national story, which is a rhetoric that elides and disavows the materiality of the warrior's body in favor of a transcendental meaning. Thus, in order to avoid a metaphoric representation of the body, I would like to examine the concrete and materialist borders of the body; to disembody the body from the transcendental sublime metaphorization and to explore the physical parts of the warrior's body, and the pleasures and anxieties they produce. By contextualizing and marking the physicality and materiality of the dematerialized national body, the enslavement of the body to the metaphysical national ideals can be challenged.

In military films such as *Paratroopers* (Judd Ne'eman, 1977), *Repeat Dive* (Shimon Dotan, 1982), *Himo, King of Jerusalem* (Amos Guttman, 1987), and *One of Us* (Uri Barbash, 1989), the Israeli male soldier masochistically seeks emotional and/or physical suffering and pain—sometimes ending in death—not to achieve a mythical national status, but rather to express a desire for lost queer attachments and identifications. He disavows, through masochistic agony, his submission to the Law of the Zionist Father and to the normative pressure of male sexuality. The hero experiences an "historical trauma" in which he is scarred by lack that prevents his reentry into the Zionist "dominant fiction."[18] The soldier's historical trauma manifests itself as a compulsion to repeat painful and agonizing experiences, which undermine the illusion of coherence and control of the dominant male order, and through which the soldier produces his masochistic pleasure.[19] In some of the films, the soldier inscribes on his flesh a subversive discourse that emphasizes the materiality of the body and of sexual desire and thus radiates negativity inimical to the submission and appropriation of the male body to the national ideology. These films focus obsessively and sometimes erotically on the physical and psychic mutilation of the soldier who fails to aspire to mastery positions of the dominant masculinity.[20] By presenting this failure, the military films of the eighties mark a crisis in Israeli male subjectivity that took place after the 1973 War and accelerated due to traumatic events, such as the war in Lebanon and the Intifada.

Masochism and Male Subjectivity

Culturally, masochism for the male means an assumption of a "feminine" position. In his attempts to solve the clinical and theoretical problems of masochism, Freud argued that the perversion of masochism situates its sufferer as a woman. Discussing male masturbation fantasies, he wrote:

> [Their] manifest content of being gagged, bound, painfully beaten, whipped, in some way maltreated, forced into unconditional obedience, dirtied, and debased. . . . [I]f one has an opportunity of studying cases in which the masochistic phantasies have been especially richly elaborated, one quickly discovers that they place the subject in a characteristically female situation.[21]

Although Freud saw in masochism a constitutive element of both male and female subjectivity, it is only female masochism that was considered natural, while male masochism was considered pathological.[22] This argument can be explained through Freud's theorization of the beating fantasies. Boys and girls are subject to unconscious fantasy that they are being beaten—that is, "loved"—and the one who beats and loves them is the father. While the girl's fantasy is accepted as normal, the boy's involves gender trouble. For the boy to be beaten/loved by the father indicates a "feminine" or a homosexual position.[23]

Theodor Reik reaches similar conclusions and argues that "the male sex is more masochistic than the female."[24] Reik suggests that, even if the woman is clinically masochistic, she still does not exceed her subjectivity. Conversely, the male masochist abandons completely his normative subjectivity, and crosses the border into the "alien" zone of womanhood. He writes:

> The woman's masochistic phantasy very seldom reaches the pitch of savage lust, of ecstasy, as does that of the man. Even the orgy in the phantasy does not ascend in so steep a curve. There is nothing in it of the wildness of the chained Prometheus, rather something of Ganymede's submission. One does not feel anything of the cyclonelike character that is so often associated with masculine masochism, that blind unrestricted lust of self-destruction. The masochistic phantasy of woman has the character of yielding and surrender rather than that of the rush ahead, of the orgiastic cumulation, of the self-abandonment of man.[25]

In his discussions about the structure and etiology of masochism, Freud clings to the argument that masochism is an integral and complementary part of sadism. He understands the mechanism of passive/active transitions as a crucial difference between masochism and sadism, and assumes that the masochist was initially a sadist, or at least experienced a sadistic pleasure. As such, Freud realizes masochism as the passive opposite of sadism. Masochism represents a change in the aim ("passive" or "active") and object ("self" or "other"), but does not reflect a change in the content of the instinct.[26]

In his study on masochism, Gilles Deleuze challenges the Freudian structure of a sadomasochistic entity. He distinguishes between sadism and masochism and considers sadomasochism to be a semiological and clinical impossibility, a mixup of qualitative and structural differences of the two perversions. "As soon as we read Masoch," he writes, "we become aware that his universe has nothing to do with that of Sade."[27] Deleuze develops a theoretical model of masochism that is focused on the suffering position of the male. Masochism involves a relationship between a man and a cold maternal figure named by Deleuze as the "oral mother." Unlike Freud, Deleuze sees the mother—and not the father—as the loved representative of the punishment. The male masochist and the oral mother establish a contract in which the male gives up his masculine potency and is reborn as a new unvirile man, while the mother gets the phallus. Deleuze emphasizes that, at the same time, it is the male who constructs the oral mother. He argues that in the male masochistic fantasy "*it is not the child but a father that is being beaten.*"[28] He writes:

> A contract is established between the hero and the woman, whereby at a precise point in time and for a determinate period she is given every right over him. By this means the masochist tries to exorcise the danger of the father and ensure that the temporal order of reality and experience will be in conformity with the symbolic order, in which the father has been abolished for all time. Through the contract . . . the masochist . . . ensures that he will be beaten . . . What is beaten, humiliated, and ridiculed in him is the image and likeness of the father, and the possibility of the father's aggressive return. . . . The masochist thus liberates himself in preparation for a rebirth in which the father will have no part.[29]

Kaja Silverman warns us of a "utopian" reading of Deleuze's concept of masochism, in which the father is forever expelled from the Symbolic and loses his authority and power over the son.[30] Thus, following Deleuze, she proposes to read male masochism as a form of suspense or deferral—masochism as a disavowal of male submission to the Law of the Father. For Silverman, this is a part of the definition of perverse sexuality that sets against normative male sexuality.

Deleuze links masochistic disavowal to fetishism. Masochistic fetishism disavows the father's functions, his authority and power over the son, and gives the phallic power to the mother. Masochistic disavowal exalts the mother to an idealized image in the son's fetishistic wish to reunite with her and to be reborn as a new sexless man who represents the denial of the father's sexuality. Hence, the masochist's obsession with fetish objects like shoes, furs, and whips. Deleuze stresses the fact that the goal of the male masochist is not to destroy the paternal authority, but rather to disavow and to suspend it in the ideal, to neutralize it in a frozen fetishistic image. He writes:

> Disavowal should perhaps be understood as the point of departure of an operation that consists neither in negating nor even destroying, but rather in radically contesting the validity of that which is: it suspends belief in and neutralizes the given in such a way that a new horizon opens beyond the given and in place of it . . . fetishism is first of all a disavowal ("No, the woman does not lack a penis"); secondly it is a defensive neutralization (since contrary to what happens with negation, the knowledge of situation as it is persists, but in the suspended, neutralized form); in the third place it is a protective and idealizing neutralization (for the belief in a female phallus is itself experienced as a protest of the ideal against the real; it remains suspended or neutralized in the ideal, the better to shield itself against the painful awareness of reality).[31]

The male masochist's disavowal of the phallic law suspends the sexual gratification that arrives with pain. The suspension of orgasmic gratification expels, as it were, the symbolic likeness to the father's genital. As Reik proposes, masochism is not so much pleasure in pain, nor even pleasure in punishment. The masochist produces his pleasure by disavowing the pain inflicted on him: He disavows pain and humiliation precisely at the moment he experiences it. The pleasure is in the disavowal of suffering which comes later and is made possible by the punishment. Suffering is not the cause of pleasure itself, but the precondition for achieving it.[32]

In this chapter, I shall focus on the masochistic practice of male soldiers who seek pain and passivity as a way to act out their queer identification with other soldiers, as well as to subvert the fixity of the phallic law. They constitute a significant political form of resistance to the phallic construction of masculinity and heterosexual power. However, masochism, as Paul Smith argued, can subvert and assert the dominant order of masculinity at the same time: "Male masochism is at first a way of not having to submit to the law, but, equally important, it turns out to be a way of not breaking (with) the law, either. Masochism might well bespeak a desire to be both sexes at once, but it depends upon the definitional parameters of masculinity and femininity that undergird our current cultural contexts."[33]

I shall discuss films that use the masochistic formation in order to reaffirm heterosexual masculinity by disavowing queerness and by exercising sadistic power on the "other." In this case, the heterosexual subject is constituted through the force of exclusion of queerness, one which produces a constitutive outside the subject, but which is, after all, "inside" the subject as its own constructing repudiation. I shall also point to films in which their heroes proclaim that their masculine meaning comes from the "other" and therefore prostrate themselves before the gaze, submitting to punishment, pain, and self-abandonment.

Male Fantasies

Paratroopers was the first film that critiqued and deconstructed Israeli male military manhood. The film is divided into two parts. The first part focuses on Wiseman (Moni Moshonov), a frightened, yet motivated soldier who longs to be a paratrooper and who is victimized and abused by his sadistic commander Yair (Gidi Gov), and the other soldiers. Wiseman fails to adjust to the normative military masculine order, collapses under the disciplinary and social pressure of the army, and eventually commits suicide by throwing himself on a live hand grenade during one of the drills. The second part of the film focuses on the emotional breakdown of Yair, who feels guilty about Wiseman's death and who is being prosecuted for it. Yair finds within himself weakness, fears, and doubts—emotions that made him abuse Wiseman—and thinks of quitting the army. However, at the end of the film, Wiseman's suicide case is covered up and Yair returns to his platoon.

As a weak and "weepy" man, Wiseman cannot stand the pressure that the military machine puts on the individual. He is motivated (he raises his army profile in order to be accepted to the paratroop unit), however he is totally unaware of his inability to perform his duty. His body is marked as "feminine," delicate, lean, light in skin color, lacking "manly" hair. He is positioned in the film as the binary opposite of another soldier, Yenoka (Moti Shiran), who has a muscular, strong, firm, dark, and hairy body. (The fact that Wiseman is Ashkenazi and Yenoka is a Sephardi Jew is crucial to the way heterosexual fears and desires are constructed in Israeli film). The difference between Yenoka's "masculine" body and Wiseman's "feminine" body is represented in one of the first scenes of the film in which the platoon doctor asks for a volunteer to demonstrate how to stop hemorrhages. "Preferably a lean

Figure 1. "Wow, what an ass!" The feminization of the male body of Wiseman (Moni Moshonov, center) in Judd Ne'eman's *Paratroopers*. Courtesy of Judd Ne'eman.

body," Yenoka volunteers first, but he is sent back because his body is too muscular. Wiseman is recommended by one of the commanders and he is asked to take off his clothes in front of the platoon. For the soldiers, Wiseman's feminized body becomes an object of sexual harassment, as well as of homoerotic attraction. The remarks that the soldiers make in reference to his body are remarks that are usually directed toward women ("Wow, what an ass!"). While pointing to Wiseman's body, the doctor says to the soldiers, "Make out with each other." He adds, "The most dangerous area is the balls." The doctor turns the soldiers' attention to one of the most sensitive and vulnerable parts of the male body and to the erotic pleasure that can be produced by exposing it to another man's touch. Little wonder, then, that the camera next cuts to a shot of Yenoka eating a cucumber—that in this context also acquires a phallic meaning—gazing with desire on Wiseman's half-naked body.

Male fantasies are inscribed on Wiseman's effeminate body. In the communal shower, the sexual harassment and the homoerotic fears and desires of the soldiers become more intense. Yenoka remarks on Wiseman's femme body: "Look what a smooth skin he has." He then grasps Wiseman's body from behind, as if he is going to fuck him, while he massages his chest and calls: "Look, he has tits." The camera presents a spectacular nude shot of the male body and focuses especially on the male penis.[34] Through songs and army slang, the soldiers mock their bodies, demystify their penises as signs of power and mastery, displaying male lack, castration, and sexual impotence. One of the soldiers calls: "Once my dick was doing something, now nothing, it became floppy." The soldiers, thus, expose the imaginary overlapping between the penis and the omniscient, and omnipotent ideal of the phallus. However, this self-contempt and self-humiliation of the male body also represents male anxieties of losing power and authority. One of the soldiers sings the following song:

> Dear commissioner, amiable commissioner
> I'm going to tell you straight to your face.
> As a result of hazing and lack of sleep all year long
> My dick that was like a cannon
> Now fails the test.
> My girlfriend that was excellent
> Now fucks with desk-job male soldiers.
> I respectfully ask you
> Please arrange that I will get a hard on.

In his song, the soldier blames military oppression for causing his impotence. However, he uses phallocentric militaristic metaphors to describe his sexual failure ("my dick that was like a cannon"). On the one hand, the military machine is imagined as granting the male soldier sexual domination, a metaphor for occupation power. On the other hand, the army authority is seen as threatening, because it demands total devotion of the soldier's body. The soldier is conflicted between his duty to sacrifice his body—in death—for the national needs and his desire for individual fulfillment. (One of the soldier says: "If I won't return home on Saturday, my dick will return on a stretcher"). Paradoxically, the soldier blames the military institution for his impotence, yet asks for its advice and solution ("I respectfully ask you / Please arrange that I will get a hard on"). This ambivalence toward the idea of self-sacrifice attests to the crisis of Israeli male subjectivity, since the mid-seventies. However, the film tries to resolve this conflict, not in political or social terms, but rather by projecting the castration threat onto the woman and other "unheroic" and "unmanly" males. Apparently, the soldier's treacherous girlfriend socializes with other men who assume his sexual functions. In other words, the gender anxieties of the Israeli heterosexual male are structured by displaced national fears.

Those male fears of emasculation are further displaced onto Wiseman's sissy body. Wiseman is ashamed to take off his underwear in front of the other soldiers and to expose his penis that presumably does not fit male standards. He is raped by the soldiers who sadistically and aggressively pull down his underwear, while Yenoka calls: "Look at his dick, you can hold it with tweezers!" Wiseman's body is fetishized by the other soldiers who examine the size of his penis. What is dramatized in the scene is the splitting of levels of belief, which Freud regarded as a key feature of the logic of disavowal in fetishism. Hence, the implication for the male soldier: "*I know* it's not true that men have a small penis," *but still,* "this man has a small dick." By disavowing their own anxiety of a small dick, the soldiers displace, through a sadistic activity, their fears of castration onto the "feminine" man who fails to aspire to the normative criteria of masculinity.

This fetishistic logic is articulated not only within the narrative, but also on the level of spectatorship. The camera appropriates the sadistic gaze of the soldiers and does not show, not even once, the gaze of the victim—Wiseman. The male spectator is mediated through the camera's gaze, sutured into this sadistic and fetishistic activity by simultaneously acknowledging and disavowing his own fears about the size of his penis. Like the fictitious characters within the film, the normative male viewer disavows his own anxiety of a small penis by displacing it onto the "feminine" man who appears on the screen and, by doing so, reduces his unconscious fears of male "irregularity." In this way, cinema produces for the male spectator an illusion of a coherent ideal male image or, in other words, produces for the male viewer the fantasy of a big penis.

The relationship between Yair and Wiseman is dialectical and simultaneously based on repulsion and attraction, fear and desire. For Wiseman, Yair, the brilliant officer with the promising career in the army, represents, on the one hand, an ideal masculinity and, on the other hand, a source of physical and emotional oppression. For Yair, Wiseman is the "other" whom he wants to repress precisely because of his resemblance to him. In the platoon meeting, Yair tells a friend who wishes to transfer Wiseman to another unit: "I was also a Wiseman when I was little and this doesn't mean anything. You can make a superb soldier out of him." Wiseman voices Yair's own passive and miserable manhood, before he was drafted into the army. He symbolizes for Yair a

Figure 2. Disciplining the "sissy" male soldier. Wiseman (Moni Moshonov, left) and Yair (Gidi Gov, right) in Judd Ne'eman's *Paratroopers*. Courtesy of Judd Ne'eman.

failed, debased, "feminine" manliness that must be repudiated through the reconstruction of the male body and mind. In this sense, Yair's words echo the Zionist ideological longing to construct a new kind of masculinity that will contradict the image of the "feminine" diasporic Jew.

The film presents a visual and narrative parallelism between the two men. In one of the scenes, they are seen marching together during a journey carrying stretchers, positioned in a medium shot on both sides of the frame. Yair turns to Wiseman and says: "If you want, you can. You see, if you want, you can. Slowly, you are starting to justify the shoes you are wearing." When Wiseman collapses later during the journey, Yair says: "I thought you were worth more, that you were not going to break like a female." As a "female," Wiseman is in opposition to the ideal Israeli military manhood marked by the red paratroopers' shoes. He is the man that Yair once, was, but had to disavow in order to justify his shoes. He is the man also must be disciplined, trained, domesticated and maybe even killed, in order to secure the imaginary coherent heterosexual masculinity of Yair. He is the other face of gender, a threatening reflection, which if not altered, must not be considered an option of manhood. Rather, it should be represented as not being a man at all—or, as in the case of Wiseman, being a "feminine" man and later in the film a dead man. Yair sees in Wiseman his own internal difference, a structural element within his own masculinity. Wiseman makes Yair feel queer from within, estranged from his own "self."

From Male Sadism to Male Masochism

In the second part of the film, feeling guilty for Wiseman's death, Yair, experiences an historical trauma in which he is compelled to repeat the disturbing event and forced to identify with his soldier's suffering. In the first part of the film, Wiseman requests his commander's permission to see the army psychiatrist, complaining that the other soldiers harass him. Yair, who ignores Wiseman's distress and called him a paranoid, finds himself now in a similar position. Not only do his soldiers threaten him (in one of the exercises one of the soldiers shoots "doubtlessly accidental" in Yair's direction), but his friends also ignore his feelings. His deputy, who took over his job after he was suspended, treats Yair in the same way he treated Wiseman. He says: "Leave me alone, I don't have time for your paranoia. . . . If you have problems go and see the army psychiatrist." A few seconds later, a platoon of soldiers approaches the two, shouting Wiseman's name. Suddenly Wiseman becomes a martyr hero, in whose name the soldiers carry out the revolt against the paternal authority of Yair.

The scene, in which Yair is being asked by the military police investigator to reconstruct the exercise during which Wiseman was killed, dramatizes the self-berating position he is forced to occupy. The investigator gives him a hand grenade, placing him in the exact position that Wiseman held. Compelled to repeat the painful memory, he imagines (in a flashback) the moment of Wiseman's death. Then he, like Wiseman, throws the hand grenade, collapses at the same spot where the body was found and requires medical attention. Identifying with Wiseman's pain, he is masochistically associated with the same "feminine" position he tried to repudiate. Moreover, he escalates his masochistic pain and self-punishment by disavowing and suspending his guilt for his soldier's death.

Yair tries to visit Wiseman's grieving parents, but escapes at the last moment, refusing to resolve the pain and preferring to torment himself from within. In a second visit, he succeeds in encountering the parents, but lies, distorts facts, and, again, does not confess. What Yair

Figure 3. Yair (Gidi Gov, right) is forced by the military police investigator (Shelomo Bar-Abba, left) to repeat the painful memory of Wiseman in Judd Ne'eman's *Paratroopers*. Courtesy of Judd Ne'eman.

masochistically beats is not so much himself as the authority of father in his male subjectivity that requires an expulsion of the "feminine" within the man. The beating of the father is directly represented in Yair's mockery of his symbolic father—his superior commander—who also expresses indifference to his suffering. By projecting the jeep's lights on his commander while he is having sex in the bushes, Yair exhibits the failure of the paternal function, exposing him in a humiliating position with his underwear is pulled down to his knees.

The film *Repeat Dive* also presents a masochistic positionality of the Israeli male soldier that is also seen in a homoerotic light. The hero of the film, Yoav (Doron Nesher), a diver in the Israeli navy commando, loses his admired friend Yochi in a military mission. Beyond the camera's homoerotic fascination with the beauty of the male body (in the opening sequence, for example, the soldiers are seen naked on the background of a sunset while they wear sensual, rubbery tight diving suits), the film stresses the homoerotic intimacy between the two men. Yoav uses the semantic field of a romantic couple to describe their special relationship. After Yochi's funeral, one of the soldiers says to Yoav: "Yochi spent more time with you than with his wife." Yoav aswers, "Yes, we are not dating any more, it's finished." At the party that the soldiers throw in Yochi's honor, Yoav confesses: "I never before had and I never will have a friend like Yochi."

His friend invites him to meet two girls, saying to him: "If you are not coming, I'm going to tell them that you are gay." The homoerotic relation between the two men is perceived as threatening and thus, in order to secure the sexual "normality" of the male protagonists, the film must fix it within a homophobic homosociality. In the girls' apartment, Yoav sings a song and then kisses his friend on the lips. This is the same song that Yochi sang on a tape that Yoav obsessively listens.

In his will, Yochi leaves Yoav objects associated with sexuality: a pack of condoms and his wife, Mira, who becomes a sexual "object" exchanged between men.[35] This inheritance is given to Yoav "as a prize for modesty and virginity," as Yochi suggests. Yoav stayed loyal and virgin for his best friend, but Yochi did not return and the promise of homosexual desire was unfulfilled. Yochi's inheritance—Mira—is a substitute and a compensation for unattainable gay male love. Her body becomes a mediating object through which Yoav tries to reach his dead lover. The relation between Mira and Yoav is seen as lifeless, clumsy, and passionless. Yoav prefers to socialize with other men rather then having sex with Mira. Little wonder that immediately after their wedding, Yoav is seen, not in bed with his new wife, but rather swimming naked with his soldier friend.

Yoav denies Yochi's death by situating himself in a masochistic and self-suffering position through which he experiences his homoerotic desire for his friend. In the apartment of the two girls he met at the party, he prefers to listen to his "lover's" disembodied voice rather than have sex with one of the girls who invites him to take a shower with her. By fetishizing the voice of the dead, he disavows and defers in the fantasy the loss of Yochi, suspending the masochistic pleasure. Within the historical trauma of Yochi's death, Yoav compulsively repeats the painful past, resisting re-assimilation into the heterosexual order, dislodging himself from the subject position which makes up the dominant fiction. In other words, the compulsive repetition of painful experiences and disavowal of loss and death are structural elements in the masochistic fantasy of the soldier.

Melancholy and Homoerotic Gender Identification

In the films *Paratroopers* and *Repeat Dive,* the heterosexuality of the soldiers is constructed through the repudiation of "femininity" within the articulation of masculinity, or through disavowal of the suggestion of male-male desire. The protagonists refuse to accept the death of a close person, refuse or foreclose grief and mourning, a refusal that takes the form of masochism. The disavowal or refusal of mourning represses representations of queerness within the military homosocial group. By mourning those lost objects, the heterosexual heroes would have been compelled to incorporate the dead within their sexual subjectivity. That is, they would have been forced to see male queerness and homosexuality as constitutive elements within the construction of their heterosexual self.

But what is the relation between refused mourning—or melancholy—and disavowed homosexuality? Judith Butler tries to link melancholic gender identification and a cultural predicament in which heterosexuality refuses to mourn or can mourn the loss of homosexual attachment only with great difficulty. She argues that gender identification is established in part through prohibitions that demand the loss of a certain sexual attachment, as well as a demand that those losses not be avowed or grieved. Her assumption is that heterosexuality is constituted through the repudiation of homosexual attachments and through enforcement of prohibition on them. Prohibition on homosexuality in heterosexual culture is one of its defining operations, thus the loss of homosexual objects are foreclosed from the start. Therefore, Butler claims that we can expect a culturally prevalent form of melancholia, one that signifies the incorporation of ungrieved and ungrievable homosexuality, a kind of refused mourning. Freud argues that melancholy is marked by the experience of self-berating. A melancholic person directs anger toward the other who was lost or died. But because melancholy is a refused grief that cannot be experienced, this anger is turned inward and becomes the substance of self-beratement, or as Butler writes, "the aggression that follows from [the] loss cannot be articulated or externalized, then it rebounds upon the ego itself."[36] Thus, according to Butler, the prohibition on homosexuality preempts the process of grief and prompts a melancholic identification, which turns homosexual desire back upon itself—that is, back upon the ego. This turning back upon itself is exactly the action of guilt and self-beratement. In this way, homosexuality is not abolished, but rather preserved and the place where homosexuality is preserved is exactly in the prohibition on homosexuality. As Butler puts it: "The act of renouncing homosexuality thus paradoxically strengthens homosexuality, but it strengthens homosexuality precisely as the power of renunciation. Renunciation becomes the aim and the vehicle of satisfaction."[37]

The heroes of *Paratroopers* and *Repeat Dive* foreclose and refuse grief and mourning of a close person, repressing his death, thus disavowing male "femininity" and sexual desire between men, constructing it as a melancholic identification that takes a form of masochism. But, those men are haunted by a queerness they cannot grieve, a melancholic disavowal of queerness that turns queerness back upon themselves in the form of a compelled repetition of unpleasurable situations. In other words, the masochism experienced by the heroes is precisely where queer attachments are not abolished, but preserved. In those films, queerness is articulated precisely in the disavowal and prohibition of queerness, a prohibition that manifests itself as male masochism.

However, this male masochism is only temporary and in the end the soldiers return to military homosociality, renewing the symbolic relation with the phallus. Both Yair and Yoav abandon their unpleasurable position and join the military group. But how does this reentry into the dominant fiction elide or heal the traumatic past of the heroes? In both films, the protagonists experienced an emotional rather than a bodily masochism. The imaginary mastery of the heroes was shattered due to the historical trauma, but their anatomical masculinity remained intact. The reconstruction of male subjectivity that can no longer take place at the level of the ego occurs instead at the level of the military group. And, because the soldier's male body remained unharmed, this return is made possible.[38]

Rectal Graves

What is the force that makes the soldier anxiously rush back to the group and how is it represented in the military film? Analyzing Israeli war films, Mihal Friedman argues that the male soldier "grows" within the male military group, tries to approach the woman and couple with her. But the woman's "otherness" evokes in him a castration anxiety and thus he returns to his male companions.[39] Friedman describes this return of the soldier to the platoon as unproblematic. Yet, I question whether this return is, in fact, unproblematic, since the male initially aspired to leave the military group. This trajectory assumes a threat and anxiety that exist for the (heterosexual) male within military homosociality. The return of the male soldier to the group is also his return to the primary fear that made him leave it, which is the potential for homosexual desire that is imagined in the military film as deviant and dreadful. Its visual and narrative representation is the act of bodily penetration or, more precisely, anal penetration.

In his essay "Is the Rectum a Grave?" Leo Bersani contends that heterosexual cultural fantasy promotes an analogy between passive anal sex, which represents a breakdown of bodily boundaries, and shattering of the male self that is equal to death. Therefore, gay men are perceived as "unable to refuse the suicidal ecstasy of being a woman,"[40] whereas being a woman, that is, being penetrated, means loss of ego, injury, and death.

In the discourse of war, Theweleit argues that the soldier's fears of menacing liquidity are also linked to anxieties of anal penetration. Anal intercourse means "deterritorialization" of the male body—the great fear of the soldier. Thus, he must penetrate the one who threatens him with penetration in order to secure his body boundaries. Theweleit writes: "Anal intercourse in its aggressive ('murderous') form may produce some form of wholeness in the persecutor. . . . The anus is identified as the site of aggression precisely because of its potential to produce vast deterritorialization. . . . It is for this reason that he pursues it to its ultimate physical location; its threat must be defused or it will indeed rip him to pieces."[41]

In the Israeli military film, the soldier's anxieties on the battlefield are associated with fears of anal assault. Military occupation and warfare aggression are deadly acts in which men penetrate other men's bodies. The act of fighting and its results in combat—for both the victors and the defeated—is eroticized as anal penetration that has destructive implications for the normative male subject. In other words, penetrating the skin and body is metaphorized and has the same effect as anal receptivity. The anus in the militarist imagination is marked as a grave, a site of sickness, humiliation, castration and loss.

Repeat Dive links the metaphoric representation of anal sexuality with the war and the enemy who penetrates and destroys the male body. The film opens with Yochi's death. Yochi was "penetrated" by the enemy during a military operation. In the scene before his funeral, his friends are seen lying on the grass, their bodies scattered and stretched out, as if dead. Yoav cynically describes the unheroic death of Yochi, who "dived and didn't emerge" and adds, "The war penetrated my ass." A few scenes later, the friends get together in an apartment that belongs to some girls they met at a party. One of the girls, dressed only in her underwear, approaches Yoav and embraces him from behind. Surprised, or rather panicked, he takes hold of her arm and throws her aggressively on her back and says: "Don't ever come at me from behind—it is dangerous!" Whether a man or a woman, the threat of anal penetration always evokes an intense phobic, even hysterical, reaction in the heterosexual male subject. In order to protect himself from the anal menace, the soldier must precede and penetrate the enemy. The equation is simple: If you are not penetrating, you will be penetrated. At the party, when introduced to two girls, Yoav's friend shouts toward him: "Assault the womb." If Yoav will not assault and penetrate, his friend threatens him that he will "tell them that you are gay."[42]

The film *Paratroopers* articulates similar heterosexual fears of anal penetration, but I would like to show how those anxieties are represented not only in the film narrative, but also how the heterosexual homophobic unconscious structures the film form. The soldiers' first remark about Wiseman's "feminine" body is in reference to his behind. While "celebrating" his death, after visiting his parents' house, one of Wiseman's commanders says: "In our platoon one of the soldiers climbed on a shack, took his clothes off, took a machine gun, plugged it in his ass, and shot." The film, then, perceives Wiseman's death as a "feminine" death, unheroic, unmanly, derogatory, and humiliating, associated with anal penetration.

Describing the paradoxical homophobic concept of the homosexual closet, D. A. Miller argues that the closet should be understood as "a homophobic, heterosexual *desire* for homosexuality, and not merely a homophobic, heterosexual *place* for it."[43] The normative heterosexual film spectator desires to see the spectacle of gay male sex—associated in heterosexual culture with anal penetration—yet at the same time is afraid to look. The desire to see homosexual intercourse is provided by mainstream cinema, but it must simultaneously be repudiated.

Wiseman's death, imagined as suicidal anality, is represented in the film in two major scenes: the scene of Wiseman's "suicide" and the scene where Yair is forced to reconstruct the soldier's death. Those scenes, through their different use of film language (mise-en-scène, editing, and camera movements) articulate the paradoxical heterosexual-homophobic concept of the homosexual closet that Miller described.

Before the scene of Wiseman's suicide, the film presents images of penetration and conquest: a medium-shot of soldiers launching phallic mortars toward a dark and smoky hole—the entrance of a concrete construction. The camera stands outside the construction, showing Wiseman who is ordered by Yair to throw a hand grenade into the "dark hole" and to follow it. The dialogue between Yair and Wiseman is shot in close-ups, where the background of Yair's head is of a sunlit desert, and the background of Wiseman's head is of the dark hole/entrance of the construction. Through the positionality of the actors in the scene, Wiseman is identified with the dark entrance—the "dark hole" that soon will become his grave when he throws himself on the hand grenade. Wiseman's death, represented verbally as a suicidal penetration to the "dark hole" of the male body—the anus—is now visualized in the image of dark hole of the construction: Wiseman's grave. This representation fits the phallocentric cultural image of the male anus as a "grave," the grave of the queer man.

In the following scene, Yair, the military doctor and other commanders are seen in close-ups examining Wiseman's body, while the other soldiers are looking through the grilled windows. The camera does not show the object of their gaze—the reverse shot—that is, Wiseman's split and dismembered body that is positioned outside the field of vision. The editing and the cuts in the film "body," omit or conceal the reverse shot—the literal cuts in the dead body, the metonyms of death. In other words, whereas Wiseman's death is imagined in the film as anal penetration, the film uses the mechanism of the cinematic cut in order not to show the "cut" in Wiseman's body—the male rectum.

This fantasmatic configuration is echoed in the words of the doctor who determines Wiseman's death: "Okay, you can close now." What is it that the doctor really wishes to close that was previously "open" in Wiseman's body? The body bag or also the phobically charged hole of the soldier's body? This is in keeping with the film's desire to close, to hide the threatening specter of the male cut/anus through the operating mechanism of the cinematic editing. The use of the cinematic cut in the film demonstrates the concept of the closet that Miller theorized. The scene presents the fantasmatic potential to see gay sexuality, imagined as anal penetration. But at the same time, by cutting away the shot of the cut body, the editing refuses and enforces the prohibition to visualize the spectacle of homosexual sex.

Contrary to the editing in the suicide scene, the scene in which Yair and the military police investigator reconstruct Wiseman's death is shot and edited in a completely different way. Instead of rapid cuts and close-up shots, the camera in a long take enters the construction that was cleaned up after Wiseman's death, looks slowly at the sooty floor and walls, exits the site in a dolly out. It reveals Yair and the investigator who are placed in opposite positions to those held by Yair and Wiseman in the previous scene. The camera approaches the two, gazes at Yair while he mimics Wiseman's suicide, follows him into the construction and shows him as he stretches out on the floor, spreading his legs. The site where Wiseman's dismembered body lay—the site of the homosexual sex—is now revealed. In other words, the film shows us the reverse-shot that was previously hidden from our sight.

In a long-take, the camera shows us an empty space where there is nothing to look at. That is, there is no gay sex to be seen; it simply does not exist. Yair identifies himself with Wiseman's fantasmatic anal death as he lies on the floor and spreads his legs, but because the camera has established the fact that there is nothing to see, the film withholds and prohibits the possible (anal) identification between the two men. The cinematic form of the long take—a long continuous shot without cuts—serves to cutaway, to conceal, the "cut" that is hidden between Yair's spread legs. The film's unconscious is voiced again through the agency of the doctor who examines Yair's body. He asks Yair about his feelings, and Yair answers that he feels "nothing," the same "nothing" that the director, through the surveillance of the camera, makes sure that we see.

As Butler has argued, "The forming of a subject requires an identification with the normative phantasm of 'sex,' and this identification takes place through a repudiation which produces a domain of abjections, a repudiation without which the subject cannot emerge. This is a repudiation which creates the valence of 'abjection' and its status for the subject as a threatening spectre."[44] In the films *Paratroopers* and *Repeat Dive,* the discursive construction of heterosexual subjectivity relies on exclusionary means that produce the "other" as an abject, as a dead body, a body that was penetrated by death, a lethal penetration imagined as anal penetration. But heterosexuality is produced not by means of a refusal to identify with the abject "other," but rather through an identification, a disavowed identification, that threatens to expose the imaginary coherence of the heterosexual subject. As Butler theorizes it: "The abjection of homosexuality can take place only through an identification that one fears to make only because one has already made it, an identification that institutes that abjection and sustains it."[45]

The heterosexuality of the male heroes in *Paratroopers* and *Repeat Dive* is purchased *through* a disavowed identification with an anally abject queerness that must never be shown, must forever remain outside the field of the cinematic vision. Further, in those films, heterosexual identity is stabilized and protected through a process of elimination and casting out of the abject body—a casting out that takes the form of an anal aggressiveness. Thus, heterosexual culture repudiates queerness through the same anality that it identifies with queerness itself. The heterosexual desire to mark and repudiate the queer body through anal activity expresses, then, the heterosexual cultural structural need for the same anal behavior to produce homophobic masculinity. This desire expresses the anal acts that are structurally inscribed within heterosexual masculinity itself. The homophobic manhood—whose very formation relies on anal repudiation—must disavow this constitutive element and project it onto the queer.

The Skin of the Film

Films such as *One of Us* and *Himo, King of Jerusalem* display a different representation of male masochism. Those films are focalized through the point of view of soldiers who were expelled or rejected from the military group because of their wounded virility and who are consciously situating themselves in an emotionally and bodily masochistic position in order to express their homoerotic desire for other soldiers. The heroes are not anxious about the "destructive" effects of bodily penetration on male subjectivity. They aim to present a version of masculinity that willingly surrenders to magnificent passivity and control, celebrating the sexual risk of self-dismissal. They desire to be penetrated, to bear masochistic physical pain, humiliation and suffering, and to suspend sexual gratification. The skin becomes the site on which the soldier heroes inscribe the discursive laws, demands and prohibitions that constitute male subjectivity. The splattered surface of the body is the place where sexual desire and male identity are enacted and performed as a material effect of surface, as a discursive practice enforced through regulative norms. The torn unsutured skin of the male body is exposed as an organic material that marks the border between the chaotic interior and the organized disciplined exterior of the body. An eruption of the messy inside onto the surface level destabilizes and deauthorizes male subjectivity, presenting it as fluid and unfixed. The cut, the wound or the scar in the skin, are metonymies for liquid, uncovering, unsutured masculinity. The heroes, thus, produce a subversive discourse on their body that challenges the idea of a coherent male identity and exposes it as a performative act, as a masquerade and as a spectacle.[46]

Furthermore, those films that present an unsutured male body critically expose not only the performativity of masculinity, but also literalize the way the cinematic apparatus produces, through operations of suture, a visual illusion of a "sutured" coherent body. The term "suture" describes "the procedures by means of which cinematic texts confer subjectivity upon their viewers."[47] Those procedures are the cinematic syntax (the shot–reverse shot technique, cuts, wipes, pans, etc.) through which the content of the film and the heterogeneous shots are given homogenous structure and rendered Symbolic, constructing the unity of the viewer's subjectivity and his/her identification with the screen.

Accordingly, the body that is represented on the screen is in fact a fragmented body composed of heterogeneous elements (close-ups, medium-shots, long-shots) stitched through the cinematic grammar and given an imaginary unified structure. The military films that display the torn unsutured body as the site where identity is written performatively on the skin, expose the imaginary representation of the sutured body that is produced by the cinema. It calls attention to the very cinematic work that discursively constructs an illusion of a coherent, unified male subjectivity and registers it on the screen. In other words, the torn skin of the soldier's male body becomes a metaphor for the "torn skin" of the cinematic body.

The Body in Pain: One of Us

The film *One of Us* is focalized through the point of view of Rafa (Sharon Alexander), a military police officer, who investigates in a paratroop unit the murder of an Arab who was responsible for the death of an Israeli soldier. As soon as he arrives, he realizes that the dead soldier is Amir (Dan Toren) and the officer in charge is Yotam (Alon Aboutbul)—both his old buddies from basic training days. The film is divided into two parts. The first part flashes back to the bonding and solidarity that the three friends formed during basic training, focusing on an incident in which Rafa photographed their commander—known as the "White Angel" (Moshe Mizrahi)—taking a shit in the bushes. Discovering the humiliating photos, the White Angel demands the negatives and the extradition of the anonymous photographer. The soldiers support Rafa and are willing to take a collective punishment. But soon the male solidarity cracks and Rafa is rejected from the group and asked to turn himself in, although nobody addresses him directly. The case ends with an anonymous denunciation, and Rafa, after being abused by the White Angel, requests to be transferred to another unit. The second part of the film focuses on Rafa's investigation of the death of the Arab, who apparently was tortured and killed in revenge for the death of Amir. Rafa is conflicted between his loyalty to Yotam as well as to the memory of their friend and his duty to expose the truth.

The psychosexual dynamic between the three friends, but also among the other soldiers, is informed by masochistic pleasure. In the first part of the film, the soldiers undergo crushing exercises, during which the warrior's body is attacked by physical and psychological pain and humiliation, aiming to produce a disciplined, coherent, and phallic military body forced to carry out military tasks. As Foucault puts it: "The body becomes a useful force only if it is both a productive and a subjected body."[48] The soldiers' motto "all for one and one for all" is heard in the opening sequence in which the fighters are seen beaten and exhausted, carrying other soldiers on stretchers, willing to inflict pain on their bodies for their fellow friends. Yotam's outcry in the end of the exercise marks the point where pain shifts to pleasure. But his pleasure cannot compete with the masochistic enjoyment of Rafa, who despite his sickness during the exercise keeps on pursuing the "Via Dolorosa."

The destruction of the male body and the masochistic pleasure it produces is linked in the film to homoerotic imagery, as the one in which the soldiers are seen doing push-ups while carrying their friends on their backs. Homoerotic masochistic pleasure is demanded from the soldiers who are ordered to smile while exercising. The motto of the film is also heard here, establishing the relation between military bonding and male homoerotic masochism. This relation is manifested especially in the scene where Yotam and Amir visit Rafa who was committed to a hospital after being tortured by the White Angel. Before this scene, the White Angel explained to the soldiers how to conquer a military target while pointing to an image of a nude female body, using sexual occupation as a metaphor for military occupation.

In the following scene, Yotam and Amir are seen breaking through Rafa's room in a parodic mimicry of a military occupation. But this time it is not a male conquest of a female body, but a male conquest of another male body, which does not end with death but rather with Yotam's passionate kiss on Rafa's lips. Furthermore, Yotam identifies Rafa as a woman when he addresses him in feminine-gendered language. "How are you?" he asks Rafa, while also appropriating to himself a feminine-gendered language, "I miss you terribly!" Shocked by Rafa's surprising announcement that he is going to leave the platoon, Yotam says,

"It's not the time to quit, Rafa, a month before it ends. You know what still awaits us? The performances, the missions. . . . My closet seems empty without your rags. You know, my balls miss your knee." In the military group, homo-eroticism is figured in masochistic terms as Yotam links military training that he wishes to experience with Rafa— that is between masochistic destruction of the male body—and his desire for homo-erotic intimacy with him.

Rafa's body becomes the site on which he himself and his fellow friends enact their homoerotic desire. His body and behavior are marked as "feminine." He has a soft and flabby body contrary to Yotam's and the other soldier's hard muscular body. In one of the scenes, he folds when the White Angel kicks him in the belly, while Yotam stays firm and erect after a similar blow. His defective physique makes the other soldiers associate him with "femininity." After he throws up during one of the exercises, a friend says to him, "Rafa, my sister, is every thing all right?" Rafa's "femininity" is linked to his sickness in the same way the nineteenth and early twenty-century medical discourse associated illness and femme males. The White Angel also uses "feminine" imagery to describe Rafa's body as he says to him: "When I order you to get up, you jump. And when I order you to lie down, you lie as a paratrooper and not as a transvestite."

But Rafa, in contrast to the other soldiers, does not remain a passive receptor of external stimuli that the military system produces in order to transform the male body into a war machine. Rather he is a dynamic subject in his need to construct systems in his own image. He constructs his relationship with his commander and with his soldier friends according to his masochistic fantasy. He takes a photo of the White Angel taking a shit in the bushes, thus humiliating the "father" figure, disavowing the phallic law through a fetishistic frozen image. The platoon stands behind Rafa, refusing to hand over the anonymous photographer, challenging the laws of masculinity of the military father, willing to bear terrible body pain and lack of sleep, some of them physically collapse. The photo becomes their secret platoon tag that they wear as soon as the White Angel is out of sight.

Masquerading as the White Angel, Yotam mimics their commander's voice, ridiculing his image and at the same time mocking his own likeness to him. In Yotam's masochistic masquerade, the power relations of sexuality are made performative and theatrical so that their "naturalness" is exposed as a cultural construct. At Yotam's command, the soldiers flip over the paratroop tag, unveiling the photo of the degraded father while looking at each other, smiling. Rafa's "feminine" gaze, marked by the photo, mediates the gazes of the soldiers, rewriting the military homosociality in masochistic terms. In another scene, threatened by the subversive look of his rebel "son," the White Angel, smashes Rafa's camera. But the camera is only an external object that Rafa uses to deauthorize the father. Thus, when the White Angel asks him if any photos or negatives are left, Rafa answers: "Only that which were inscribed in memory." Little wonder that Yotam and Amir buy Rafa a new camera, returning to him the look taken by the father.

As the sadistic father, the White Angel has a strong super-ego that represents the phallic laws of the military institution that enforces repudiation of "femininity" within the articulation of masculinity.[49] But, as a sadist, he has no ego other than that of his victims—the reason why he does not have a name that defines his "self," but only a nickname that the soldiers gave him. As a masochist, Rafa has a weak superego but has a strong ego that humiliates and manipulates the paternal authority of the White Angel to perform his masochist fantasy. Rafa's actions, as well as his subversive humor, are designed to undermine the paternal function which makes the White Angel say, "You know what will kill you? Your shitty humor along with some help from me." However, the psychosexual dynamic between Rafa and the White Angel does not produce the masochistic or sadistic pleasure of any of them. As Deleuze has argued, the sadist will never tolerate a masochistic victim who produces pleasure from pain and vice versa. As a pure superego, the sadist exercises his sexuality by inflicting pain on his victims who submit to, rather then challenge, sadistic pleasure. By torturing the soldiers' bodies—but not the bodies of Yotam and Amir and especially not Rafa's body—the White Angel produces his sadistic fantasy.

This is why the other soldiers quickly break the masochistic solidarity with Rafa and demand that he turn himself in. Rafa's masochistic fantasy threatens to expose homosexual elements within the military group. By submitting to their commander's sadism, the soldiers repudiate and displace the homosexual threat onto the masochist who is expelled from the male homosociality. When Rafa tries to sit near his friends, one of them says, "It's starting to stink in here." Rafa is perceived, as Mary Douglas wrote, as a polluting person: "A polluting person is always in the wrong. He has developed some wrong condition or simply crossed some line which should not have been crossed and this displacement unleashes danger for someone."[50] Rafa crosses the line between masculinity and femininity, between pain and pleasure. He threatens the heterosexual social order and breaks the taboo of the normative male body.

Unlike the other soldiers, Yotam and Amir stay loyal to the homo-erotic masochistic camaraderie. Amir scolds his friends, including Yotam, for asking Rafa to hand himself over and interprets masochis-tic suffering as an inherent part of the character and demands of mas-culinity: "What do you want? To feel like men because you back him up but not to pay the price that this decision demands from you." Yotam manifests his masochistic identification with Rafa when he asks the White Angel to join in Rafa's body penalty. When his request is declined, Yotam refuses to take off the heavy army gear as a sign of masochistic solidarity with his friend.

Rafa's masochistic pleasure is more complex. He masochistically seeks the punishment of the White Angel in order to beat and humil-iate the father in his male subjectivity. (He decides to inform on him-self anonymously—information revealed in the second part of the film). However, pain itself is not what he desires. There are certain effects associated with pain that are pleasurable for him. When the White Angel asks him why he does not cry from the great pain he inflicts on him, Rafa answers, "I cry only from things that are really painful," and adds, "With me, pain is associated only with love." The sadistic torments of the White Angel do not make Rafa feel any real pain, because he feels contempt and not love toward him. His love is devoted to his friends who are being beaten because of him. He produces his homoerotic masochistic pleasure through guilt feelings for the suffer-ing of his friends. The masochist, as Deleuze argued, "stands guilt on its head by making punishment into a condition that makes possible the forbidden pleasure."[51] By causing them to be beaten and at the same time feeling guilty for the pain inflicted on them, Rafa expresses his forbidden homoerotic love for Yotam and Amir. He wishes to suspend this guilt, to defer the homoerotic masochistic enjoyment and this is precisely why he chooses to inform on himself anonymously. Rafa could have openly exposed himself as the photographer and received the deserved punishment. Indeed, he chooses to get the punishment but he does so anonymously, because in this way he can suspend his guilt feelings toward his friends who assume that one of them betrayed Rafa. In other words, Rafa aims for pleasure, but the sexual gratifica-tion is detoured in order to achieve a subversive triumph in what

appears to be a defeat. Rafa manipulates sacred military ideals of sacrifice and male solidarity to perform the role he assigned to them in
his masochistic scenario. He causes his self-expulsion from the military group and constitutes his masochistic fantasy. In the hospital, saying goodbye to his friends, he cries for forbidden love. He cries because
of the pain associated with love.

In the second part of the film, pressure is put on Rafa to close the
investigation and to leave the base. As before, he is projected as a "feminine" male (he is directed to sleep in the girls' residence) and as a polluting person (the soldiers are disgusted to eat with him). But now his
constructed bodily anomaly is figured as a national threat as his investigation is perceived as subversive ("he burrows like a tapeworm"), vin-
dictive ("he has a long history with this unit"), and antinationalist ("all
this fuss for a terrorist who killed your friend"). He threatens to expose
the lies that structure the myth of Israeli military male solidarity by
unmasking not only the cover-up of the murder of the Palestinian, but
also his own expulsion from the military group. The site of the inquiry
is the site of the body: the abject bodies of both Rafa and the Palestinian,
who were sadistically repudiated from the military space. Images and
rituals of cleaning that appear throughout the film (the washing of
the car in the opening sequence, the whitewashing of the base, and

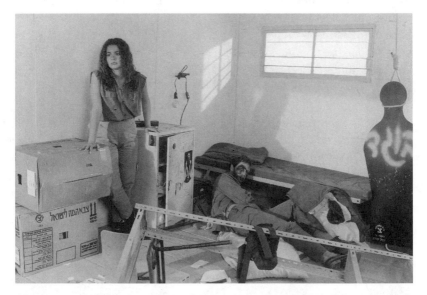

Figure 4. A soldier is being beaten. Rafa (Sharon Alexander) and Tamar (Daliah
Shimko) in Uri Barbash's *One of Us*. Courtesy of Uri Barbash.

especially the cleaning of the blood after the brutal murder) mark the compulsive repression of abject bodies that threaten to contaminate the homosocial space, as well as demarcate the body boundaries of the military brotherhood. Rafa's return is thus the return of the repressed abject who comes to investigate the national as well as the sexual suppression by painfully inscribing on his flesh the suffering of both. He threatens to destabilize the national and sexual oppressive hierarchies on which the soldiers' solidarity is based.

The relationship between Rafa and Yotam in the second part of the film also articulates the interweaving of the national and the homoerotic discourses. Yotam expresses ambivalence toward Rafa. On the one hand, he clings to the military paternal authority that he is now a part of, seeing in Rafa's inquiry a desecration of Amir's memory. On the other hand, he convinces his superior officer to allow Rafa to conduct the investigation ("I specifically need him to investigate"). By giving Rafa the power to investigate, he seeks self-punishment. He desires to reenact with him the homoerotic masochistic fantasy though which he could beat his own military parental authority that is responsible for both the national repression of the Palestinian and the sexual repression of his desire for his loved friend. Rafa is made to bear the conflicted desire of Yotam who beats him for questioning his girlfriend, Tamar (Daliah Shimko), about the murder. Seconds later, he lies on a bed in Rafa's arms, putting his head on his chest as they nostalgically look together on the image of the humiliated father—the image of the White Angel taking a shit that Rafa kept—deferring phallic masculinity, renewing their masochistic homoerotic relation. By beating his friend, and at the same time feeling guilty for it, Yotam writes on Rafa's submissive body the lies, the crimes, and the desires that compose the Israeli national masculinity.

Tamar says to Yotam, "It hurts me to see you like this . . . weak, so dependent on him, like he needs to approve something that you began to doubt." Yotam doubts his very own masculinity that requires a national and sexual repudiation without which the Israeli heterosexual subjectivity cannot emerge. He makes love with Tamar against a projected slide of the three friends, as her body mediates his homoerotic desire for his friends. He disavows the paternal presence through the fetishistic image of the masochistic bonding, positioning masochistic homoerotic desire as an internal difference within his manliness. In this scene, the boundary between the screen and the skin, between representation and reality, is blurred, literalizing the idea that desire is only skin deep.

The Oral Mother and Male Homoeroticism: Himmo, King of Jerusalem

While in *One of Us* the woman is produced only as a mediating object of male homoeroticism, in the film *Himmo, King of Jerusalem,* the female figure has a more central and active role in the male masochistic fantasy.[52] Set during the siege of Jerusalem in the War of Independence, the film focuses on a young nurse, Hamutal (Alona Kimchi), who volunteers to work in a temporary hospital, which has been established in a monastery. The wounded soldiers see her as a kind of ideal oral mother. They choose her as the loving and confronting mother over the other nurse, Shoshana, who is expelled from the monastery's belfry where they lie. She gives the suffering men an attention that exceeds her professional duty, listens to their stories, identifying with their pain—qualities that lift her to a level of a Christian saint. (In one of the scenes, the monastery nun caresses Hamutal's hair in an image that evokes the iconography of the pièta.) Hamutal dedicates most of her attention to Himmo, a gruesomely maimed soldier, blind and dismembered, with whom she falls in love. She takes him out into the sunlight despite the doctor's prohibition; talks with him although he cannot answer her back; objects to placing his bed near the door—a sign for his forthcoming death—and eventually sleeps beside him at night.

Along with her image as an ideal maternal figure, the soldiers perceive her as a cold and cruel mother who neglects them in favor of Himmo. (Franji, one of the wounded, says to her, "Leave Himmo alone; there are others also"). They seek her cruelty, asking her to inflict pain on their tortured flesh, insisting that she penetrate their castrated bodies with injections. When she forgets to perform her role as the torturing mother, they complain. Assa asks, "Why does everybody love her? An average girl." And to Franji, he says: "She likes to feel like a martyr. It's a sexy feeling, Franji, it's the peak of pleasure." The soldiers doubt her purity in order to project Hamutal as the cruel oral mother through which they produce their masochistic pleasure that challenges their phallic power. Himmo also seeks her coldness and brutality. The only words he can say to her are "shoot me, shoot me," a masochistic death wish he desires her to exercise. The film associates Hamutal with the ideal divas of Hollywood cinema, such as Greta Garbo, Betty Grable, Esther Williams, and Elizabeth Taylor, an association that recalls Marlene Dietrich's representation as a mythical powerful female

Figure 5. "She is like a movie star from your cinema—a frozen fire." Assa (Dov Navon), Hamutal (Alona Kimchi), and Dr. Abayov (Yossi Graber) in Amos Gutmann's *Himmo, King of Jerusalem.* Courtesy of Miri Gutmann.

figure in Josef von Sternberg's masochistic screen fantasies, as Gaylyn Studlar has shown.[53] In Sternberg's films, as in *Himmo, King of Jerusalem,* the admired Hollywood star is represented as a source of vitality and as a lifesaver. Marco, Himmo's brother, shows Hamutal a picture of Betty Grable that he hangs around his neck, that saved him from death when "a bullet stuck between her legs." Hamutal's styled blond hair and slender body give her a glamorous look of the cinematic goddesses of the forties. The monastery nun describes her: "She is like a movie star from your cinema—a frozen fire. She touches everyone and nobody can touch her."

Hamutal is a source of male masochistic identification with phallic femininity through which the soldiers subvert their paternal heritage, presenting male lack and loss that demystify the heroic aura assigned to the fighters of the War of Independence. However, their wounded male identity is especially defined through negated identification with Himmo's ultimate suffering body. They aspire to reach Himmo's masochistic ideal, trying to deepen their body pains, masochistically inscribing on their flesh their castration in order to compare themselves and identify with the exalted agony of Himmo. But his ideal suffering leaves them, as the doctor says to Assa, "not properly wounded." Assa himself complains: "Before they brought Himmo, we were totally miserable, but we knew how to complain, like one who lies near an amputee and his leg hurts. Compared to him we are crumbs that fell off the table, zero, nothing, not even properly wounded. Even she [Hamutal] prefers him over us." His dissected body and dark gaze—"darker then the soul of the angel of death," as Marco describes—make them masochistic subjects, yet at the same time they are afraid to be totally consumed as he desires. Listening to nationalist pathos songs on the radio, they try in vain to blur his death outcries that disturb their sleep at night. Paradoxically, they come into being only through the one that threatens to destroy them. Thus, Himmo represents not so much male lack, but a loss of fixed male identity and coherent ego boundaries.

It is not accidental that Himmo, who is called "King of Jerusalem," is associated in the film with the masochistic image of Jesus, "King of the Jews." The wounded soldiers, like Christian masochists, seek to remake themselves according to the model of the suffering Christ/Himmo, the embodiment of earthly divestiture and loss. The Christian lives his/her life in perpetual anticipation of the Second Coming of Christ, an anticipation that makes the present suffering enjoyable.[54] The soldiers construct their masochistic identity according to the suffering spectacle of Himmo, anticipating his resurrection. (Franji asks Hamutal to marry Himmo in order to bring him back to life.)

The masochistic attraction of the soldiers to Himmo is figured also in homoerotic terms. Once, Franji says admiringly, Himmo's glorious masculinity was famous all over Jerusalem: "Girls have fainted over him . . . Women tourists came to see him." However, Himmo is haunted by a dark past, marked as feminine. He was named after a woman, Himma, his grandmother's young sister who was caught in the cellar during the great earthquake in the city of Zfat when she wanted to try on her wedding dress. She survived in the cellar for fifteen days and then died. Bearing her name as well as her fate, Himmo, like Himma, relives her story, doomed to die in a similar way—in siege, within the darkness of his blindness.

Identified with the same feminine destiny, Himmo's castrated "feminine" body becomes an object for the soldiers' homoerotic desire, marked mainly by the fetishization of his mouth—Himmo's "sacred mouth," as Franji describes it. Diana Fuss argues:

> If, in the popular imaginary, gay male homosexuality can be said
> to have an erotogenic zone of its own, its corporeal "repository"
> may well be the spectacularized site of the anus. . . . I would like
> to suggest that alongside the scene of intercourse *per anum*
> between men, modernist culture offers quite another spectacle of
> male homosexuality, one based on oral, rather then anal eroti-
> cism. . . . Notions of anal incorporation cannot help but invoke
> tropes of orality.[55]

Fuss claims that for Freud, the mouth is the most archaic of sexual
organs and the least developed of the libidinal zones, which provides
us with our earlier sexual experience of sucking the mother's breast.
The mouth and the anus must be abandoned in favor of the genitalia
if the subject is to attain (hetero)sexual maturity. Failure to do so
accounts for the appearance of what Freud calls human sexual perversion. In his psychoanalytic biography of Leonardo da Vinci, Freud
sees oral eroticism as the principal drive that organizes and sustains
homosexual identity formation. Thus, for Fuss, oral eroticism is
another "sodomitical scene . . . [that] extend[s] and stretch[es] the pri-
ority accorded to anality in symbolic configurations of male homosexuality."[56]

Contrary to Freud's demonization of "oral" male homosexuality,
Himmo, King of Jerusalem presents the mouth as the site of sexual pleasure between men. Franji, who was once Himmo's best friend, always
envied his manhood, an envy involved with sexual adoration and
attraction. ("I love him more than you do," he says to Hamutal). In one
of the scenes, he describes, in explicit erotic terms, Himmo's beauty,
emphasizing especially his magical and sensual mouth, his "sacred
mouth," and then bursts into crying. Hearing his words, Himmo
empathizes with his lost friend and cries. Possessing the phallic
power, Hamutal mediates the homoerotic relation between the wounded
soldiers and Himmo. She erotically penetrates her finger into Himmo's
mouth in a kind of oral suction or anal penetration figuration, while
the men look at the specter with desire. Franji lives in suspense for the
second coming of Himmo via Hamutal and the promise of redemptive
homoerotic end-pleasure with him. This suspension makes it possible
for him to experience the present pain and suffering as future pleasures.
Thus, he asks Assa to draw on his cast "two mouths, one like a stone
and one like a flower, and they kiss"—Himmo's mouth of death and
Hamutal's mouth of life. None of the "castrated" men are able to exer-

cise Himmo's death wish that will make their gratification possible, and they urge the oral mother to inject him with the lethal dose. Even Marco, who keeps in his pocket a phallic gun designed to fulfil Himmo's desire, gives the task to Hamutal, and then kisses his brother goodbye on his sacred lips.

The homoerotic discourse in the film subverts the national myth of the "living-dead" that Himmo, the zombie, the Jewish Golem, literalizes. His "living-dead" body does not represent a transcendental national ideal, but rather individual sexual homoerotic desire. Assa mocks Hamutal's desire to make Himmo's body meaningful: "There is something comforting about the thought that you are bonded to this Golem. There is a hope that, when we are sick and ugly, someone would find through us a spiritual uplifting and meanwhile wipe our ass." This critique of Israeli national death culture is presented also when Assa tells Franji about the "heroic" death of Hamutal's former lover: "He blew himself up on an explosive in order to save his friends," and cynically adds, "But there is no proof that he was a hero. He might have fallen by accident on the explosive. However, one thing is certain: he is more hero then you, because he is more dead then you." At the end of the film, while Hamutal executes her lover, Franji says: "Once, we walked in the street and shouted, 'If we die, they will bury us in the mountains of Bab-el-Wad.' And an old Yeke shouted, 'You are not going to die in Bab-el-Wad. You are going to die in King George.'" Bab-el-Wad refers to the famous Israeli convoys of provisions that were shelled on their way to besieged Jerusalem during the War of Independence. In the film, the privilege of a heroic death is denied the soldiers, who are destined to die a meaningless death in the monastery, or as the old man suggested on King George Street—a death without national redemption. The fact that they are mocked by an old *yeke* (a nickname for a German Jew) and not by a Sabra, as they are, also undermines their authority as national heroes.

Death is homoeroticized in the film. The soldiers' homoerotic desire for Himmo is presented as a sexual identification with an anti-ideal masculinity that seeks to destroy itself. Thus, the end-pleasure of sexual desire can be fulfilled only masochistically through violence, murder, and death. Neither death nor sex is associated with liberation and transcendence, but with abjection and denial. In this sense, the film manifests a radical and highly critical position of the (hetero)sexual and national norms of Israeli society.

3 | The Invention of Mizrahi Masculinity

The interethnic tension between Ashkenazim and Mizrahim emerged in Israel after the period of mass immigration (1948–1954) during which approximately seven hundred thousand immigrants arrived after the establishment of the state, doubling the Jewish population in Israel. The Mizrahi immigrants were transported to Israel from Arab and Muslim countries such as Iraq, Morocco, Iran, Syria, Yemen, Turkey, India, Algeria, and Egypt by Zionist and state organized operations, following the Israeli Independence War (1954). The mass importation of Arab-Jews was motivated by the state's demographic, economic, and political necessities, defined by Levy Eshkol, head of the Settlement Department of the Jewish Agency, as "the need for working and fighting hands." However, for David Ben-Gurion, the first Israeli prime minister, the Jews of Europe were the first candidates for citizenship in Israel and, after the Jews of America politely declined his proposal to immigrate to Israel, he turned unwillingly to the Jews of Islam Nations. Ben-Gurion wrote: "Hitler, more than hurt the Jewish people, whom he knew and detested, [he] hurt the Jewish State, whose coming he did not foresee. He destroyed the substance, the main and essential building force of the state. The state arose and did not find the nation which had waited for it."[1]

Ben-Gurion's Eurocentric approach toward the Orient, which he saw as "pre-modern," "barbaric," one that endangered the civilized and modern features of the new Westernized State of Israeli, informed his view on the Mizrahim: "We do not want Israelis to become Arabs. We are in duty bound to fight against the spirit of the Levant, which corrupts individuals and societies, and preserve the authentic Jewish values as they crystallized in the diaspora."[2] Clearly, for Ben-Gurion, Zionism was a liberation movement of the European Jewish diaspora and his comparison between Mizrahim and black Africans who were brought to America as slaves only underlines the social oppression that Oriental Jews have experienced in Israel. According to the official discourse on the Mizrahim, as Ella Shohat best describes it:

> European Zionism "saved" Sephardi Jews from the harsh rule of their Arab "captors." It took them out of "primitive condition" of poverty and superstition and ushered them gently into a modern Western society characterized by tolerance, democracy, and "human values," values with which they were but vaguely and erratically familiar due to the "Levantine environments" from which they came. Within Israel, of course, they have suffered not simply from the problem of "the gap," that between their standard of living and that of European Jews, but also from the problem of their "incomplete integration" into Israeli liberalism and prosperity, handicapped as they have been by their Oriental, illiterate, despotic, sexist, and generally pre-modern formation in their lands of origin, as well as by their propensity for generating large families. Fortunately, however, the political establishment, the welfare institutions, and the educational system have done all in their power to "reduce this gap" by initiating the Oriental Jews into ways of a civilized, modern society. Fortunately as well, intermarriage is proceeding apace, and the Sephardim have won new appreciation for their "traditional cultural values," their folkloric music, their rich cuisine, and warm hospitality. A serious problem persists, however. Due to their inadequate education and "lack of experience with democracy," the Jews of Asia and Africa tend to be extremely conservative, even reactionary, and religiously fanatic, in contrast to the liberal, secular, and educated European Jews. Antisocialist, they form the base of support for the right-wing parties. Given their "cruel experience in Arab lands," furthermore, they tend to be "Arab-haters," and in this sense they have been an "obstacle to peace," preventing the efforts of the "peace camp" to make a "reasonable settlement" with the Arabs.[3]

This Zionist discourse has had effects on the construction of the Mizrahi body and, more specifically, on the Mizrahi male body and sexuality in the dominant Ashkenazi imagination and its particular representation in Israeli cinema. The Zionist discourse exercised parallel practices of homogenization and differentiation that elided the experience of the Mizrahi body.[4] According to the official Zionist historiography, the immigration of the Arab-Jews was the result of messianic longing for the land of Zion and a long history of anti-Semitic persecutions in their countries of origin. However, this narrative masked the Zionist political and economic interests in bringing the Jews of Islam Nations to Israel. The Mizrahi body was nationalized as part of a "universal" national subject and was melted into a modern social so-called "neutral" collectivity. The Zionist movement exploited Mizrahi bodies as cheap labor and evicted Mizrahim into small settlements along the state's borders and into "deserted" Palestinian urban neighborhoods, creating a living deference wall against military Arab attacks, as well as blocking any attempts of Palestinian refugees to return to their homeland. The Jewish national body was established as the binary opposition of the Arab "other" by this incorporation of the Mizrahi body into the Zionist Ashkenazi order. Mizrahim were forced to chose between anti-Zionist Arab identity and pro-Zionist Jewish identity and thus, for the first time in the history of the Arab-Jews, as Shohat noted, their "Arabness and Jewishness were posed as antonyms."[5]

At the same time, on the interior-ethnic Jewish level, Zionism exercised practices of differentiation over the Mizrahi body, marking it as the sexual "other" of the Zionist-Ashkenazi body ideal. In terms of the male body, the discursive construction of Arab-Jews men as violent savages and primitives reproduces certain Zionist-Ashkenazi ideological fictions and psychic fixations about the sexual "nature" of Oriental masculinity and the "otherness" it is constructed to embody. Assigned the role of embodying ethnic/sexual difference within an Ashkenazi metaphorics of representation, the Mizrahi man becomes for the Ashkenazi man the repository of his repressed fantasies, similar to the way in which the Western colonialist projected his own desires onto the "native." As Frantz Fanon has already described: "The civilized white man retains an irrational longing for unusual eras of sexual license. . . . Projecting his own desires onto the Negro, the white man behaves 'as if' the Negro really has them."[6] Those fictions about Mizrahi manhood were fabricated in order to allay the Ashkenazi subject's own fears and desires, as well as to provide a means to justify the regulation of Mizrahi men's bodies and absolve any sense of guilt.

The Ashkenazi colonial fantasy fixed Mizrahi males to a narrow spectrum of sexual stereotypes. The Mizrahi male was represented as a sexual "savage" and a hypersexual stud who "does it more" and even better, hence the Ashkenazi fear of engulfment, of being swamped by "primitive" Mizrahi multitudes. Abba Eben, a prestigious member of Israeli Parliament, said: "One of the great apprehensions which afflict us . . . is the danger lest the predominance of immigrants of Oriental origin force Israel to equalize its cultural level with that of the neighboring world."[7] The myth about over-reproduction and hypersexuality locked the Mizrahi male into his body, reinforcing the racist notion that Oriental males are inferior in mind and morality on account of their bodies. Israeli physicians determined that the Mizrahim's "primitive" and "backward" nature is driven from their heredity/genetic structure. "How can we build a future of a people on these ruins of man's psyche?" asked one doctor.[8] Thus, the journalist Eliezer Livne urgently requested to constitute a selection policy in which only strong and healthy Oriental bodies will be transported to Israel. He said: "We definitely cannot agree that the morally or physically retarded and dubious part [of the population] will immigrate to the country. Specifically when the strong and rooted Jewish class remained in the Diaspora . . . Israel is not a refuge for the unproductive backward cycles of the Diaspora, but a center for the best of them."[9]

In Morocco, Jews were forced to pass physical and gymnastic tests in order to determine their bodily qualification before arriving in Israel.[10] Mizrahi males were entangled within the Israeli body apparatus that classified, regulated and disciplined their bodies, produced them as better, normalized, approved men. However, unlike the European Jewish workers who have been presented as "idealists, able to devote to the ideal, to create new moulds and new content of life," Arab-Jews have been described as "merely workers" and "primitive matter."[11] In one of his essays, Ben-Gurion wrote:

The majority of these Jews [Oriental Jews] are poor. They do not have property which was taken for them and do not have education and culture that was never given to them. . . . The diasporas that have been eliminated and gathered in Israel do not yet constitute a people, but a riffraff and human dust without a

language, without education, without roots . . . [in] the vision of
the state. The transformation of this human dust to a cultural, independent and visionary nation—is uneasy work.[12]

Ben-Gurion uses the term "human dust" to describe the Mizrahim, the
same term which he used to describe Holocaust survivors. But while
the "degenerated" mind and body of the Eastern European Jew could
be fixed and changed, the Mizrahi Jew was destined to be enslaved to
his flesh, reduced to his corporeality. He was perceived as lacking an
enlightened awareness of higher visionary meanings, lacking national
consciousness, assigned only to Ashkenazim.

This discourse about the Mizrahi body sometimes took a more
"humanist" form, as in K. Shabetay's so-called critique of the Ashkenazi
racist discourse. The journalist said:

We suffer from a burden of intelligence, from brain workers and
brain work. The emotional background of Zionism, and especially the working Zionism—was a desire to escape from the
exaggerated burden of intelligent inquiry into a simple, natural,
better life. We need . . . overfull "injections" of neutrality, simplicity, and bodily common people. These naïve, child-like Jews,
with their simplicity, with their intelligence, which is . . . not like
Einstein,' are the spice of life against our excessive brainy inquiry.[13]

The notion that the Arab-Jew has only a body and no mind echoes
Fanon's description of the raced body under the colonial gaze: "There
are times when the black man is locked into his body. Now for a being
who has acquired consciousness of himself and of his body, who has
attained the dialectic of subject and object, the body is no longer a cause
of structure of consciousness, it has become an object of consciousness."[14] The Mizrahi man, then, is all body. He cannot attain the dialectic of subject-object, cannot transcend his materiality.

Along the image of the hypervirile Mizrahi male, the Israeli-
Ashkenazi gaze was also fascinated by the delicate, noble, and "exotic"
beauty of Mizrahi male bodies. A member of the Jewish Agency emis-
sary in Libya described the male Arab-Jew as if he were trading in
horses: "They are handsome as far as their physique and outward
appearance are concerned, but I found it very difficult to tell them apart
from the good quality Arab type."[15] The Mizrahi man was invented and
classified as a "type" of racial man, a racial form, with recognizable psychological and physiological qualities and morphology. New immigrants

were organized into categorical types according to their countries of origin, in the same way that European colonial missions categorized the populations of the Third World in their sociological, anthropological, and medical diagnostic manuals. In official and journalistic reports, Mizrahim's bodies were associated with the unsanitary, plagues, sexual diseases, and sexual perversity. In a series of notorious racist articles, published in 1949, the journalist Arye Gelblum described the Mizrahi immigrants in these terms:

> This is a race unlike any we have seen before . . . The primitiveness of these people is unsurpassable. They have almost no education at all, and what is worse is their inability to comprehend anything intellectual. As a rule, they are only slightly more advanced than the better than the Arabs, Negroes, and Berbers in their countries. . . . In the [North] Africans corners of the camps you find filth, gambling, drunkenness, and prostitution. Many of them suffer from serious eye diseases, as well skin and venereal diseases.[16]

Zionist medical discourse also associated the pathologized body and sexuality of the Mizrahi man with homosexuality. Pseudo-scientific psychological reports traced "unnatural" sexual relations among Mizrahi males. Hedda Grossmann, an Israeli psychologist who was sent to explore the Mizrahim's mental condition in transit camps (*mahabarot*), argued that because of the immigration process that separated Mizrahi men from their natural families and friends, they tended to gather in same-sex male groups and to develop homoerotic relations. She wrote: "There were expressions of physical affection very close to homosexuality, whose origins are easily understood in the context of the relationship between the sexes in this community."[17] While Mizrahi men are usually associated with sexism and homophobia— resulting from the "primitive" societies they originated from—they were, simultaneously and paradoxically, characterized by freedom of licentious sex unobtainable in the West. Grossmann is concerned that those expressions of homoeroticism between Mizrahi men "will no doubt cause trouble when they arrive, in view of the fact that there are very few girls and the sexual ratio being so unequal among the Oriental immigrants. In our group, for example, there was not a single girl."[18] Grossman's anxiety expresses the Zionist fear of homosexuality that threatens to undo the compulsory heterosexual Zionist national gendering project.

The image of the Mizrahi man as having "unfit" corporality was enforced by Ben-Gurion himself. Referring specifically to the Yemenite-Jewish male, the Zionist leader wrote:

> This tribe is in some ways more easily absorbed, both culturally and economically, than any other. It is hardworking, it is not attracted to the city life, it has—or at least, the male part has—a good grounding in Hebrew and Jewish heritage. Yet in other ways it may be the most problematic of all. It is thousand of years behind us, perhaps even more. It lacks the most basic and primary concepts of civilization (as distinct from culture). Its attitude toward women and children is primitive. Its physical condition [is] poor. Its bodily strength is depleted and does not have the minimal notions of hygiene. For thousands of years, it lived in one of the most benighted and improvised lands, under a rule even more backward than an ordinary feudal and theocratic regime.[19]

The Arab-Jews as a "race" were imagined as a threat to Israeli body hygiene and to the national survival of the Ashkenazi "race." This pathologicalization of the Mizrahi body and sexuality was institutionalized by the Israeli absorption apparatus that "purified" the Mizrahim's "contaminated" Oriental bodies by spraying them with DDT disinfection powder.[20] The Ashkenazi-Israeli biopower discourse created Mizrahim as an internal biological degenerated "enemy within," against which Israeli society must defend itself to secure its life and existence. In order to exercise and elaborate its own power, the Israeli regulation regime generated the very pathological object it sought to control.

Practices of homogenization of the Mizrahi body, dissolving the Mizrahi male on the national level into the Jewish heteronormative order, were exercised along practices of differentiation that produced and fixed the sexual difference of Mizrahi masculinity on the interior Jewish ethnic level. The Mizrahi man was trapped within his threatening "otherness," his bodily difference, left outside of the ideal masculinity of the handsome Ashkenazi Sabra—an ideal that by definition the Mizrahi body could not fully assume. The parallel practices of homogenization and differentiation, which positioned the Mizrahi man in and out of Jewish-Israeli collectivity, produced a split and fragmented the Mizrahi male body, estranged from his own body image. This dialectic of homogenization and differentiation that structures the colonial gaze of Ashkenazi Zionism posed difficulties for establishing a Mizrahi male subjectivity.

This chapter explores the construction of the Mizrahi body and sexuality in mainstream Israeli cinema. It also examines the practices of resistance used by Mizrahi filmmakers to the discourses of Zionist-Ashkenazi manhood during two historical decades that played an important role in the forming of the Mizrahi male subject. The emergence of a new Mizrahi social-political consciousness in the seventies gave rise to a new male Mizrahi macho image aimed to challenge the positions of dependency and powerlessness which Ashkenazi hegemony enforced. Both Ashkenazi mainstream and Mizrahi independent cinema reacted to this Mizrahi macho style. On the one hand, the film *Casablan* (Menachem Golan, 1973), part of the popular "Bourekas" genre that focused on the ethnic tension between Mizrahi and Ashkenazim, expressed an anxiety about the growth of the new Mizrahi hypermasculinity. It also made an effort to normalize and domesticate Mizrahi males by disavowing ethnic differences, using a practice of mimicry that forced Sephardi men to represent the image of the Ashkenazi heteronormativity. Mizrahi men were obliged to inhabit an inhabitable zone of ambivalence that grants them neither identity nor difference. Inspired by the new Mizrahi resistance, the Mizrahi independent filmmaker, Nissim Dayan, in his film *Light Out of Nowhere* (1973), critiqued Ashkenazi discrimination inflicted on Mizrahi men. However, by adopting the new Mizrahi macho image, the film reproduced the Ashkenazi dominant definitions of Mizrahi masculinity as violent and aggressive as well as visualized its social ethnic consciousness through an oppressive rhetoric of misogyny and gender/sexual binaries enforced by compulsory heterosexuality.

In the end of the 1970s and the 1980s—along with the coming to power of the Likud right party (1977) and the war in Lebanon (1982)—filmmakers, who were identified with the liberal Left, expressed discontent with the state's policies, especially those regarding the Palestinian problem. The interethnic tension, which took central stage in the seventies Israeli cinema, was now marginalized and neglected by films that focused on the Israeli-Palestinian conflict. In these films, the interethnic issue was labeled as an "interior social problem" that must be solved only after achieving peace. At the same time, Mizrahi people were represented in these films as Arab-hating nationalists who pose a major obstacle for peace. On the one hand, the eighties political films incorporated the Mizrahi question and the interethnic social conflict into the Israeli-Palestinian political conflict; on the other hand, the Ashkenazi Left produced the

threatening "otherness" of the Mizrahim as violent fanatics and as enemies of peace.

Behind the Walls (Uri Barbash, 1986), the most famous film produced in the eighties about the Israeli-Palestinian conflict, exercises
practices of homogenization and differentiation over the Mizrahi man
in order to erase the interethnic conflict and to establish Ashkenazi leftist ideological identity. The film produces the image of the Mizrahi male
as a homophobe in direct signifying relation to his cinematic representation as an Arab-hating nationalist.[21] However, in order to create
an Israeli-Palestinian national solidarity, within which the Mizrahi
is incorporated, the film displaces the pathological sexuality/Arab-
hating of the Mizrahi man onto an ethnically unmarked homosexual
male figure.

Exceptional is the cinematic work of the Mizrahi director Ze'ev
Revach who continued to produce social-ethnic Bourekas comedies from
the seventies to the nineties. Revach extends the politics of representation of Mizrahi males beyond the "negative/positive" dead-end
dichotomy that has been constructed by both mainstream and independent filmmakers. He uses subversive strategies of passing and the
grotesque which enable the recognition of a new Mizrahi ethnicity.
Revach's films cross visible boundaries of racial and sexual difference
and present a version of Mizrahi masculinity that exposes the masquerade of Mizrahi manhood as spectacle.

Reconstructing Mizrahi Masculinity

The Mizrahi body, whether male or female, is a sub-
ordinated body. Specifically, for Mizrahi men, the regulation of body
and sexuality signifies a loss of access to positions of power and mastery that are regarded as the essence of masculinity in patriarchy.
Under Ashkenazi oppression, the Mizrahi man cannot fully assume the
role of the "father." Ben-Gurion himself dismissed the paternal functions of the Mizrahi man: "The Yemenite father does not look after his
children and family as we do. . . . He is not accustomed to feed his child
properly before eating himself."[22] In the process of *aliya* [immigration],
the Mizrahi father lost his familial prestige and authority, as he was
forced not only to erase his cultural identity which was regarded as backward and primitive, but he was also economically restrained, incapable
of giving his children better living conditions.

In David Benchetrit documentary film *Kaddim Wind: Moroccan
Chronicle* (2002), some of the male interviewees of Moroccan descent

tell about the humiliations of Mizrahi father who arrived in Israel in the fifties. The former leader of Shas, the Jewish-Sephardic Orthodox Movement, Arye Derei describes:

> I have good memories from Morocco. . . . everything seemed like a dream. When we came to Israel . . . [the] problem started. [We] came to Israel . . . to a small apartment . . . [with] difficult living conditions. But the most vivid memory that I have is the crisis that my father experienced. Father, who had a business in Morocco, suddenly [became] a worker in a governmental factory, earning a minimum wage. Can you understand what this does to a man in his thirties? Nobody appreciated his work. [The result was] a broken father and broken children.

Reuven Abergel, a leader of the Mizrahi Black Panthers, tells: "I love him [my father] a lot. My anger was great. I lost my childhood. I needed to separate myself from the family and to leave for the kibbutz. I saw his weakness, his bent back. . . . I saw him defeated."

In another film, *Samir* (1997), also directed by Benchetrit, the Iraqi-Jewish author Sami Michael describes the humiliating process of absorption for his father:

> I admired my father. I loved him greatly. . . . I remember, my father was crashed as a proud man who was a provider. They gave him a feeling that there was no hope; he lost all that he once represented. [Everyone] who was over a certain age, and who had a certain heritage, a certain language, a certain mentality, was dangerous [for Zionism]. He must not be destroyed physically, but he was doomed. . . . [He] decided not to immigrant to Israel [that is, not to adjust to the Zionist society] and to remain a new immigrant all his life."

Along with the undermining of Mizrahi father's economical status, the selection policy of the Jewish Agency, according to which only a chosen part of the Moroccan family was permitted immigration, split and dismantled the patriarchal nuclear Mizrahi family. The social activist Sami Shalom-Chetrit states in *Kaddim*: "We became cared for so quickly. You become cared for. You stop being an independent person. You stop being human. You become a creature who loses control over his destiny. From that moment, your parents are not your parents anymore. You have a teacher, a therapist, a social worker." Derei states:

> The solution was to go to a boarding school at the age of nine . . .
> outside of town. The thing that it did at home . . . I remember my
> mother . . . [how can she] send [away] her two adult boys . . . ?
> We were in heaven in Morocco; we were sons of kings. And sud-
> denly [we] had to leave. To leave behind frustrated parents and
> come for a visit once a month. . . . And from this [experience], you
> realize that you have a problem. And gradually, as I grew to
> understood more, I realized that I was not brought up like other
> kids.

The fury against the Ashkenazi establishment that degraded the
Mizrahi father and the anger against the Mizrahi father himself, who
did not resist oppression, produced the social revolutionary awareness
of second-generation Mizrahim. Mizrahi social activist men constructed the narrative of the defeated "castrated" father in order to constitute their resistance to Ashkenazi supremacy and to produce the
image of a new Mizrahi man. The desire for a new kind of strong, brave,
tough heterosexual Mizrahi masculinity was predicted by the need to
contest the conditions of dependency and enslavement that the
Ashkenazi oppressive regime enforced.[23]

In the seventies, the Mizrahi Black Panthers Movement—dominated
by men—rebelled against Ashkenazi ethnic discrimination. The establishment, alarmed by the Panthers' protest (especially the famous
May 1972 demonstration in which Molotov cocktails were launched
against the police), arrested its leaders and explained their political
action as a result of the "violent nature" of Mizrahim. The provocative
choice of name for the Israeli Mizrahi resistance was an ironic rever-
sal of the Ashkenazi stereotype of Mizrahim as "black animals," as well
as a reference to the American Black Panthers.[24]

The inspiration of the American Black resistance was not only by
name, but also by image. Mizrahi Black Panthers adopted the highly
sexualized macho look of the Black Americans: clenched fists, long
sideburns, and Afro hairstyle. This macho look could be described as
the "cool pose." "Cool pose," as Richard Majors explains it in the context of African American masculinity, is the way raced men have
learned "to mistrust the words and actions of dominant white people,
[and thus] black males have learned to make great use of 'poses' and
'postures' which connote control, toughness, and detachment."[25] The
Panthers' cool pose was an attempt to restore the injured Mizrahi male
body and to protect it from injury. However, while the Mizrahi cool
pose represents a safeguard against oppression from the dominant

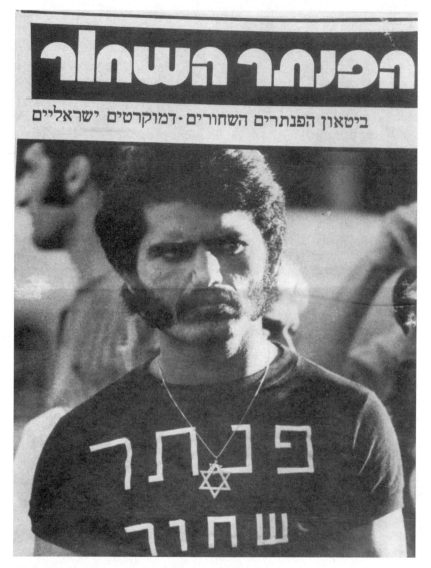

הפנתר השחור

ביטאון הפנתרים השחורים·דמוקרטים ישראליים

Figure 6. The new sexualized macho look of the Mizrahi Black Panthers from the cover of the Black Panthers' journal. Courtesy of the Musrara School of Photography and New Media.

Ashkenazi society, it is also an aggressive assertion of phallocentric masculinity.

The Mizrahi Panthers often used the term *defukim veshehorim* [fucked and black] in reference to Black-American nationalists. But "fucked and black" also articulates their racial and class discrimination in sexual terms. The Panthers identified male sexual "passivity" with the oppressed social class and male sexual "activity" with the racist practice of the Ashkenazi establishment. This association is explicitly manifested in one of the Panthers' criticism of the Ministry of Welfare: "We need to eliminate the institutions for criminal juveniles that become a hothouse for future criminals. In an institution for criminal juveniles, I saw an instructor having sexual intercourse with a boy. . . . This is the treatment that those institutes provide."[26]

The brutalization of Mizrahim by Ashkenazi supremacist domination is figured as a homosexual rape. Homosexuality comes into focus as the undoing of one man's authority by another, as humiliation of one man by another. It signifies merely a failed, debased, or inadequate masculinity. Viewing this relationship as one between a Mizrahi boy and an Ashkenazi male adult—and not between two adult men—emphasizes the asymmetrical social and sexual power relations (a "pervert" Ashkenazi man and a "innocent" Mizrahi boy) and the idea of forced sex. This construction is important for the new male Mizrahi discourse, because as long as the sexual act is performed unvoluntarily on the part of the Mizrahi male (and not out of homosexual desire between two adult men), Mizrahi men can be cured from this social-social trauma and rebuild their injured heteromasculinity. This narrative also justifies the right for a new "active," empowered, upright, Mizrahi heterosexual manhood that is dependent on self-definition against a phobic specter of sex between men, wherein the phallus serves as signifier.

This Mizrahi phallic sexual politics appears in the contemporary writing of Shalom-Chetrit. In his radical book *The Ashkenazi Revolution Is Dead* (a reference to the 1964 Kalman Katznelson's racist book, *The Ashkenazi Revolution*), Shalom-Chetrit, critiques the Mizrahi fathers' generation for groveling and subordinating themselves to the "gods of European Zionism" in order to gain access to imaginary positions of power and honor. "This generation," he argues, "produced those who want to be more Zionist than the Zionists themselves, more nationalist than the nationalists, in order to win the identity of the strong, the Zionist-Ashkenazi identity." Shalom-Chetrit claims that this generation is a "castrated Mizrahi generation."[27] In Shalom-Chetrit's protest discourse, the Zionist-Ashkenazi domination is imagined through the metaphor of male castration that culturally connotes a so-called humiliating and "feminine" positionality of the male body. The submission of the "castrated" Mizrahi fathers' generation to Zionist authority positions them as "passive" sexual objects of the Ashkenazi "active" masculine power. For Shalom-Chetrit, the fathers' generation's lack of social and political self-consciousness is articulated in terms of gender and sexual active/passive binarisms. In order to be a "real" Mizrahi man and to reclaim and construct his "active" and phallic masculinity, Shalom-Chetrit must repudiate and demonize "femininity" within men. As bell hooks so eloquently puts it in another context, Shalom-Chetrit shares "the patriarchal belief that revolutionary struggle [is] really about the erect phallus."[28]

Fifty years after the immigration of Mizrahim to Israel, a different, more emphatic tone is heard among Mizrahi men in relation to the "castrated" father. In *Kaddim,* Abergel says: "If he were an oak tree with all the strong winds that blow in the state he would break into pieces; and he was forced to turn himself into a low grass in order for the winds to blow over him without him and his family being injured." In *Samir,* Michael states: "When there is no milk and no bread to give to the children . . . [how can he be asked] to get up and fight for his culture and for his ancestors' poetry? He was . . . in a state of helplessness and felt that everyone despised him. It is a very painful process." The submissiveness and vulnerability of the father is imagined here as a form of power, as resistance and protest against Zionist oppression.

However, the oedipal struggle of second-generation Mizrahi men was not with the Mizrahi father, since he was already removed from his patriarchal power position by Ashkenazi Zionism and perceived as defeated, passive and "castrated," but with the "white" colonial father, David Ben-Gurion. In *Kaddim,* Shalom-Chetrit states: "I was brought up with a picture of Ben-Gurion hanged on the wall. . . . [He] was the new king of the Jews. . . . He turned the Moroccan into children. He was their father and they adopted him because they were lost. He was the great papa." But for Mizrahi men, argues the film *Kaddim,* Ben-Gurion turn out to be a traitorous, racist, and violent father, who sent his aggressive forces against the Mizrahi protest of Wadi-Salib in the fifties. In this revolutionary event, the Mizrahi demonstrators yelled: "We are the sons of the king of Morocco and not the sons of Ben-Gurion."

In the male Mizrahi discourse from the seventies to today, the pain of Ashkenazi oppression is imagined as the pain of men inflicted by other men. Healing of that pain takes place only within an oedipal conflict between men. The relation between the Mizrahi man and the Ashkenazi father is perceived as the only space for Mizrahi struggle. Mizrahi men linked Mizrahi liberation with the desire to create a social structure wherein they could constitute themselves as patriarchs. On the one hand, Mizrahi men expressed contempt for Ashkenazi men; yet, they also envied them for their access to patriarchal power. The Mizrahi male believed in the fantasy that patriarchy and phallocentrism might heal the wounds inflicted by Ashkenazi discrimination. This Mizrahi politics may be seen as a challenge to the oppressive Ashkenazi hegemony, but it also assumes a form which is oppressive to women and gays.[29]

The Bourekas Film and the Politics of Heteronormativity: Casablan

Casablan was one of first films to address the growing force of the Mizrahi Black Panthers and the new Mizrahi consciousness. The film is a musical, part of the Bourekas genre (named after a Sephardi pastry), a cycle of films that mostly flourished after the success of the 1967 War and specifically focused on the ethnic tension between Mizrahim and Ashkenazim in Israeli society. In most Bourekas films, the interethnic tension is resolved through an erotic reunion, or a marriage, of the heterosexual mixed couple. Israeli film scholarship has already critiqued this imagined social integration that disavows and silences any kind of representation of Mizrahi struggle through the Ashkenazi ideology of the melting pot. As Ella Shohat wrote: "Like Israeli politicians and social scientists who hail the trend . . . toward mixed marriage as a sign that the ethnic problem is disappearing, so the happy endings of the 'bourekas' film foster a 'mythical' solution which in fact buttresses the status quo."[30]

However, while Israeli film scholars were critical about the fictive erotic solution of the Bourekas film in terms of Mizrahi ethnicity, they avoided critiquing the heterocentrism and heteronormativity enforced by this narrative. Michael Warner discusses the ways heteronormative culture—a public culture, juridical, economic, and aesthetic—is organized for the promotion of heterosexuality. He writes: "Het[erosexual] culture thinks of itself as the elemental form of human association, as the very model of intergender relations, as the indivisible basis of all community, and as the means of reproduction without which society wouldn't exist. Materialist thinking about society has in many cases reinforced these tendencies, inherent in heterosexual ideology, toward totalized view of the social."[31] One of the tasks of the Bourekas genre was to propagate and enforce heterosexuality, naturalized through the concept of reproduction and erotic biethnic male-female union and masked by terms such as "family values" and "exile-gathering" [*kibbutz galuyut*]—exclusive and privileged means of the Zionist heterosexual culture through which it could interpret itself as society.

The film *Casablan* promotes not just any heterosexuality, but specifically Ashkenazi heterosexuality. Threaten by the rise of a new Mizrahi heterosexual masculinity, the film tries to disavow ethnic differences by enforcing practices of mimicry in which the Mizrahi male hero was made to reflect the image of Ashkenazi heteronormativity. As Homi Bhabha has explained, colonial mimicry is a "desire for a reformed, recognizable Other as a subject of difference that is almost the same, but not quite."[32] In *Casablan,* the male identity of the Mizrahi "panthers" is policed and controlled by a practice of Ashkenazi mimicry that was institutionalized and legitimized by biethnic heterosexual marriage and the military.[33]

Known by his nickname Casablan, or in short Casa (Yehoram Gaon), Yossef Siman-Tov is a Moroccan Jew, born in Casablanca, a leader of a gang of young Mizrahi men who "terrorizes" the streets of Jafa. Casa and his friends are associated in the film with the Black Panthers on levels of both visual and narrative representation. The gang's Afro hairstyles, the long and thick sideburns, the muscular bodies, as well as Casa's heavy gold chain with a big Star of David are all inspired by the Panthers' sexualized macho image. Casa's cool pose is emphasized in a scene in which the gang and he strike cool and tough poses before the mirror, trying on different clothes, a moment before Casa's anxious encounter with the threatening Ashkenazi world, represented by the family of Rachel (Efrat Lavie), the Ashkenazi girl with whom he is in love. The choreography in the scene uses frozen body postures that perfectly fit the "cool pose" esthetic, as it controls and toughens the Mizrahi male body, asserting it as a discrete identity. The association between the Mizrahi Black Panthers and Casa is made explicit in the narrative when Rachel's father, who rejects Casa's courting of his daughter, says to him: "You should be in jail with the criminals. Go back to your Panthers; there you can be a big hero." Like in the official discourse on Black Panthers, Casa's Oriental masculinity is considered hostile and violent, which enables the film to ignore and disregard the Panthers' social outcry, as well as to justify the force used to oppress the Mizrahi resistance.

At the same time, the film presents Casa's distress, loneliness, and alienation from the racist Ashkenazi society. (When Rachel expresses indifference to his provocations, Casa asks, "Why? Because I'm a

Figure 7. The re-hetero-masculinization of the Mizrahi male. Casa (Yehoram Gaon) in Menachem Golan's *Casablan*. Courtesy of G. G. Studios LTD.

Moroccan?"). Apparently, he uses violence only to cover his sensitivity and vulnerability. ("You broke our Casa," one neighbor says to Rachel). Behind the tough and violent exterior hides an honest and noble person. Hurt for being marked as violent and criminal, his pride is really cracked when he is falsely accused by the neighbors and Rachel of stealing money designated to renovate the condemned neighborhood. He prefers to stay in jail rather than to refute the false accusations, although he knows who the real thief is. Those qualities of pride, toughness, self-control, and self-respect are romanticized attributes that are mythologically regarded as the essence of the patriarchal hetero-sexual male. When Rachel's father accuses him of not having self-respect ("Respect, honor, [you] wouldn't even know that something like this exists."), of not being a "real man," Casa nostalgically remembers the proud masculinity that he had in Morocco. He sings:

> At the Kasbah, at high noon . . .
> I'd walk around by myself
> Alone but tall and proud
> And people said 'now look at him'
> And what do you expect
> And they would wave from every door with due respect
> And they would know just then and there
> That I, just I, have self-respect.

In another episode, he sings:

> My home is there, beyond the sea
> Oh I remember how the Sabbath's candles glowed
> And my father looked at me.
> Nothing was said.

The songs express a nostalgia for the original Arab homeland, fantasies of return and memories of home, that were, as Shohat argued, repressed and forbidden by Zionism, ignoring the complex cultural history and community life shared by Jews and Muslims in Arab countries and universalizing it to Western ideals of Jewish persecution in Europe.[34] The film forecloses these cultural reminiscences and explains Casa's "failed" masculinity by the absence of the Moroccan father who stayed in Casablanca. The narrative forces Casa to forget his father and homeland and offers him the opportunity to reconstruct his self-respect through the military, the ideal of Ashkenazi heterosexual masculinity.

The film, unexpectedly, reveals that Casa won an honor medal in the 1967 Six Days War, one of the most heroic and vigorous Israeli wars in which the Israeli army defeated five Arab armies in six days. Casa's military heroism comes to legitimize his masculinity and to establish the fact that he became a criminal only because he lost his relationship to the Law of the military Father after the war was over. The film disavows the Ashkenazi social oppression that probably led Casa into crime and violence and offers to Mizrahi men an imaginary access to patriarchal power, a fantasy—shared by Mizrahi activists—that phallocentrism will contest their position of dependency, but which in fact only reinforces the Ashkenazi patriarchal domination. Little wonder that toward the end of the film, Casa reunites with his symbolic father—his army commander who now serves as a police officer and investigates Casa for the crime that he did not commit. When Casa says that he felt abandoned after he was released from the army ("I didn't have a home to go back to. You were my home."), his commander scolds him for his weakness, bitterness, and what he calls his "inferiority complex," commanding him to be a "man" again. Assigned to a position of "dependency" and "inferiority," the Mizrahi male is infantilized as an Oriental childlike man who needs an Ashkenazi trusteeship that will gently guide him into "adult" society.[35] Reflecting on his commander's comments, Casa sings: "Stop raging at the world/ you're no saint/ get a grip on yourself/ clean up your act/ don't be like a woman/ see what a shame." The Mizrahi man's inferiority complex is associated with failed, deteriorated, feminized masculinity, marked as an inferior stage of male sexuality that must be disavowed and repudiated, if he is to submit to the imperative of Ashkenazi heterosexual manhood.

The patriarchal institutions of the military and interethnic marriage join forces together in order to reinvent the new "Ashkenazied" masculinity of the Mizrahi man. The film constructs for Casa a macho "rescue fantasy," in which he will save Rachel from the rape attempt by a repellent Hungarian neighbor, Yanus, who is in love with Rachel and actually stole the money. This produces the male Oriental Jew as an eligible and suitable citizen and heterosexual man for Ashkenazi girl. Heterosexuality thus becomes a pre-condition for the "proper" citizenship of the Mizrahi male.

The Mizrahi man's forced submission to the imperative norms of Ashkenazi heterosexual masculinity also enables the "whitening" of his ethnic identity. Richard Dyer argues that whiteness is always about the reproduction of white bodies through heterosexuality. The white anxiety surrounding interracial heterosexuality that threatens the purity of the white race only emphasizes the centrality and structural importance of reproduction and heterosexuality to the existence and continuity of whiteness. However, Dyer notes that in some cases interracial sex was "encouraged on the grounds that the population would gradually become whiter and the black and the native elements would be bred out. Both approaches make the same assumption: that it is better to be white and that sexual reproduction is the key to achieving whiteness."[36]

Although the case of interethnic sexual reproduction in Israel is different from both the approaches that Dyer mentions—due to the fact that both sides of the mixed heterosexual couple are Jewish—there still exists a parallel ideological motivation of the Israeli establishment to promote ethnic sexual integration. The dominant ideology of exile-gathering and ethnic (sexual) integration that the Bourekas films expressed and promoted, aimed to disavow ethnic differences to "Ashkenazied" Mizrahim. The best way to achieve that was through heterosexuality and reproduction of "whiter" Ashkenazi bodies. Hence, heterosexuality and reproduction are structural elements in the construction of Ashkenazi "whiteness" and in the "Ashkenization" of the Mizrahim.

The film opens and ends with a subplot about the pregnancy and labor of one of the neighbors. The family wishes for the expectant woman to have a boy, or as one puts it: "Be it a boy or a girl, it's all the same to me, providing there is a *brit* (the Jewish circumcision ritual)." The birth of the new male boy, a product of an interethnic marriage, symbolizes the rebirth of Casa's new "Ashkenazied" heterosexual masculinity. In the *brit* scene, Casa becomes the godfather of the newborn who is even named after him (Yossef)—notions that underline the signifying relationship between heterosexual reproduction and the "whitening" of the Mizrahi man. The film disavows ethnic differences by practice of mimicry that reinforces the Ashkenazi hetero-masculinity domination. Paradoxically, the ethnic borders of the Ashkenazi people cannot be constituted without Mizrahim and without the constant disavowal of their relation to them. Ashkenazi heteronormativity is established through the very production of its Mizrahi "others" which it excludes.

Between Mizrahi Men:
Light Out of Nowhere

The film *Light Out of Nowhere* is focalized through the eyes of Shaul Chetrit (Nissim Levy), a seventeen-year-old Mizrahi boy, who is torn between two members of his crumbling family. On the one hand, there is his older brother Baruch (Avi Saltzberg), a criminal who despises the establishment and especially his own father, and who submits himself to Ashkenazi domination. On the other hand, there is the father himself (Shlomo Bassan), a simple, hard-working man, who forces Shaul to look for a job and to conform to the establishment's laws. While Shaul does not see in his brother's "rebellion" an alternative for social or individual change, he refuses to submit himself to a hopeless future offered to him by his father. Shaul, like his girlfriend Daliya and his brother, longs for a better future, some kind of hope, or as he puts it, "there must be something, some place." As Shohat has argued, Shaul's lack of motivation to work is represented in the film, in contrast to other Israeli films, not "as a problem of Oriental mentality but rather as a symptom of a political structure."[37]

Shaul's story is contextualized within social events that took place in Israel during the early seventies. Although the name of the Black Panthers is not mentioned directly, the film nevertheless presents a Mizrahi social struggle against the Ashkenazi discriminatory hegemony that evokes the movement's protest. In one of the film's most powerful scenes, municipal inspectors and the police execute a destruction order for a neighbor's illegal constructions. A female neighbor shouts toward them: "Go and destroy the Ashkenazim's houses. . . . Our children fight against the Arabs, but that there should be a place for the child to live, that is impossible! Since when has this government cared [about us]? Go on, bring those *vuzvuzim* [slang for Askenazim] from Russia." After torching one of the police vehicles, she is forcefully evicted and arrested. At other times, the rebellion against the establishment is expressed in the film in more comic form, as in the scene in which a gang of street boys mocks Zionist and Israeli national figures like Herzl, Golda Meir, and Abba Eben.

Shaul is a young man who is caught not only between two oppressed family members and between two ways of social existence, but also between two (presumably) conflicted perspectives on masculinity: his father's feminized unheroic manhood and his brother's hypermasculinity. Baruch sees proud and strong manhood as a precondition for survival in discriminatory Israeli society, a defense and rebellion against the passive and powerless positions that the Ashkenazi domination enforces on Mizrahi males. He tells his brother: "You better know, either you fuck or are fucked. This is life. It will take you a long time to understand how shitty life can be here. You are still 'green.'" Baruch's words evoke not only the Black Panthers' slogan "fucked and black," but also their compulsory heterosexual discourse. Baruch's self-empowered heterosexual phallic Mizrahi male identity is established on the binary oppositions of active/passive, whereas the

Figure 8. Caught between two conflicted perspectives on Mizrahi masculinity. Shaul (Nissim Levy, center) in Nissim Dayan's *Light Out of Nowhere*. Courtesy of Nissim Dayan.

Ashkenazi male hegemony emasculates and submits Mizrahi men to their authority.

As in the Black Panthers' discourse of masculinity, male passivity is demonized, signifying incompetent, humiliated, and violated masculinity. Baruch sees his own father as such an unmanly man, a colonized man who grovels to the Ashkenzai establishment. The film opens with a quarrel between the two, where Baruch says to his father: "I'm not a coward like you. When people see me, they feel courageous. Look at you, soon you will cry." Ironically, in the background, the radio plays a gymnastics broadcast, one of the morning exercise programs on Israeli radio in the years following the establishment of the state that served the national mission of constructing a new manly Zionist body. Through Baruch, the film critiques the father's "sissy" manliness and the Zionist-Ashkenazi body culture that emasculated Mizrahi males, excluding them from its discourse of masculinity and denying them access to positions of power, authority and equal citizenship. On the other hand, the film reinforces the (Zionist) phallocentric notion of manhood by marking the Mizrahi "feminine" male as a having a failed, debased or inadequate body that must be deflected to make way for a new Oriental heterosexual masculinity.

The image of the weak, submissive father is also represented through Shaul's eyes. In one of the scenes, the father forces his son to meet his friend, a government official, who can help Shaul find a job. The father disdains his son's professional abilities in front of the establishment representative ("he knows nothing"), lights the latter's cigarette, grovels before his power and authority, and admiringly says, "A man like you . . . in such an office." The Mizrahi man's passive feminized submission before the Ashkenazi establishment is also expressed in another scene in which a group of young Mizrahi boys ridicule their friend who has joined the army; they snatch his army hat, use it for handball and say, "He runs like a woman." Here, again, is the paradoxical discourse of the new Mizrahi heteromasculinity. The boys mock the heroic myth of the army and the illusion of empowered masculinity that it produces for Mizrahi men. Yet Mizrahi subversion and protest against the Ashkenazi hegemony becomes visible only through a compulsory heterosexual rhetoric that mocks and degrades "femininity" within men.

The film also produces the myth of Mizrahi phallic maleness through the representation of Baruch's sexual potency. The film represents Baruch as a tough and virile man: tight undershirt and jeans, hard muscles, and hairy manly chest. The film also emphasizes his sexual capacity and success, especially among Ashkenazi women ("I snap my fingers and I have them in my pocket!"). However, the myth of Mizrahi men's sexual potency arises from the core Orientalist beliefs of Zionist racist ideology, which held Mizrahim to be invested less in their minds and more in their bodies. Thus, the film not only reproduces this racist myth, but also, like many Mizrahi men, does not want to demystify it. The realm of sex offers for Mizrahi males a space for emotional and bodily expression, self-encouragement and self-affirmation that contests the oppressive conditions of Israeli social reality. For Baruch, instrumentalization of sex and sexuality becomes a necessary step for masculine survival and self-definition. In one moment in the film, the brothers stand on each side of the frame, separated by a fetishistic image of a nude woman. Baruch asks Shaul if he has succeeded in getting his girlfriend into bed, and when Shaul responds negatively, Baruch says, "You better know, a woman never makes the

decisions, it is the man who decides." His lack of sexual experience
and his brother's superior virility place Shaul in a "feminine" position
associated with failed manhood. His employer says to him, "If not for
your brother, you would not dream of working here. You are worse than
a woman!"). As compensation for his lack of phallic power, (read as
social dependency), he fantasizes about a Scandinavian girl he sees on
the street who represents his longing for the recognition of the
Ashkenazi "white" society. ("This one loves Ashkenazim," his brother
testifies about him.) Fanon, in another context, described this fantasy
of the colonized man:

> By loving me she proves that I am worthy of white love. I am loved
> like a white man.
> I am a white man.
> Her love takes me onto the noble road that leads to total
> realization . . .
> I marry white culture, white beauty, and white whiteness.
> When my restless hands caress those white breasts, they
> grasp white civilization and dignity and make them mine.[38]

The film attempts to critique this macho fantasy of the Mizrahi male,
exposing its imaginary access to power which it produces for Mizrahi
men. Shaul witnesses his brother's friends coming out of a deserted
building after they have had serial sex with the Scandinavian girl. When
he enters the building he finds her sitting exhausted on the floor, asking him in Swedish, "You too?" Shaul's fantasy is shattered. He understands now that having sex with the white girl will not lead to any real
change in his life and that his brother's so-called revolutionary struggle is an illusionary one. However, the film visualizes Shaul's insight
through a misogynistic discourse wherein the (white) woman's body
becomes a site for the elaboration of Mizrahi male's social consciousness. The film, therefore, does not attempt to deconstruct the normative patriarchal thinking, but rather accepts its sexist parameters.

Shaul's double identity finds a certain expression in W.E.B. Du
Bois's concept of the "double-consciousness" of the American black
man:

> It is a peculiar sensation, this double-consciousness, this sense of
> always looking at one's self through the eyes of others, of measuring
> one's soul by the tape of a world that looks on in amused contempt
> and pity. One ever feels this two-ness—an American, a Negro; two

souls, two thoughts, two unreconciled strivings; two warring
ideals in one dark body, whose dogged strength alone keeps it from
being torn asunder.[39]

For Du Bois, a precondition of "true self-consciousness" of a racialized
and national subject position is first gaining male heterosexual self-
consciousness.[40] In *Light Out of Nowhere,* Shaul does not succeed in
gaining "true" Mizrahi male self-consciousness. The film ends with an
image of the hero sitting on the sidewalk with his head in his hands.
In the background, the radio again plays a gymnastics broadcast. Shaul
feels alienated from his own male duality that he cannot reconcile,
estranged from his own conflicted identification with the male identities enforced upon his father and brother by Zionist-Ashkenazi ideology. The film, in a sense, understands this Mizrahi spilt masculine
identity as a contradiction that cannot but should eventually be
resolved, a conflicted gendered subjectivity that threatens to sunder
the hero's "self" from within. Understanding the Mizrahi male self-
identity in this way, the film still assumes and reinforces the femi-
nine/masculine, active/passive binary equations of Zionist compulsory
heterosexual discourse and does not exploit the structural contradictions of those imagined differences in order to deconstruct the Zionist
dominant regime of "truth."

From Arab Hatred to Homophobia: Beyond the Walls

The sexuality of the Mizrahi man in the film *Beyond
the Walls* is constructed within the socio-political framework of the
Israeli/Palestinian conflict. The film describes the relationship between
Israelis and Palestinians in a maximum-security Israeli prison, allegorized as a microcosm of Israeli society. The two main protagonists—
Uri (Arnon Zadok), a Mizrahi criminal imprisoned for armed robbery,
and Issam (Muhammad Bakri), a political prisoner imprisoned for
terrorist activity—overcome their political differences during the film.
Together with Assaf (Asi Dayan), a peace activist who is imprisoned
for contacting PLO agents and the other prisoners, they join in a struggle against establishment domination, represented by the corrupt
Ashkenazi chief warden (Hillel Ne'eman). The film constructs an alle-
gorical camaraderie of the oppressed. However, as Ella Shohat has
argued, "Since the film alludes to Palestinian contextual reality but
elides that of the Sephardi, its didactic allegory lacks reciprocity." While

Uri eventually follows the Peace Camp line "he does not take the additional pedagogical step which would manifest awareness of his situation as an Oriental Jew. He does not reach the recognition that the very same historical process that created the 'Palestinian problem' also created the 'Oriental Jewish problem.' Because of his lack of awareness, he never presents his problem as a collective one; he interacts with Issam as an Israeli-Jew and not as a Sephardi."[41]

In the first part of the film, Uri and his Mizrahi friends are imagined as Arab-haters, differentiated from Assaf, the peaceable Leftist. The film establishes a signifying relation between the Mizrahi men's fanatic nationalism and their pathological homophobic sexuality—that is, their repressed homosexuality.[42] However, in order to constitute a political alliance between the Jewish and the Arab prisoners, the film, in the second part, displaces the homophobia/Arab-hating of the Mizrahim to another prisoner—the ethnically unmarked homosexual male. The film homogenizes and disavows the sexual "otherness" of the Mizrahi male—as an allegory for his constructed ethnic "otherness"—in order to produce a political Leftist (Ashkenazi) agenda.

The film opens with an image of the nude body of Uri as he slowly takes his clothes off. What seems to be an "objective" shot is revealed, a few seconds later, as the subjective point of view of the wardens (Mizrahim in this case), who inspect Uri's body parts—mouth, armpit, genitals, bottom—for lethal objects, examining his body for visible signs of criminality. The Mizrahi male body is fragmented and anatomized to locate parts that can be appropriated and made to testify for the "truth" of the whole racial identity. This practice of synecdoche and metonyms that characterizes the visual logic of racism, submits the racialized body to interpretation and textualization.[43] The dominant gaze seeks to read the Mizrahi male body that now itself becomes a lethal object, a phobic spectacle, regulated and disciplined through a racist visual economy. Further, once subject to interpretation, as Lee Edelman argued, the spectacularized male body becomes representational, unnatural, questionable, and even "feminine" in the sense that it is opposed to the ideological construction of heterosexual masculinity as the antithesis of representation.[44]

The "feminine" positionality of the Mizrahi male body is even more emphasized, a few shots later, when Uri hears the horrified screams of another prisoner in the next room who is being subject to an enema examination. The threatening rustle of the plastic glove that the prison's male nurse wears on his hand, and the warden who commands

Uri to "lay down on the couch or we will help you lay down," present a horrific spectacle of male anal penetration, wherein the Ashkenazi domination is figured as a violent force that threatens to violate the bodily integrity of the Mizrahi male in order to reinscribe his social humiliation. The Mizrahi man is compelled, through the threat of anal penetration, to "lay down" in front of the Ashkenazi domination that towers over him physically and denies his male agency, transforming him into a "feminine" receptacle for Ashkenazi male power. Neither of the characters is homosexual, but homosexuality, as it is configured in the heterocentric view as the humiliating anal penetration of one man by another, is registered in the homophobic optic vision of the film as a violent disappropriation of masculine authority that evokes the paranoid relation of the Mizrahi heterosexual male subject. Hence, in direct response to this threat of the catastrophic undoing of his masculinity, Uri holds the male nurse and threatens him with a knife. According to the film, it is the figurative homosexuality and not homophobia that poses a central threat for Mizrahi men. The sexual oppression, allegorized as Mizrahi social oppression, is disavowed and projected onto the Oriental man, marked as a homophobe.

The sexually allegorized social oppression of the Sephardi Jews is further displaced by the film onto a political conflict between the Ashkenazi and the Mizrahi that revolves around the Palestinian ques-

Figure 9. Imagining the Mizrahi man's homophobia. Uri (Arnon Zadok) in Uri Barbash's *Beyond the Walls.* Courtesy of Uri Barbash.

tion, in which the Mizrahi men themselves are constructed as homophobic—a metaphor for their violent antagonism toward the Peace Camp. For the prisoners, Assaf is an Arab-lover who "fucks in the ass" with Palestinians. When Assaf enters the cell, Fitussi (Rami Danon), one of the prisoners, feminizes him and the other prisoners when he addresses them as women: "Girls, girls, look who came in from the cold." "Enter, sweetie," he calls to Assaf, "we will defrost you a little." While one of the prisoners holds him from behind, Fitussi unbuttons Assaf's shirt and pants and commands him to spread his legs. ("Open so everybody can come in.") Fittusi, then, asks one of the prisoners to play an "Eastern chord" on the guitar and while rubbing his ass against Assaf's groin he says: "Do you like the Orient, baby? I'm going to teach you something new about the East that you never knew. Let's start with Turkey."

The film represents the Mizrahi men's hostility toward the peaceable Ashkenazi as a brutal homosexual rape associated with the "nature" of Eastern male sexuality. Mizrahi men are constructed as homophobic—that is, as repressed homosexuals—who project their pathological sexuality onto the Ashkenazi Peace Camp and the Palestinians. In the deviant mind of the Mizrahi man, any attempt of Israelis to negotiate with the Palestinians is seen as a homosexual rape of Jews by Arabs. By displacing the sexually allegorized social oppression of the Ashkenazi establishment onto the pathological sexual nature of the Mizrahi man and by associating this Oriental sexual "hostility" in the Palestinian context, the film disavows ethnic power relations in Israeli society and blocks any Mizrahi social awareness.

However, the stigmatization of the male Oriental Jew as homophobe poses a problem for the utopian collaboration between the Mizrahi men, the Ashkenazi Assaf and the Palestinian prisoners. In order to establish this multi-ethnic male homosociality, the film projects the Mizrahi pathological sexuality onto the stigmatized body of another prisoner, Menashe, assigned to the role of homosexual perversity. Menashe's ethnicity is unmarked. The film focuses on his cooperation with the corrupted chief warden, his hatred for the Palestinian prisoners and mainly his abused sexual relation with another prisoner, Doron, an effeminate young male, whom he violently raped. Doron hangs himself after refusing to lie for the chief warden who wants him to testify that it was the Palestinians who murdered one of the Israeli prisoners. The chief warden threatens Doron that he will be sent back to Menashe.

When the prisoners discover the chief warden's conspiracy, Doron becomes a kind of a martyred hero who, in his death, enabled solidarity of the oppressed. The homosexual sadistic Menashe now takes the projected role of the anti-Palestinian homophobe—a role assigned before to the Mizrahi men. Menashe must be positioned outside the joint struggle and outside the film's Leftist discourse, in order to displace homosexuality onto his body and to establish the prisoners' multi-ethnic hetero-solidarity. The film disavows ethnic differences and neutralizes the constructed sexual/political threat posed by Mizrahi men by displacing it onto the homosexual male, thus establishing its Ashkenazi Leftist vision, based upon homophobic repudiation of homosexuality.

Strategies of Subversion: The Films of Ze'ev Revach

The Mizrahi male body is forced to represent, to mimic, to be a stand-in, or mirror image upon which the Israeli Ashkenazi "self" projects itself. Caught between ambivalent and conflicted body images, the Mizrahi man cannot attain full cultural signification. He is excluded from the cultural field of symbolization, denied the entry into the realm of subjectivity itself. Unlike the child in front of the mirror for whom the specular reflection returns as the basis of the body image, when Mizrahim are made to bear the repressed fantasies of the Ashkenazi hegemony, they are denied entry into the alterity, which Lacan sees as grounding the necessary fiction of the unified "self." Thus, to use Fanon's observation from another context, the Mizrahi man is "forever in combat with his own image."[45]

Breaking through this impasse of the body-image dichotomies, Ze'ev Revach in his Bourekas comedies (which he directed and starred in), such as *Wrong Number* (1979), *Ladies Hairdresser* (1984), *Batito* (1987), and *Double Buskilla* (1998), is aware of the objectification of the Mizrahi male body under the Ashkenazi gaze and performs a version of Mizrahi masculinity that resists any ontological fixity.[46] He displays a post-essentialist conception of Mizrahi male subjectivity in which he theatrically stages a "self" whose authentic identity gives way to subversive practices of the grotesque, mimicry, and passing. Revach's body fits perfectly with Mikhail Bakhtin's concept of the grotesque body, in which the body "is not something completed and finished, but open and uncompleted."[47] Contrary to the representation of the self-controlled, self-restrained, cool, posed male body in films like *Casablan,* Revach often makes a spectacle of himself with his grotesque laughter, exaggerated facial and bodily gestures, and loose behavior.[48] Revach's body is an open, liquid, out-of-control body that transgresses its own limits by eating too much (in *Charlie and a Half* [1974]), or drinking too much (in *Ladies Hairdresser*), or both (in *Batito*), or by challenging his bodily elastic. (In *Batito,* he falls into a washing machine and spins himself to oblivion.) His body is always in the process of becoming, of metamorphosis; hence, the emphasis in his films on changed identifies, masquerade, and cross-dressing. He also emphasizes bodily fluids and discharges, such as sweat (in *Ladies Hairdresser,* his wife tells him, "I get pregnant by smelling your sweat") and excrement (in *Ladies Hairdresser,* he plays a cleaning servant who "cleans the shit of the world"), as well as "the lower stratum of the body" by playing the role of a hypervirile stud who, in *Only Today* (1976), for example, exercises his sexual skills on rich Ashkenazi married women.

Bakhtin writes: "The grotesque body . . . is a body in the becoming. It is never finished, never complete: it is continually built, created, and builds and creates another body. Moreover, the body swallows the world and is itself swallowed by the world. . . . All these convexities

Figure 10. "Cleaning the shit of the world." Sasson (Ze'ev Revach, left) in Ze'ev Revach's *Ladies Hairdresser.* Courtesy of Shapira Films LTD.

and orifices between bodies and between the body and the world are overcome: there is an interchange and interorientation."[49] Bakthin stresses the interplay between the body and the world. Only within the realm of the social does the body become meaningful and intelligible.

Revach's male body is always in relation to the world, to the social reality of deprivation and poverty that the Ashkenazi hegemony enforced on Mizrahim. His grotesque body is a result of, but also a critical response to and a weapon against, the ethno-economic discrimination in Israeli society, and the specific implications it has for the Mizrahi man. He manifests a male subjectivity that is always deauthorized by its attempt to maintain mastery. He works out the tension between trying to be a heterosexual Mizrahi man in a prejudiced social environment and the problems of identity that this project embodies.

Ladies Hairdresser is a film about Mizrahi heterosexual male identity in crisis. The film opens with the facial image of Victor (Revach), checking his reflection in the mirror, preparing himself for love-making with his wife. But the task is not easy. Victor, a working-class cleaner who lives in a small wretched apartment with his seven noisy children (ironically named after Israeli national leaders such as Ben-Gurion, Golda, and Weitzman) cannot find a moment of privacy. His specular mirror reflection is estranged, as he faces the poverty and the disgraceful living conditions. He is unable to fulfill his heterosexual needs. Unsuccessful in achieving a unified "self," his body "bursts" and splits apart when his estranged twin brother, Michelle (also played by Revach), enters his life. Michelle, a successful gay hairdresser, comes to rescue Victor who got into trouble for stealing money from the company for which he works. The two decide to switch identities: Victor will pass as a gay hairstylist and Michelle will pass as a straight family man. By passing as each other, the brothers hope to trick the police who will not be able match the fingerprints Victor left on the safe with those of Michelle.

But by passing, the Mizrahi twins also challenge the notion that identity categories of gender, sex, class, and ethnicity are inherent and unalterable essences, disclosing the "truth" that identities are not singularly true or false, but multiple and contingent. Amazed by the "authenticity" of his brother's passing as himself, Michelle says: "If I didn't know that this is you, I would think that this is me—but more manly." Passing as Victor, Michelle fools the police polygraph that tries to fix identities, telling us the "truth" about them, enforcing the cultural logic that the body is the site of identity intelligibility. "Are you

Figure 11. Mizrahi heterosexual male identity in crisis. Michelle (Ze'ev Revach, right) as the gay hairdresser in Ze'ev Revach's *Ladies Hairdresser*. Courtesy of Shapira Films LTD.

a male?" the police officer asks Michelle and the machine indicators run wild. Mimicking his straight brother and being gay himself, Michelle embodies seemingly contradictory notions of sexual and gender identity: male or female, homosexual or heterosexual. He inhabits an apparently impossible threshold between sexes and genders and represents a bodily anomaly. When the policeman asks him if he wants to return to his wife and children, the machine literally explodes.

This incident represents not only Michelle's dread of heterosexual lifestyle, as he has already tasted the distress his brother lives in, but also—if we understand the film as Victor's hetero-fantasy of escaping *his* miserable life—expresses the Mizrahi straight male's desire to liberate his oppressed masculinity. For Victor, passing as his brother gives him not only access to wealth and better living conditions, but also to a liberated (hetero)sexuality, attainable only in the upper-class Ashkenazi circles (as a hairdresser he has a semi-affair with a rich and beautiful Ashkenazi woman).

The fact that discloses that this film is a heterosexual fantasy is that Michelle does not get anything by passing as his brother, only the satisfaction of helping his identical twin, while Victor enjoys the pleasures of the bourgeois life. The idea that Michelle is constituted as Victor's sexual extension is visualized in the scene where Victor calls his brother, after years of detachment, from a payphone positioned, of all places, at the groin of a giant male body painted on a building's wall. Michelle, thus, is a projected image of Victor's desires that include also an unexpected brief gay encounter, when Michelle's lover joins Victor in the Jacuzzi, mistaking him for his brother.

In fact, many Bourekas films have used techniques of passing to describe Mizrahi infiltration into Ashkenazi enclosed society. In *Charlie and a Half,* for example, the Mizrahi hero passes as a wealthy Ashkenazi man in order to win the heart of an upper-class Ashkenazi girl, fooling her family and her boyfriend. However, toward the end of the film, the girl unveils his true Mizrahi identity, exposing him as a con man working on the streets. Passing here appears to be a temporary condition in which the Mizrahi enjoys the privileges of the Ashkenazi world, but more importantly, questions the very notion of ethnicity as biological essence, foregrounding the social contexts of racial and class vision by challenging the epistemological "truth" of identity itself. However, this form of subversion quickly becomes a form of surveillance as the "real" essence of the Mizrahi identity is disclosed. The Bourekas films in many cases blur the distinction between Ashkenazi and Mizrahi, not as a strategy of resistance, but only in order to reinforce Ashkenazi control. Shohat has pointed to the fact that most of the Mizrahi characters in the Bourekas films are played by Ashkenazi actors (such as Haim Topol, Yehuda Barkan, Gila Almagor), thus denying Mizrahi self-representation.[50] By passing as Mizrahim, these actors not only regulate Mizrahi cultural identity but also become better Mizrahim than the Mizrahim themselves. I am not suggesting that there is an "authentic" way to represent Mizrahim or that there is a Mizrahi essence of representation. Nor am I suggesting that Mizrahi actors could have done the job better. I argue that the Ashkenazi passing for Mizrahim in some Bourekas films can be seen as an allegory of the Ashkenazi control over Mizrahi cultural visibility.

In these terms, are Revach's strategies of passing subversive or are they techniques of surveillance? Anne McClintock argues that "privileged groups can, on occasion, display their privilege precisely by extravagant display of their *right to ambiguity.*"[51] In other words, by passing as gay, the heterosexual could better govern and regulate homosexuality, thus making passing an allegory of heterosexual power. I believe that Revach displays here a unique performance of queer heterosexual Mizrahi male identity. For Victor, Michelle becomes a kind of an "ego ideal," which places Victor in a narcissistic male position.

In his essay "Homo-Narcissism; or, Heterosexuality," Michael Warner points out that "the modern system of sex and gender would not be possible without a disposition to interpret the difference between genders as the difference between self and Other." According to this disposition, difference is always an allegory of gender and "having a sexual object of the opposite gender is taken to be the normal and paradigmatic form of an interest in the Other or, more generally, in others."[52] Contrary to that, according to heterocentric thinking, if one's sexual object is of the same gender as oneself, then one has presumably failed to distinguish between "self" and "other," and between identification and desire. Therefore, homosexuality is defined as a form of auto-eroticism and narcissism. Warner's strong claim is that the construction of homosexuality as narcissism actually *"allows the constitution of heterosexuality as such."*[53] In other words, heterosexuality needs to construct homosexuality as narcissism in order to constitute the heterosexist self-understanding of gender as a difference. As such, homo-narcissism is a structural element within the construction of heterosexuality. But heterosexuality must disavow this constitutive condition and project it onto the queer.

I would like to suggest that Revach does not disavow his own narcissism, but celebrates it within his own heterosexuality. This is due to the fact that Victor's narcissistic image—Michelle—is already he, himself. And Revach himself is both of them. Moreover, Michelle is not excluded nor repudiated from the narrative as soon as Victor's heterosexuality is reconstituted, as happens in most popular films. On the contrary, the two are seen at the end of the film, working together in Michelle's beauty salon, side-by-side, two sides of the same mirror (they are literally cutting hair on both sides of the same mirror), reflecting one another in an endless mirror play. Their multiple personalities are projected onto the other characters in the film—Victor's wife and his mother-in-law are masquerading and passing as Ashkenazi upper-class people—who cross fixed identity boundaries. Revach resists the normative understanding of sexual difference as difference itself, questioning the dominant assumptions of identity intelligibility that produce his and others' sexual subjectivity. As such, he could qualify as a heterosexual queer.

4 | Homoland
Interracial Sex and the Israeli/Palestinian Conflict

Narratives of biracial sexual unions are common in Israeli cinema, from the early Zionist cinema of the thirties to today. Among them are *Sabra* (Alexander Ford, 1933), *My Michael* (Dan Wolman, 1975), *Hide and Seek* (Wolman, 1980), *Hamsin* (Daniel Wachsmann, 1982), *Drifting* (Amos Guttman, 1983), *On a Narrow Bridge* (Nissim Dayan, 1985), *The Lover* (Michal Bat-Adam, 1986), *Nadia* (Amnon Rubinstein, 1986), *Ricochets* (Eli Cohen, 1986), *Lookout* (Dina Zvi-Riklis, 1990), and *Day after Day* (Amos Gitai, 1998).

In the Israeli social psyche, miscegenation gives rise to fears of racial, sexual, moral, physiological, and national decay and degeneracy, because it poses a threat to Jewish "purity" and dominance. Thus it fuels the desire to maintain the binary oppositions between colonizer and colonized, "civilized" and "savage," Israeli and Palestinian. Specifically, sexual relations between a Jewish woman and an Arab man (as opposed to those between a Jewish man and an Arab woman) evoke the greatest fears for Jewish racial purity, inasmuch as the Jewish woman, and not the Jewish man, is the origin of Jewish identity for any offspring. Hence the strict religious and cultural prohibition against such relationships. This anxiety, as an indicator of the sexual activity of the Arab man, pathologizes him as a sexual deviant, criminal, and a barbarian. The Arab man, as the Israeli member of Parliament Rabbi Meir Khanna put it in his racist diatribes of the early eighties, threatens "to steal our wives and daughters."[1] The

Israeli female body is perceived in this context as national property beck-
oning to the enemy within. Like the primitive male "other," women are
seen as a threat to the very existence of the Jewish nation.

Anxieties about racial sexual hybridity arise from the desire to reinforce racial dichotomies. Yet the very existence of those dichotomies
indicates the mutual dependence and construction of Israeli and
Palestinian subjectivities. The Jewish Israeli fear of hybridization and
the Jewish insistence on racial difference mask a latent fascination with
the Arab subject, a desire for forbidden love, an array of sexual fantasies.
For the Palestinian subject, sexual relations with an Israeli man or
woman may represent an attempt to move from the cultural margins
to the center and so to gain access to socioeconomic opportunities.[2]

In the official Jewish Israeli discourse, the attempt of Palestinians
to pass as Israeli Jews is depicted as an effort to assume a false status
and the privileges accruing to it. Palestinian passing challenges the
notion that the Jewish Israeli identity is an innate, unchangeable
essence, thereby questioning the privileges on which Jewish Israeli racial
subjectivity in founded. Sexual hybridization in this situation breaks
down the symmetry and duality of "self" and "other," inside and outside. Hybridity, as Homi Bhabha argues, is a problem of "colonial
representation and individuation that reverses the effects of the colonialist disavowal, so that other 'denied' knowledges enter upon the dominant discourse and estrange the basis of its authority."[3] In other
words, what is disavowed is not repressed but repeated in the hybrid.

Most of the films that focus on interracial romance were produced in the eighties, after the Six Day War (1967), the Yom Kippur
War (1973), and after the occupation of the West Bank. The critical tone
of Israeli cinema of the eighties is inseparably intertwined with the economic, political and social changes that followed these events.[4] Cheap
Palestinian labor, along with the transition from a socialist to a capi-
talist economy, enabled the Jewish Israeli working class, mostly made
up of Sephardi Jews who had endured social and cultural oppression
from Ashkenazi Zionism, to improve their standards of living and
political position. In reaction to the discriminatory policies of the
Avodah (the labor party), they affiliated themselves with the Likud
(the nationalist right-wing party), and the Avodah's thirty years of hegemony came to an end. The cultural elite—writers, artists, academics,
and film directors, among others—who were identified with the Avodah
were cut off from their economic and moral base of support. Object-
ing strongly to the Likud's occupation policy in the West Bank and

disappointed by the Avodah's inability to stop the occupation, the cultural elite took up a new ethical and political position based on resistance to the occupation and on promotion of negotiations with the Palestine Liberation Organization. As the Israeli-Palestinian conflict became more violent, with the explosion of the Intifada in the Occupied Territories, more films transgressed the taboo of interracial sex, trying, in some cases, to critique and subvert antimiscegenation discourses.

The majority of these films focus on heterosexual racial mixing, usually between a Palestinian man and an Israeli woman.[5] The emphasis on this kind of coupling in Israeli cinema may be explained not only by the strong taboo against such relationships, but also by the domination of heterosexuality in narratives of hybridization. As Robert Young argues, hybridity will always carry with it an implicit politics of heterosexuality, because "anxiety about hybridity reflect[s] the desire to keep races separate, which mean[s] that attention [is] immediately focused on the mixed race offspring that result[s] from interracial sexual intercourse."[6] In other words, homosexuality poses little threat, because it produces no children. Nevertheless, Young emphasizes the paradox of homosexuality and hybridity:

> On the face of it . . . hybridity must always be a resolutely heterosexual category. In fact, in historical terms, concern about racial amalgamation tended if anything to encourage same-sex sex (playing the imperial game was, after all, already an implicitly homo-erotic practice). Moreover, *at one point,* hybridity and homosexuality did coincide to become *identified* with each other, namely as forms of degeneration. The norm/deviation model of race as of sexuality meant that "perversions" such as homosexuality became associated with degenerate products of miscegenation.[7]

Young's argument remains enclosed in a conspicuously heterocentric interpretive framework. His historicization and theorization of hybridity lean heavily on the concept of heterosexual reproduction. Rather than expose the discursive ways that heteroculture naturalizes itself and imagines itself exclusively and totally as society through the idea of reproduction, Young accepts heterosexuality as an essentialist sexual category of identity that is "naturally" different from homosexuality. From this perspective, it is impossible to conceptualize homosexuality and hybridity or heterosexuality as interdependent or as reciprocally constituted.[8]

This chapter examines constructions of interracial sexual unions, especially male-male unions, in cinematic and cultural representations of the Israeli-Palestinian conflict. It will trace structural analogies between heterosexual interracial sexuality and homoerotic fears and desires. Both heterosexual and homosexual interracial sexual relations are represented as "abnormal," "degenerate" forms of desire that threaten to cause the catastrophic undoing of Jewish Israeli national and racial sovereignty. Miscegenation and homosexuality mobilize fears of racial decline in the population, evoking anxieties about the future of the Jewish race, inasmuch as they threaten not only to pollute the Jewish state but to put an end to it.

Sabra and *Hamsin* are examples of films in which cultural anxieties over miscegenation and homoerotic sexuality overlap and shape one another. In *Sabra*—the first Zionist film that focuses on the Jewish-Arab conflict—the male pioneer is suspended between a fantasy of heterosexual domination and anxiety about queer emasculation. These fears and desires are projected onto the Arabs, who in turn are produced both as objects of sexual fascination (figured in the quasi romance between the pioneer and an Arab woman) and as bearers of a queer threat (associated with the violent attack launched by the Arab masses). In this way, the film's sexualization of the conflict leads to a splitting of sexual fears and desires within Zionist heteromasculinity.

Hamsin presents a different view of heterosexual and homoerotic interracial sexuality. In the film, the Israeli colonial heterosexual male subject's fears about miscegenation mirror anxieties of homoeroticism. Hybridity is marked by traces of homoerotic desires that threaten to deconstruct the imagined homogeneity of the Israeli male heterosexual's national, political, and racial domination. In this sense, *Hamsin* encourages us to reevaluate and re-theorize the discourse of hybridity in terms of homophobia. The structural analogies between hetero-biracial sex and homoerotic desires and anxieties suggest that homosexuality is not only identified with hybridity, but also structurally part of it.

Representations of interracial sexual desire between Israeli and Palestinian men are also explored. The films *Hide and Seek* and *Drifting* use representations of biracial same-sex sexual relations to critique the heteronormative national ideology and, in *Drifting*'s case, also the identity politics of the Israeli gay community. But this critique is limited. *Hide and Seek* productively uses interracial homosexual

coupling to construct its Leftist vision, at the cost of leaving racial mixing almost invisible, while *Drifting* exploits male-male biracial eroticism to demonstrate the extension of colonial power over the
homosexualized Palestinian male "other."

Finally, I consider the meanings of interracial male-male sex for
Palestinian men. So long as they maintain an "active" role in biracial
sexual relations with Israeli men, anal sex becomes for some Palestinian
men a practice of resistance to Israeli domination.

Nation, Narration, and Penetration

Early Zionist cinema played a major role in the
invention of Jewish male heterosexual subjectivity. In the montage
sequence of a well-drilling scene in the film *Avodah* (Helmar Lerski,
1935) close-ups of muscular half-naked male pioneers are linked with
close-ups of a drilling machine. Shots of active men's bodies, hard muscles, sweaty tanned skins, and proud faces, seen from a low angle, intertwine with shots of gears and transmissions. Man and machine, flesh
and iron, organic and mechanical merge in a magnificent masculine
work harmony. This staging of Zionist heteromasculinity is articulated
through the symbolic feminization of the conquered land, which is associated with female genitalia. Cinematic fascination with male bodies
is colored by emphatic eroticism when the phallic drill penetrates the
vagina-like well, which ejaculates a jet of water.[9] The pioneers penetrate "Mother Earth," fertilizing her body, staking their sovereign ter-
ritorial rights on her flesh. In Western Orientalist discourse, as Edward
Said observes, the Eastern land is feminized and represented as available for penetration by the European man.[10] The Eastern territory and
people are figured as contained by the "superior" rationality of the
Western mind.

However, Said's metaphor of the Western sexual appropriation of
the East remains enclosed in a heterocentric matrix. According to this
scenario, the castration complex that determines (compulsory) sexual
identities structures the relationships between the Western (Zionist)
figurative penis and the Eastern vagina. But in this psychosexual
dynamic, as Joseph A. Boone claims, "that which appears alluringly
feminine is not always, or necessarily, female."[11] Put somewhat differently, that which appears for the male European Jewish pioneer to
be an inviting vagina is sometimes a luscious male anus. This is a case
not simply of mistaken sexual identities but of unconscious fantasy and
anxiety on the part of the male subject who witnesses the sexual

scene, as in Freud's case history of the Wolf Man. In his childhood fantasy, the Wolf Man witnesses his parents engaging in a sexual act that, he believes, is being performed from behind, that is, in his mother's anus. In a dazzling analysis of the Wolf Man case, Lee Edelman argues that the anus evokes castration anxiety in the male subject, because it marks on his own body the anatomo-phantasmic potential of being in his mother's place. The anus operates as a "phobically charged" orifice that the male subject must "repudiate" in order to submit to "the law of castration" and to the imperative of heterosexualization. Edelman writes:

> Obedient to the law of castration . . . the male . . . must repudiate the pleasures of the anus because their fulfillment allegedly presupposes, and inflicts, the loss or "wound" that serves as the very definition of the female's castration. Thus the male who is terrorized into heterosexuality through his internalization of this determining narrative must embrace with all his narcissistic energy the phantom of hierarchically inflected binarism always to be defended zealously. His anus, in turn, will be phobically charged as the site at which he traumatically confronts the possibility of becoming "like his mother," while the female genitalia will always be informed by their signifying relation to the anal eroticism he has been made to disavow.[12]

The "signifying relation" between the vagina and the anus is underlined by the Wolf Man's reference to the vagina as "front bottom." For Edelman, the real trauma of this "sodomitical scene" lies in its potential for ruining the fixed positionality of sexual difference inaugurated and sustained by the castration complex.[13]

The Zionist story presents a new scenario for Edelman's theorization of the role the anus plays in castration anxiety. As a site of penetration, it must be repudiated by the heterosexual Zionist male subject, if he wishes to escape not only the possibility of becoming "like his mother," but the possibility of becoming like his *father*. For the anus in the Zionist discourse is associated with the feminized father—the "penetrated," homosexualized diasporic male Jew. In other words, the Zionist male subject must disavow the anus to avoid being like his mother's "front bottom" *and* like his father's "behind," if he is to submit to the narrative of castration and thus to the narrative of the nation. Through this narrative of castration, Zionist compulsory male heterosexuality is sustained and reinforced.

The Zionist need for a double repudiation of the anus may explain the excessive, even hysterical, Zionist demand for the construction of a new heterosexual Jewish masculinity. The overwrought cinematic imagery—the clenched fists, the hard muscles, the masochistically hard pioneering work, the proliferation of phallic symbols—signifies Zionist male heterosexuality's painful and difficult repression of its identification with the so-called passive position of the "castrated" woman and homosexualized male Jew.

Indeed, many Zionist films follow the heterosexual narrative of castration and, in so doing, establish Zionist heteronormativity. However, the colonial scene of conquest is structured not only by male fantasies of unlimited heterosexual power, but also by the dread, associated with fears of impotence, emasculation, and death, that the male body's boundaries will be catastrophically undone. The film *Sabra* presents a different but still anxious vision of well drilling that presents difficulties for the submission of Zionist men to the narrative of castration. This film focuses on the pioneers' futile efforts to drill a well in "sterile," "unproductive" Palestine. The deep, dark, vagina-like hole that they dig yields no water. Not only does the land's "vagina" not respond to the men's "penetration," but the pleasures of the act of vaginally penetrating the opposite sex are foreclosed to them, due to the absence of women from their homosocial group. The male subject's self-denial makes it impossible for him to submit to the law of castration and thereby to confirm his heterosexuality. The result is male heterosexual anxiety, manifested in the film by the collapse into the well of one of the pioneers, who is thus placed in a passive position, no longer able to project castration anxiety, with all the force of binary opposition, onto the woman's or the land's vagina.

In the patriarchal gender sign system, for a man to be in a nonheterosexual and sexual passive position connotes his feminization and sexual penetrability. The well now becomes a "phobically charged . . . site," a threatening (ass)hole that traumatically evokes the possibility of emasculation and homosexualization, the possibility of the Zionist male's body becoming like his mother's "front bottom" and his father's "behind." Bearing the mark of penetration, the pioneer fears the figurative possibility of being "fucked."

A few minutes before his death, the pioneer who falls down the well hallucinates about the dreamy figure of a woman, superimposed on images of fertile land, who kisses him, and then he envisions streams of water flowing over his pleasured body as he dies. The fem-

inized pioneer, who has failed to perform the masculine act of penetration, experiences and confirms through fantasy the heterosexual pleasures he has been denied. Zionist masculinity is presented, then, as a
fantasy that the male subject attains with great difficulty and with dev-
astating results for his subjectivity, to the point of his total destruction.

This heterosexual panic is emphasized even more in the following scenes. Immediately after the fantasy scene, the pioneers' wives
arrive suddenly out of the desert, in effect coming to reinforce the
national narrative of castration and therefore the narrative of heterosexuality. Rescued from their dread of passivity and from the figurative potential of anal eroticism, the male pioneers welcome their
wives with enthusiasm, or with relief: "Our wives! Our wives!" Des-
perate to make love to their women, the men hysterically rush to submit to the law of castration and heterosexuality, hurrying to protect
themselves from suffering the metaphorical fate of their dead, feminized,
queered friend. Only after the women arrive and heterosexuality is
reconfirmed does the water spout from the land.

Thus *Sabra* is less about omnipotent Zionist colonization than it
is about the crisis of Zionist male heterosexual subjectivity. The Zionist
male is suspended between a fantasy of heterosexual conquest and the
fear of queer emasculation. The gendering of Palestine as both submissive and castrating represents a splitting of the Zionist male "self,"
which is disavowed and projected onto the sexualized colonial space.
On the one hand, fantasies of heterosexual domination are displaced
onto an erotic romance between a beautiful Arab girl, Fatima, and a pioneer. On the other, anxieties about queer emasculation are projected
onto the bodies of the Arab warriors, who attack the Zionist settlement
from behind. Close-ups of waving swords and menacing faces mark the
anxious specter of the Arab force that threatens to violate the bodily
integrity of the Zionist male settlers. For the Zionist heterosexual
male to be emasculated means a "passive" and "feminine" positioning of his body, an inability to produce children, a failure to reproduce
the race. Therefore the charging Arab multitudes embody the fear of
racial engulfment and male castration and impotence.

The film establishes a direct signifying relationship between
Zionist national domination and heterosexual domination. The Arabs
are exploited by their own sheikh, who forces them to pay exorbitant
prices for water. He agrees to let his community have water only if one
of his people will sell his young daughter, Fatima, to him. When the
father refuses, the sheikh incites his people to believe that the Zionists

are responsible for the scarcity of water, provoking the Arab attack on the Jewish settlement. The Arab violence is constructed as a release of libidinal energy, threatening to undo (from behind) the Zionist male body, and must therefore be deflected to make way for the triumphant law of the symbolic. The pioneers' triumph over the Arab masses not only establishes the Zionist "white man's burden" of saving the Arabs from their own corrupt leader, initiating a sort of Arab-Jewish coexistence, but also symbolizes the Zionists' victory over the Arabs' threat of racial and sexual emasculation and the sheikh's heterosexual desire for Fatima. The narrative of the Zionist conquest is structurally intertwined with the regulation of Arab male sexuality. Once they have quelled the fear of racial engulfment and emasculation, the pioneers can establish their heterosexual sovereign authority, figured in the romance between Fatima and the pioneer. Little wonder, then, that immediately after the battle scene, Fatima salves the wounds of her Zionist lover and gives him water. The forming of Zionist heteromasculinity requires the submission of the Zionist male, as well as of the racial "other's" sexuality, to the law of castration. The erotization of the Arabs as both sexually dreadful and desirable articulates disavowed and displaced split aspects of the male pioneer himself, representing a suspended doubling of sexual and racial fear and fantasy within Zionist male heterosexual identity.

White Man Saving a Brown Man
from White and Brown Men

The film *Hamsin* displays the intersectionality of homoeroticism and miscegenation, critically exposing the ambivalence of the sexual and racial fears and desires that structure Israeli national domination. Male homoeroticism is represented by the friendship between Gedalia, an Israeli cattle breeder in a village in Galilee, and his Palestinian worker, Khaled, who becomes the lover of Gedalia's sister, Hava. Such relations between Jewish women and Arab men evoke in the Israeli male subject racial, national, and sexual anxieties. Given that the Israeli occupation compelled Palestinians to make a living in Israeli cities and settlements, the "dangers" posed to the health of the Jewish race and nationality by interracial sex were almost inevitable. One of the reasons for the Israeli man's intense anxieties is the fear of the dissolution of the "self," represented by fusion with the "other." That fusion destabilizes the racial Manichaean dichotomies constructed by Zionist ideology (the dichotomies between Arab and Jew, Palestinian and Israeli, East and West).

Gedalia's violent reaction to his sister's choice of an Arab lover seems to be founded on such a fear. In the film, liquid imagery signifies the dissolution of the Israeli "self" in a return to the imaginary phase of psychic formation, when the borders between "self" and "other" are not yet in place. Oceanic imagery, as Lola Young notes, characterizes antimiscegenation discourses in which the "self" is threatened with dissolution by the invasion of "waves," "tides," and "floods" of immigrants.[14] In *Hamsin,* the Palestinian man is the alien intruder who threatens to destabilize racial binaries. Miscegenation is perceived as a violent invasion, or (sexual) penetration, of the family and of the national body. The anxious sight of miscegenation mirrors the Israeli man's own fears and fantasies of biracial sex with the Palestinian male "other." To protect himself, Gedalia must spill blood outside— that is, must kill Khaled—to calm his internal anxiety. In this sense, homoeroticism is not antithetical to the discourse of heterosexual miscegenation, but rather a structural condition of it.

When Gedalia hears that the Israeli government plans to confiscate Arab land in Galilee, he attempts to buy it from his Arab neighbors, the Adass family, hoping to construct a dream farm on it and to continue his grandfather and father's legacy. In the process, he alienates himself both from Palestinian nationalists—who would rather have Israeli nationalization imposed on them than sell the land "by choice"— and from his Israeli friends—who want to take part in this project of expropriation, but whose help he rejects. ("I work alone," he replies to Gidi, a friend who offers him partnership.) Gedalia's only ally is Khaled, to whom he reveals his ambitions and with whom he plans a cooperative future.

Gedalia's close relationship to Khaled can be seen in a homoerotic light: The film says nothing about Gedalia's heterosexual history and he has no love interest in the present. The few moments in the film that refer to his sexuality are devoted to the erotic affection he shows Khaled as they shower together. Standing half-naked in the field, the men splash water on each other, laughing and touching each other's bodies. Both Palestinians and Israelis understand the "strange" relationship of the two in terms of emotional and bodily closeness that exceeds the normative relations between Arab and Jewish men. While the Israelis call Gedalia "an Arab lover," the nationalist Palestinians

Figure 12. Homoerotic desire and the Israeli-Palestinian conflict. Gedalia (Shlomo Tarshish, left) and Khaled (Yasin Shawap, right) in Daniel Wachsmann's *Hamsin*. Courtesy of Daniel Wachsmann.

say of Khaled, "Look at him, driving Gedalia's jeep as if they're partners. He lives there, eats at [his] table; he'll end up licking his ass."

But this "ideal" male companionship masks deeper power and knowledge relations between Gedalia and Khaled. Khaled's socioeconomic and political condition—indeed, his whole selfhood—is controlled and policed by his master's authoritative so-called kindness, friendship, and hospitality. (Khaled lives in an isolated shack on the farm, Gedalia forbids him to associate with his Palestinian friends or with Hava.) As Khaled's taskmaster, Gedalia not only regulates Khaled's sociopolitical position, but monitors his body and sexuality. By "rescuing" him both from the Israeli farmers, who rage about the damage caused to the plantations by the nationalist Palestinians, and from the nationalist Palestinians themselves, who try to convince Khaled to participate in their subversive activity, Gedalia establishes Khaled's body as a thing—an instrument available for economic domination—and as an object for his homoerotic pleasure. To paraphrase Gayatri Chakravorty Spivak's famous formulation of the colonial fantasy— "White men are saving brown women from brown men"—Gedalia produces a homoerotic colonial rescue fantasy, in which a white man saves a brown man from white and brown men for his own sexual consumption.[15]

Hamsin examines an apparently sharp conflict of interest between Hava and Gedalia. Having left her piano studies in Jerusalem over her mother's objections, she is settled in her grandfather's house on the farm, the same house that Gedalia wishes to sell in order to buy Arab lands. Moreover, her forbidden relations with Khaled threaten Gedalia's patriarchal domination over her (he commands her not to ride a horse at night; that is, he restricts and monitors her movements and agency), as well as his domination over Khaled. In short, brother and sister constitute obstacles to each other's desires, be they national, social, or sexual.

However, the film also reflects the brother's and sister's doubled desires on narrative and visual levels. Each sibling wants to settle down on the family's ancestral land, maintaining the pioneers' patriarchal heritage. Gedalia wishes to maintain their father's heritage, Hava their grandfather's). Hava, like Gedalia, rejects the attempts of other villagers to come between her and her ambitions. She dismisses Gidi, a childhood friend and now a farmer who romantically courts her, just as Gedalia rejects Gidi's business proposal. But the most striking resemblance between brother and sister is expressed in Hava's relationship to Khaled. Like Khaled and Gedalia, Khaled and Hava develop a unique relationship that challenges the traditional form of relations between Arab men and Jewish women. She gives him a ride home; allows him, and him alone, to help her clean her grandfather's house; and eventually becomes his lover.

Her "unfit" behavior provokes intense reactions from the people around her, reactions similar to those that Gedalia has received because of his relationship with Khaled, yet much stronger, since she and Khaled are breaking a taboo. The Israeli villagers note her "going with Arabs"—that is, sleeping with one—and her mother is shocked and disgusted by her sexual behavior: "Such a thing never happened here! It's going to turn out very bad!" Indeed, Gedalia will murder Khaled in the end. Finally, since her name "Hava" (Eve) bears the emblem of Jewish femininity, the source of Jewish female identity, her forbidden love story takes on a mythological dimension.

Outrageous and subversive of Israeli domination as it is, Hava and Khaled's relationship cannot escape the imprint of national and racial power/knowledge relations. As the representative of the "superior" race, the Israeli woman exercises power over the Palestinian man. In colonial texts, as Ella Shohat notes, the white woman "can be granted an ephemeral 'positional superiority.' In a film like *The Sheik* (1921), the 'norms of the text' . . . are represented by the western male but in the moments of his absence, the white woman becomes the civilising center of the film."[16] Khaled becomes an object of desire for Hava, as she gazes at his muscular half-naked body while he washes himself. The film does not grant the Arab male the power of looking that is part of the visual economy of mainstream cinema, in which the man is the subject and the woman the object of the gaze. When Khaled tries to glance at Hava's naked body while she undresses, she returns his look and thus prevents him from constructing her as the object of his gaze; at the same time, she constructs him as the object of *her* gaze. For Hava, as for Gedalia, Khaled is an object of sexual consumption, a means by which to rebel against maternal authority. (Forced to study piano, she "slept the whole year in Jerusalem," she tells her mother, defiantly.) As a privileged subject, Hava will always have Khaled available to her. For Khaled, sexual intercourse with a Jewish woman is an honor. (His friends admire and envy him for his "privilege".) It is a way of entering the forbidden zone of Israeli hegemony and escaping, if only illusorily, from his oppressed condition. In the context of the Israeli-Palestinian conflict, interracial sex might be an instrument of the colonized for achieving "liberated" national and political selfhood, as well as a means for reconstructing a proud, upright, and empowered Palestinian masculinity. Yet this representation, more than teaching us about Arab male sexuality, exposes the film's anxiety about Palestinian men responding to their oppression by "steal[ing] our wives and daughters."

The relationship between Hava and Gedalia is constructed around ambivalence. On one hand, Gedalia must block Hava's desires to settle down and see Khaled in order to establish his position of sovereignty. On the other, her desires mirror his own conscious and unconscious fantasies. Imitating her brother, Hava becomes, as Bhabha puts it, a mimic (wo)man, at once "resemblance and menace."[17] Khaled and Hava's act of miscegenation makes Gedalia feel his own painful fluid sense of or need for "otherness"; it unmasks the fixity of his identity and authority; it makes him feel estranged from himself, sick with desire for the "other." His own repressed fantasies for "otherness" puts into question the "natural" authority of Israeli domination.

The idea that miscegenation repeats Gedalia's disavowed queer desires for Khaled is articulated also by the film's formal construction. During one episode Khaled is thrown out of the village's movie theater: He is denied the viewing position, usually occupied by the Israeli subject. So he decides to appropriate this position by force, by staring through Hava's window at her naked body. A tracking shot shows Khaled approaching the window, seeing only what an Israeli man would be allowed to see. Spotting his voyeuristic gaze, Hava does not panic or get angry, as she might be expected to do, but responds positively, returning Khaled's look while continuing to undress. This scene of visual miscegenation is followed by a scene marked by emphatic homoerotic imagery: Gedalia and Khaled working half-naked in the field, their bodies sweating as they penetrate the earth with a drill. In the next scene, the men splash water on each other with a hose. In other words, the film links miscegenation and homoeroticism, heterosexual and same-sex interracial desire. Little wonder that the film is suffused with liquid imagery: bottles of water, a water main that explodes, showers, sweat, rain. Even the film's Hebrew title, *Hamsin,* refers to the hot desert wind that flows through the Middle East (the reason that the characters in the film sweat so much). The liquid imagery symbolizes the desire for and fear of interracial sex.

A similar analogy between miscegenation and homoeroticism is implied through cinematic form, in the last two scenes of the film. In another tracking shot, Gedalia is seen approaching Hava's window, occupying the same position as Khaled when he gazed at Hava. Feeling fear and desire now in response to the sight of Hava and Khaled making love, Gedalia, in the following scene, homoerotically penetrates Khaled

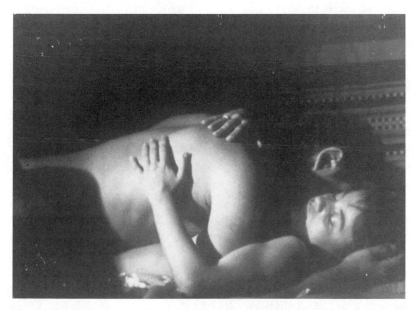

Figure 13. The specter of Arab-Jewish miscegenation. Khaled (Yasin Shawap) and Hava (Hemeda Levi) in Daniel Wachsmann's *Hamsin.* Courtesy of Daniel Wachsmann.

by releasing a bull that gores him to death. Through the window he has seen both what he longs for and what he fears. Suddenly, witnessing this act of miscegenation, he feels estranged and deauthorized from the inside. He can no longer pretend to be the voice of colonial authority, because the sight of hybridity repeats what he disavows. Bhabha writes that "in the objectification of the scopic drive there is always the threatened return of the look; in the identification of the imaginary relation there is always the alienating other (or mirror) which crucially returns its image to the subject."[18] The observer becomes the observed. Gedalia's look of surveillance returns to him and haunts him with his own repressed desires. Gedalia, the observer, is already inscribed in the observed sexual scene; it is the point from which the sight of miscegenation itself looks back at him. This is menacing to him precisely because his essence and authority are alienated. In self-defense, he must dam the subversive floods that threaten him both from inside and from outside. It is no coincidence that, after he has penetrated Khaled with the bull, rain pours down—a signifier for his uncontrolled libidinal energies—breaking the heat, washing away the blood.

Anal Israel

Hide and Seek (1980) was the first Israeli film that referred directly to interracial male-male sexual desire. Against the background of 1946 Jerusalem during the British Mandate, the film presents the story of Uri, a young boy left with his grandfather after his parents are sent on a political mission to Europe. Uri and his friends form a secret society that aspires to help Jewish armed underground organizations, such as the Haganah, in their war against both British rule and the Arab enemy. At the same time, he develops a warm and trusting relationship with his schoolteacher, Balaban, an man who is unconventional not only because of his informal teaching methods but because of his refusal to join any underground organization. When Uri spots Balaban exchanging words and notes with Arab men, he and the other boys suspect him of being a spy. While the members of the Haganah find him not guilty of espionage, they nevertheless discover his secret—he is having sex with an Arab man—and decide to punish him for his "treason." Wanting to protect Balaban, Uri rushes to his apartment and, through the window, witnesses him and his Arab partner making love. A few seconds later, the Haganah members break open the door and beat them up.

Figure 14. Biracial homosexuality in 1946 Jerusalem. Balaban (Doron Tavori, left) and his nameless Arab lover (Rafi Mualam, right) in Dan Wolman's *Hide and Seek.* Courtesy of Dan Wolman.

The film critically links pre-state nationalist anxieties and fears of biracial homosexuality. Male-male desire is perceived as a threat to national security and as alien, unnatural behavior because of its "un-Zionist" practice, its sexual entanglement with the Arab enemy. The film conflates homosexuality and fears of Arab infiltration to show that homophobia and nationalist ideology are closely intertwined. The ability of the homosexual, like the spy, to "pass" produces anxiety for heterosexuals—especially for heterosexual men or, in this case, boys—about the undetected pervasiveness of sexuality and the subversive activities of the enemy within. For this reason, the homosexual/spy must be identified, made visible, marked, tracked and regulated. Furthermore, the reading of the homosexual, like the spy, as both visibly different (Balaban "doesn't look like a man at all," says one of the boys) and totally invisible produces in the heterosexual child, Uri, a simultaneous desire to see the "secret world" of homosexuality and a fear of the spectacle of male-male sex. Indeed, he dreads this sight precisely because of his desire to look at, to make visible and to control the visibility of homosexual difference. He desires to see but, paradoxically, cannot afford to see. The glimpsed vision of male-male sex marks the threatened return of (anal) pregenital pleasures that the heterosexual subject must disavow in order to submit to the triumphant Law of the Father. Thus the sight of two men fucking must be visible only through its repudiation, figured in the Haganah's homophobic violence. Through this repudiation, the heterosexual boy comes into being.

Although *Hide and Seek* critiques nationalist ideology for denying the possibility of interracial sexual expression, it avoids representing the actual relationship between Balaban and his nameless Arab lover. Their presence is expressly staged as an allegory of the nationalist fanaticism engulfing Israeli society. Their queer voice is never heard; we always witness them from a distance, through Uri's gaze. Images of biracial male-male sexual desire appear only in the last moments of the film, which eschews the complexities and tensions inherent in the construction of racial homosexual subjectivities in the context of the Israeli-Palestinian conflict. Interracial (homo)sexuality, then, remains at the fringes of, or is excluded from, both the film and the official nationalist discourse.

Amos Guttman was the first filmmaker to produce queer Israeli cinema. *Drifting* (1983), his first feature film, presents sexual relations between Israeli and Palestinian men and suggests a critique of both the official nationalist ideology and the sexual politics of Israeli gay subculture. Generally, representations of (homo)sexuality in Guttman's films offer no redemptive vision. The protagonists seek, through the sexual act, the thrill of demeaning of the "self," of self-dismissal. They perform a version of sexuality that acts out, what Leo Bersani terms, the "radical disintegration and humiliation of the self."[19] Guttman's radical visions of sexuality were rejected by the Aguda, the Israeli association of gay men, lesbian, bisexuals, and transgendered people that in the seventies began to demand more "positive" images of Jewish Israeli gay life. He was accused of incorporating into his films a "depressing," "alienating," even homophobic imagery of gay social existence. (These issues will be further discussed in Chapter Five.)

In *Drifting*, Guttman's subversive sexual politics is dramatized through the sexual relationship between Robby and two Palestinian "terrorists," as his grandmother calls them, whom he invites into his home. He feeds them, bandages the wound of one of them, and even pleasures them by summoning a female prostitute to the house. (It is implied that they are running away from the Israeli police.) In the middle of the night, he wakes one of them—an attractive, hypermasculine

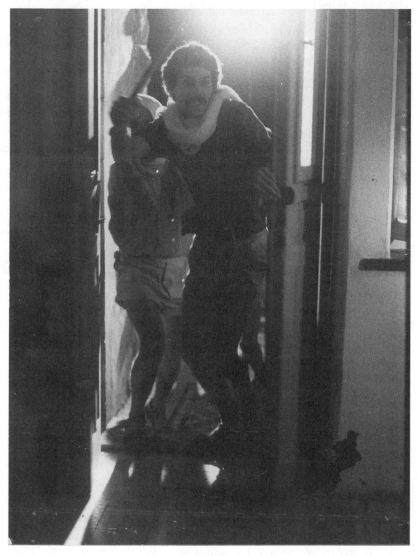

Figure 15. Imaging the Haganah's homophobic violence in Dan Wolman's *Hide and Seek*. Courtesy of Dan Wolman.

man—leans against the wall, pulls down his underwear, and asks the Palestinian to fuck him.

Gay anal receptivity is associated in phallocentric culture with the abdication of power, with insatiable feminine sexuality. Gay men who embrace this understanding of anal sex represent to others, according to Bersani, a desire to abandon positions of mastery and the coherence of the "self": "Male homosexuality advertises the risk of the sexual itself as the risk of self-dismissal, of *losing sight* of the self, and in so doing it proposes and dangerously represents *jouissance* as a mode of ascesis."[20] Contrary to Gedalia in *Hamsin,* for example, Robby willingly renounces his self-mastery, submits to the domination of the racial "other," and positions himself as the object of an Arab male's anal penetration. He yearns for dissolution of the psychic boundaries of the "self," forfeits his authority as the oppressor, relinquishes his sovereign status, attempts to become the "other," rather than the colonizer. For Robby, only at the moment of merging—at the sexualized political and racial moment of mixing, in the terrible and pleasurable shattering of the subject—is *jouissance* to be found. By willingly submitting in this way, however, he passionately and compulsively seeks an antiredemptive self-shattering of ego boundaries and national identity, thereby demonstrating his hostility toward the Israeli political and national order. At the same time, by celebrating the sexual pleasure found in anti-identificatory self-annihilation, *Drifting* challenges the Aguda's sexual identity politics and its imperious demand for a "respectful" representation of homosexuality. Thus the film articulates a radical and highly critical position versus the sexual and nationalist norms of (gay and straight) Israeli society.

Guttman achieves this complex critique of the nationalist discourse and the sexual politics of the Aguda through the narrative of male-male sex between Israeli and Palestinian. But what does this sexual agenda imply for *Drifting*'s representation of the Palestinian men? Guttman's radical vision of (homo)sexuality comes at the price of a racist construction of the Arab male, who is compelled to inhabit an uninhabitable zone of ambivalence that denies his identity.[21]

In *Drifting,* Robby does not (and we do not) know much about his Palestinian companions: They have no names, no history. It is not clear (and it seems not to matter) whether they are Israeli citizens or Palestinians from Gaza or the West Bank. They simply came from "the village." The film thereby maintains the long tradition of repressive and discriminatory politics in the representation of Arabs and Palestinians in Israeli cinema. Their identity is elided, dismissed, stripped of its uniqueness, becoming an abstract object for Israeli examination, knowledge, and sexual pleasure.[22] The homogenization of their subjectivity and history not only makes Israeli discursive domination easier, but enables the construction of an Israeli (male homo-

sexual) authority and sovereign consciousness in which, and in relation to which, the Palestinian people emerge.

Arab masculinity is associated in the film with hypersexuality and
virility, embodying for the Israeli orientalist gaze, to put it in Said's
terms, a promise of "excessive 'freedom of intercourse,'" suggesting the
"escapism of sexual fantasy" and "untiring sensuality, unlimited
desire, deep generative energies."[23] Palestinian men are held to engage
in not just any sex, but licentious same-sex sex, reinforcing the Israeli
homophobic belief that "all Arab men are homosexuals" or at least participate in homosexual sex. At the same time, they are represented in
the film as coming from a backward, primitive, and conservative
Islamic society. "In our village, someone like you would be dead by
now," the Palestinian with whom Robby has had sex says to him.

The stereotype of homophobically violent "Islamic fundamental-
ist" Palestinian men is embedded in *Drifting,* along with their image
as terrorists. Once their assumed homosexuality is displaced onto
homophobia and terrorism, *Drifting* can rehearse the Israeli national
(anal) anxiety that "the Arabs want to fuck us in the ass," an allegory
for the constructed Palestinian desire to eliminate Israel. In Israeli cultural representation, the Arab anal threat is figured in terms of the
enemy's sexual pathology and anti-Semitism, not in terms of Palestinian
resistance to Israeli occupation. The paradox that "all Arab men are
homosexuals" and "all Arabs are homophobic terrorists" enables
Israeli cultural discourse not only to regulate the Arab male body and
Arab sexuality, but to deny Israel's own colonialist practices and racist
(sexual anal) aggressiveness by assigning them to the inimical body of
the Palestinian man.[24] This ambivalent representation of Palestinian masculinity allows *Drifting* to exploit the Arab male body and sexuality,
absolving itself of guilt by associating the Palestinian man with homophobic and nationalistic violence and, at the same time, aligning itself
with presumably Western attitudes of tolerance and progressiveness
toward racial and sexual issues. In this way, fears of and desires for the
Arab male body that structure the homophobic discourse of the Orient
help constitute the construction of the Israeli/Western (homo)sexual
"self."

Robby's sexual *jouissance* and ego shattering could be achieved not
in spite of or in contrast to Israeli domination, but because of it. The
Israeli gay man is allowed the privilege of sex with Palestinian men
because of certain historical and economic factors, such as the Israeli
colonization of the Occupied Territories. Palestinian bodies are

exploited not only for cheap labor but as objects of (homo)sexual desire. Looking through his window with desire at the Palestinian male's half-nude muscular body, Robby's friend asks him, "Should I buy him for you?"[25]

Fixed by the Israeli male homosexual gaze, the Palestinian male body becomes a product, a commodity for the consumption and visual pleasure of the young Israeli film director, as well as for the Israeli new queer cinema and its viewers. No matter how much Robby subverts the Israeli sexual and national order, he still enjoys the privileges of Israeli occupation. Under the sheltering sky of Israeli colonization, the anally penetrated male does not necessarily occupy a position of powerlessness or submission, or the penetrator one of mastery and domination. Rather, anal-sex power relations are affected and structured by race, class, and national privilege.

Sex and Resistance

The ironies and paradoxes of the colonial psychosexual dynamic also appear in other Israeli cultural representations. In interviews conducted by Jehoeda Sofer in Israel and the Occupied Territories, Shmuel, an Israeli gay man, talks about his sexual experiences with Palestinian men. Once, after he had been "fucked . . . three times in two hours," his partner demanded that he pay for the services:

> When I answered that I [wouldn't], and he could forget about it, he became angry and threatened me. There was nobody around, and I felt a bit insecure. However I walked in the direction of Jaffa Gate. He started being louder. I told him that he should not forget that he is an Arab, and that under Israeli rule he had no case against a Jew, and that he'd better leave me alone. I never would have dared to go to the police, but it worked. I also knew that he was deeply insulted, as he realized that the fuckee is not powerless, as he assumed.[26]

Smuel decided not to go to the police, not out of pity for the Palestinian, but because it is not an attractive option for an Israeli man to admit that he has been fucked by an Arab. Loath to seek help from a heterocentric institution that often discriminates against Israeli gays and Arabs alike, Smuel nevertheless used his privileged status and tapped into the discriminatory rhetoric of Israeli hegemony, because it granted him a position of relative power. The paradox faced by Israeli gay men is that they struggle against categories of manliness and nationalism that oppress them and others, yet they use those categories to exercise their authority over Palestinian men.

From a Palestinian point of view, the power relations in interracial anal sex have different, sometimes contrary, meanings. Fucking Jewish "bottoms" does not necessarily express a gay identity or even garner sexual pleasure for Palestinian "tops." Anal sex is often practiced by Arab men to humiliate and resist the Jewish Israeli enemy. In Sofer's interviews, a Palestinian man, quoted by an Israeli gay man, describes the psychosexual dynamic of such encounters: "If the Arabs would have had war with the Israelis using our cocks, we would have defeated them easily. The Israelis are a bunch of feminine males who want [to] and should be fucked by Arabs. Israelis have no self-respect, they let themselves and their females be fucked. . . . An Arab man will never let himself be fucked."[27] In this extraordinary testimonial, the Israeli-Palestinian conflict is homosexualized and understood in terms of sexual occupation. The male body becomes a battlefield where victory or defeat is defined, on both sides of the conflict, by the position one takes in anal male-male sex. Anal sex is regarded as a form of warfare, and penises (whether Israeli or Palestinian) are regarded as weapons that can enslave or kill. The Arab male, in this representation, wants to avenge his people for the shame they have suffered through Israeli occupation. His refusal to let himself be fucked can be understood in terms of national resistance, pride, and honor.

Notions of shame, honor, and anal submission have a further significance in Islamic discourses of homosexuality. In Arab culture, seeking sexual contact with people of the same sex does not necessarily express gay identity or desire; much depends on the relationship between the partners. For a sexual contact to be deemed honorable, a man should not find himself at the receiving end of anal intercourse. A man who penetrates another man does not suffer the same shame as the man penetrated, if indeed he suffers any at all. A man who gets fucked risks shame and social sanction. If he was penetrated as a boy but does not allow himself to be as an adult, no one will mention his sexual past, as his male honor depends on the suppression of that history.[28] Getting fucked as an adult male is not tolerable in traditional Muslim societies. As Jim Wafer argues, "The reason that Arab cultures have so much difficulty dealing with sex between males is that [a] man's masculinity is compromised by taking the 'passive' role in sexual relations; and for an Arab male to have his masculinity doubted is 'a supreme affront.' "[29]

Some Muslim men penetrate others less for sexual pleasure than to humiliate their partners. In several Islamic texts, argues Wafer, anal submission is linked to the submission of male non-believers to Islam ("Islam" literally means "submission"). Non-Muslim elements are sometimes conceived of as effeminate and must be made to submit through *jihad,* the holy war that in this context acquires an erotic meaning. Therefore, Wafer writes, "the West is regarded as 'decadent' by Muslims not just because it is becoming more accepting of homosexuality . . . but because, according to the initiatory symbolism of Islam, it *has* to be seen as effeminate."[30]

These arguments can help us comprehend the nationalistic rhetoric and the feminization of Israeli males by the Palestinian man quoted in Sofer's interview, as well as his fear of being anally penetrated. Similar notions of interracial sex between men can be found in another testimonial cited by Sofer. The subject is Salim, a twenty-two-year-old Palestinian who lives in East Jerusalem:

> He [Salim] told me that he fucks men because it is his only chance to have sex, but that, needless to say, he prefers women. However, meeting a Palestinian woman for sex before marriage is almost impossible. Jewish women, he says, do not go with Palestinians. Even female Jewish prostitutes discriminate against Arabs: they charge prices Salim cannot pay, or reject them totally. So he looks for sexual satisfaction with men in the park in Tel Aviv and West Jerusalem. Mostly he does not ask for payment, but if the man is old or looks rich he does. He is not interested in a lasting relationship with a man, because "I am not a homosexual. I was never fucked, and I will never let anybody fuck me. As soon as I have enough money and get married, I will stop coming here. Men who let themselves get fucked are not men. They have lost their respect. Among Arabs, this is a shame for the whole family."[31]

This description refers to the moral and political norms governing sexual relations between men in Palestinian society.[32] In the context of the Israeli-Palestinian conflict, the lack of reciprocity in national relations is reflected in the sexual contact, but with a different structuring of power relations. Interracial sexual relations between men must be hierarchical. For the Palestinian man to maintain his masculine and national integrity, he must not stand in a sexually symmetrical relation to the Israeli gay man; he must obtain sexual pleasure solely by penetrating the body of his Jewish partner. At the same time, the sexually superior partner, the Palestinian, is socioeconomically inferior to sexually "passive" Israeli men. Asking for money from old or rich Jews and enjoying the "active" part in the sexual act give the Palestinian man temporary male mastery that ostensibly rescues his national pride. Anal sex is configured in this vision as a disappropriation of Israeli masculine authority, transforming the Jewish male body into a "feminine" receptacle for Palestinian power.

Interracial sex between men has a different meaning for Palestinian men who define themselves as gay. The marginalized status of Palestinian gay men in both Palestinian and Israeli societies, as well as in the Israeli gay community itself,[33] leads Palestinian queers to identify with Western notions of homosexuality in reaction to the traditional Palestinian social structure, which does not legitimize same-sex desire, and, at the same time, leads them to refuse this identification by clinging to traditional Muslim social roles as a means of resisting Israeli's practical and discursive domination of Palestinian society. But Palestinian gay men's attitudes toward the heterosexual and homosexual Palestinian and Israeli societies remain to be explored. The Israeli-Palestinian conflict offers a complex, fluid, and paradoxical network of interracial sexual relationships between males from the perspectives of both Israeli and Palestinian men. Multiple cultural notions of masculinity and femininity, homo and hetero, "active" and "passive," power and submission, "top" and "bottom," honor and shame together produce ambivalent intersectionalities of race, sex, gender, and nationalism.

5 The New Queers

Sexual Orientation in the Eighties and Nineties

> [G]iven the historical and contemporary force of
> prohibitions against every same-sex expression,
> for anyone to disavow those meanings, or to dis-
> place them from the term's [that is, "queer"] defi-
> nitional center, would be to dematerialize any
> possibility of queerness itself.
>   At the same time . . . "queer" . . . spins . . .
> along dimensions that can't be subsumed under
> gender and sexuality at all: the way race, ethnic-
> ity, postcolonial nationality criss-cross with these
> and other identity-constituting, identity-fracturing
> discourse, for example.
>   —Eve Kosofsky Sedgwick, *Tendencies* (1993)

Israeli gay and lesbian consciousness emerged in the seventies with the establishment of the Aguda—the association of gay men, lesbian, bisexuals, and trans-genders in Israel (1975). The struggle of queer activists to achieve representation was predicated on a critique of the absence, marginality, and negative stereotypical character of gay and lesbian experience in Israeli society. The Aguda's political goal was to gain access to rights of representation, as well as to counter the homophobic quality of images of gays and lesbians with "positive" queer imagery. In a book documenting the history of the gay community in Israel, Lee Walzer points to a radical shift that took place in gay cultural visibility between 1988 and 1993.[1] The political and legal successes of activists—the 1988 repeal of Israel's anti-sodomy law and passage of an amendment to the Equal Workplace Opportunities Law that took into account sexual orientation, as well as the Knesset's (Israel's parliament) first conference on gay and lesbian issues in 1993—legitimized, to some extent, gay and lesbian representation in mainstream media. It also gave rise to a new queer culture that grew safely within the Israeli consensus.

The demand for "positive" images of gay lifestyle emphasized by the Israeli gay community in the seventies and eighties caused the rejection of fringe gay groups, such as transsexuals, bisexuals and queer Palestinians. This sexual politics of the Aguda, supported by queer journalists and other gay cultural personas, also had an effect on the reception of Amos Guttman's films. Guttman was accused of incorporating into his films a "depressing," "alienating," even homophobic imagery of the gay social existence. Indeed, Guttman, the first filmmaker to produce queer Israeli cinema, portrays in his films an obvious contempt for the demand for politically correct, idealized, and sanitized depictions of (homo)sexuality. He refuses to provide "positive" images of either gay or straight sex. Contrary to the Zionist project of redeeming the male body, male (homo)sexuality is associated in his films with power and domination, with violence and death. His male heroes slip into a delicious passivity, into an uncontainable agitation; they passionately and compulsively seek to lose their ego boundaries and to shatter their self-identity and the way it is constructed by the national heteronormativity.

Before he joined the mainstream media in his hit TV show *Florentin* (1997), Eytan Fox made a short film *Time Off* (1990) that also challenges the dominant national heteromasculinity by signifying gay male eroticism in the Israeli army through the disembodied cinematic voice. The queer disembodied voice functions in the film as a necessary vessel of homosexual desire and identification and as a force that undermines the imaginary stability and homogeneity of the male sexual subjectivity.

However, these new queer visions of gay (Ashkenazi) filmmakers are marked by an absence of any political awareness of ethnicity. Moreover, they repeat the colonial fantasy of the dominant discourse in which Mizrahi men are fixed into a narrow repertoire of "types"—the Eastern sexual stud, and the delicate exotic Oriental boy. The disavowal of ethnicity in Ashkenazi gay sexual politics and the incorporation of Mizrahi men into stereotyping and sexual objectification enable the construction of an Ashkenazi gay identity, whose repudiated structural element is the image of the Mizrahi gay man.

Amos Guttman's Laws of Desire

Guttman died of an AIDS related disease on February 1993. In his short filmic career, he made three short films: *Repeat Premiers* (1977), *A Safe Place* (1977), and *Drifting* (1979). *Drifting* was later made as a feature film (1983), followed by three more features, *Bar 51* (1986), *Himmo, King of Jerusalem* (1987), and *Amazing Grace* (1992). His films are influenced by the style and the themes of the Hollywood melodramas of the forties and fifties, especially those of Douglas Sirk, but also by the silent melodramas of D. W. Griffith as well as by Rainer Werner Fassbinder's cinema. (Originally, Guttman wanted to name his film *Bar 51* after Griffith's 1922 film *Orphans of the Storm*.)

Representations of (homo)sexuality in Guttman's films offer no redemptive vision. The protagonists are hopelessly caught in vicious circles of sexual and emotional exploitation. They depend on each other for their social, economic, and emotional existence—for their very identity—but cannot bear the incursions of others in their lives. They are oppressed, manipulated, and betrayed, but at the same time they exercise power and domination over others. In *Drifting* (feature version), Ilan (Ami Traub) is a married gay man who has sex with his wife ("You close your eyes and think about the national anthem"), only because he is afraid to be without economic support. Yet, he mocks his one-night-stand soldier lover, who "gets a dick up his ass and immediately talks about a relationship." In another scene at a gay club, Robby (Jonathan Segal), a young filmmaker who wants to make "the first Jewish gay movie," follows an attractive man into the bathroom, hoping for casual sex. Rejected on the spot, he gives a blowjob to another young man whom he does not desire and whom he himself rejects a minute later. Robby finds out that an old man who had promised to sponsor his new film never had money to begin with. "He asked me not to leave him because he doesn't have anyone," Robby says. "He asked me to sleep with him . . . I slept with him. I don't know how."

In *Amazing Grace,* Yonatan (Gal Hoyberger) falls in love with Thomas, who continually rejects him, but eventually has sex with him. He then returns to New York, leaving Yonatan alone with the HIV virus. In the same film, Miki (Aki Avni), an army defector who tries to commit suicide after his mother hands him over to the military police, says sadly, "Whatever I do, I am always left alone."

This pessimism, inflated to the point of self-annihilation, is interspersed with flashes of ecstatic optimism and sexual fantasies, most of them unattainable. Guttman depicts threatening emotional situations as well as moments of self-sacrificing and unconditional love in an aesthetically pleasing, camp form that make the psychic and social existence tolerable. Most of his films present a dancing ritual that dramatizes the power relations of sex. In those rituals of subjection and possession, men challenge and fight one another, seduce and touch one another, play games of domination and submission, of weakness and dependency, performing the mechanisms of control expressed in the sexual act. In *Drifting,* Robbi takes three runaways into his home, convincing them that he will give them roles in his new film if they obey him. Sitting masterfully in his "director chair," he orders them to take off their clothes and perform oral sex. In this scene, the hierarchical authority inherent in cinematic production dramatizes the power relations and the self-abasement in sexuality itself. Guttmann rejects the illusory, redemptive account of sexual desire in favor of what Leo Bersani terms "the inestimable value of sex as—at least in certain of its ineradicable aspects—anticommunal, antiegalitarian, antinurturing, antiloving."[2]

Bersani's argument is part of a broad project he names "the *redemptive reinvention of sex,*"[3] which critiques a long line of theorists of sexuality, such as Andrea Dworkin, Catherine MacKinnon, Pat Califa, Gayle Robin, Simon Watney, Jeffrey Weeks, and Michel Foucault. For Bersani, "The immense body of contemporary discourse that argues for a radically revised imagination of the body's capacity for pleasure . . . has as its very condition of possibility a certain refusal of sex as we know it, and frequently hidden agreement about sexuality as being, in its essence, less disturbing, less socially abrasive, less violent, more respectful of 'personhood,' than it has been in a male-dominated phallocentric culture."[4] Sexuality, or "sex as we know it" involves, "a shattering of psychic structures themselves that are the precondition of the very establishment of a relation to others."[5] Drawing on Georges Bataille and Freud, Bersani critiques the humanist understanding of sex as an act that completes the "self" in the "other," and instead suggests that sex acts out a "radical disintegration and humiliation of the self."[6] According to Bersani, "The sexual emerges as the *jouissance* of exploded limits, as the ecstatic suffering into which the human organism momentarily plunges when it is 'pressed' beyond a certain threshold of endurance. Sexuality, at least in the mode in which it is constituted, may be a tautology for masochism."[7] This version of sexuality is highly problematic to a phallocentric culture because male-dominated culture disavows the value of powerlessness in both men and women: "The oppression of women disguises a fearful male response to the seductiveness of an image of sexual powerlessness."[8] Sexuality, Bersani claims, advertises and celebrates the risk of loss of "self" on which phallocentrism depends. For Bersani, gay sex—and in particular gay anal sex—challenges the phantasmatic construction of the "self" and has potential for dissolution. Gay anal receptivity is associated in the phallocentric culture with abdication of power, with insatiable feminine sexuality. Gay men who embrace this cultural understanding of anal sex, represent to others, according to Bersani, a desire to abandon positions of mastery and coherence of the "self": "Male homosexuality advertises the risk of the sexual itself as the risk of self-dismissal, of *losing sight* of the self, and in so doing it proposes and dangerously represents *jouissance* as a mode of ascesis."[9]

I shall return to Bersani's theory of sexuality in a moment, but for now I would like to suggest that Guttman's disturbing and violent vision of sexuality could be seen as a critique on "the redemptive reinvention of sex" of the phallic masculinity of Zionist culture as well as of the Aguda's imperative demand for a "respectful" representation of homosexuality. Yair Qedar, a journalist associated with the Aguda's cultural activism, wrote the following critique of Guttman's *Amazing Grace*:

> Guttman's film presents a world in which, because of original sin, the sin of love of men, tragic punishment inevitably comes. The heroes of the film are condemned to death or loneliness because they choose or are born into a different existence, in which the equation homosexuality = AIDS = death is assumed, an existence whose essential tragic force can be compared only with [the film's] decadent aesthetic, *which is so charming* (my emphasis).[10]

Qedar is aware of the seductiveness of Guttman's images of sexual powerlessness, but he disavows this tempting force of ecstatic sexual suffering in favor of a "redemptive" reading of sexuality. In *Drifting*, Guttmann's most autobiographical film, Robby says: "Even the Gay Association doesn't want to hear about the short films I've made. They're not positive films; they don't put homosexuality in the desired light."

Guttman's queer cinema presents a vision of a disintegrated and debased nuclear family. Fathers are absent (with one exception in *Drifting* in which the father appears in a short scene "in an impulse of sentimentality," as Robby describes it) and the male heroes are associated with their mothers, who are usually depressed and suicidal. The great divas of the silver screen—such as Anna Magnani, Marlene Dietrich, Greta Garbo, and Joan Crawford—are the source for a primal identification with the maternal and femininity. Gay men's identification with maternal rather then paternal figures, argues Kaja Silverman, "negate[s] the most fundamental premise of male subjectivity—an identification with masculinity—and in so doing . . . obstruct[s] paternal lineality."[11] According to Silverman, by refusing to identify with the father, male homosexuals relinquish phallic power and mastery positions and embrace features such as lack, specularity and receptivity—in short, castration—that the phallic construction of manliness disavows and externalizes.

However, as Brett Farmer noted, though the "gay male subject may make a foundational identification with psychic femininity—whether by accepting those tropes of castration culturally defined as feminine, or by identifying with 'femininity' of the maternal image—'he' is still required to negotiate a psychocultural relation with the category of masculinity that, by definition, plays a determinative role in the organization of *male* homosexuality."[12] In other words, phallic manhood is a repudiated structural element within gay masculinity.

Bersani took such a notion even further and claimed that "[t]he logic of homosexual desire includes the potential for loving identification with gay man's enemies."[13] Gay men's internalization of certain codes of cultural masculinity, specifically the gay macho style, "is in part constitutive of male homosexual desire, which, like all sexual desire, combines and confuses impulses to appropriate and to identify with the object of desire."[14] For Bersani, gay men's adoption of these codes arises from the fact that "a sexual desire for men can't be merely a kind of culturally neutral attraction to a Platonic Idea of the male body; the object of that desire necessarily includes a socially determined and socially pervasive definition of what it means to be a man."[15]

The hypervirile male Sabra appears in Guttman's films as the loved object of desire. His idealized muscular body is a source of sexual excitement for the gay protagonists who, despite their alienation from the straight macho culture, never stop feeling uncontrolled fascination and attraction. The lack of interest of the gay hero in participating in gym class in the film *A Safe Place* express his rejection of the Zionist body culture and its compulsive demand for heterosexual masculinity. However, in the locker room, he produces erotic pleasure by touching

Figure 16. Stripping Israeli phallic masculinity in Amos Gutmann's *Amazing Grace*. Courtesy of Dagan Price.

the fetishized items of clothing of his classmates. Identification with macho masculinity takes place in the heroes' fantasies where the phallic male is stripped, literally and figuratively, of his masterful virility and pictured in passive, vulnerable eroticized positions. The hero of *Repeat Premiers* is a puppeteer who imagined that his desired masculine co-worker moves his arms slowly, as pulled by invisible threads. In *Amazing Grace,* as Yonatan lies in his bed masturbating, he fantasizes that muscular male models in a magazine underwear advertisement come to life, tenderly and sensually caressing one another.

The gay man, Bersani argues, "never stops representing the internalized phallic male as infinitely loved object of sacrifice."[16] This psychic identification is literalized in both *Repeat Premiers* and *A Safe Place,* in which the protagonists fantasize the phallic man lying naked, bathing in chiaroscuro lighting, in a pose that recalls the iconography of Saint Sebastian. This process of identification and incorporation means that paternal masculinity is figured in the libidinal construction of male homosexuality as a site of transgression and negation. Phallic masculinity in Guttman's films is a primary source of desire for gay men; however this desire is structured by constitutive ambivalence of cathexis and displacement. "Gay men," to quote Bersani again, "'gnaw at the roots of a male heterosexual identity' . . . because, from within their nearly mad identification with it, *they never cease to feel the appeal of its being violated.*"[17]

In Guttman's films, fantasies of power and control give way, in anticipatory excitement or in the orgasmic shattering of the body, to degrading self-abolition. Representations of sex emphasize the sexual act as a symbolic embodiment of abdication of mastery, of a desire to abandon the "self" in favor of communicating with what Bersani calls "'lower' orders of being."[18] Tragically, AIDS literalized this fantasmatic potential of gay sex as an actual death. In heterosexual media, the epidemic is figured as somehow caused by gay sexual practices. Homosexuality itself was imagined as death-bearing practice; however this is hardly new. Jeff Nunokawa argues that long before the AIDS era, the history of the homosexual man for the dominant culture has been one of death, doom, and extinction. This long-standing discursive tradition figured the gay man as already dying, as one whose desire is incipient dying. For the straight mind, he claims, "AIDS is a gay disease, and it means death, because AIDS has been made the most recent chapter in our culture's history of gay male, a history which, from its beginning, has read like a book of funerals."[19] However, according to

Nunokawa, this construction of the gay man is not restricted to the lurid heterosexism but also reproduced by gay culture itself: "The gay community is thus taxed during its sad time by a double burden: the variegated regime of heterosexism not only inhibits the work of acknowledging the loss of a gay man, it also exacts the incessant reproduction of this labor, by casting his death as his definition."[20]

Rather than expelling the figure of the doomed homosexual, the film *Amazing Grace* confronts it. I would like to suggest that the film stages such a confrontation by critically linking the recent queer history of AIDS and Israel's national culture of death. The majority of the Israeli gay community attacked Guttman's film for its internalized homophobia, for, as Qedar argues in his critique cited above, reproducing and reinforcing the association between homosexuality and death. Gay activism in Israel from the eighties into the mid nineties, tried to disconnect AIDS from discussions of homosexuality. At that time, the Aguda pursued a mainstream strategy and image, stating that gays and lesbians are "just like everyone else."[21] However, gay activists' demand for "positive" images of homosexuality assumes a refusal to acknowledge the materiality of AIDS and the death of friends, sons, and lovers. By eliding and disavowing the doomed image of the gay man, gay activism shared with heterosexism a similar ideology of masking the dead and living AIDS body. In a documentary film about the making of *Amazing Grace,* Guttman says, "What characterizes the disease and makes it a social disease is the terrible solitude. I knew that some of my friends died because I read the obituaries in the paper. Nobody told me. They all died as Unknown Soldiers, quietly and alone." Guttman uses the national trope of the "Unknown Soldier" to describe the casualties of AIDS. Death is decontextualized from the AIDS body of the "Unknown (homosexual) Soldier" in order to produce the national (read straight) as well as the gay imagined community.

More than any other social group in the Israeli national community, mothers—who did not actively participate in wars and whose husbands and sons were killed in combat—were forced by the Israeli national ideology to accept their loss in terms of national redemption. It is not surprising that in *Amazing Grace* Guttmann gives voice to Thomas's mother, who expresses the combined pain of her son's future death from AIDS, her personal history of loss as a Holocaust survivor and Israel's national history of death:

> I wanted to keep together what was left from our family. . . . I tried
> to take care of Thomas as much as it was possible. I didn't want

him to experience the things that I experienced. This is why I wanted to come to Israel. But there is always something going on: war, new diseases. No, I'm not sorry that Thomas has no children. . . . But it hurts me, if I think about it, that I cannot do anything for him. I don't know how I can help him. I don't know what I can do.[22]

By blurring the private death of European Jews in the Holocaust with Israeli soldiers on the battlefield, the official cultural discourse produced and legitimized the Israeli national collectivity. Specifically, the disavowal of the materiality of AIDS was needed to invent and enforce the image of a heterosexual Israeli national community. Male homosexuals who, in the dominant imagination, were associated exclusively with the disease were not only left outside of the national discourse, but were also imagined as not existing at all. By marking and linking the death from AIDS with "official" national deaths, Guttman not only resists the dematerialization and decontextualization of *all* deaths in Israeli nationalism and the imagined community it produces, but also specifically challenges heteronormative ideology and the way it polices death in national culture.

Throughout his films, the dominant national discourse was a prime target for Guttman's critique of the "redemptive reinvention of sex." In *Drifting,* a group of gays walking in the Independence Park— a site for gay male cruising in Tel Aviv constituting a sharp contrast to the idealized Zionist dream—ironically sings a famous Israeli folk song about the "beautiful and blooming land of Israel." Communal singing, one of Israel's distinctive cultural marks, is critiqued in *Bar 51* for producing an imagined national solidarity by disavowing not only the expression of (sexual) individualism but also for eliding the pain, loss, alienation, and despair that are part of the Israeli existence.

In one scene in the film, Marianna (Smadar Kalchinsky), a naïve homeless orphan girl who is involved in a "forbidden" love relationship with her brother, watches on television Sara'le Sharrone, a famous Israeli kibbutznik folk singer of the eighties, who says in an excited voice, "There are those days that you think all sorts of thoughts, and you want to cry, and instead of crying you sing, and when you sing together, you feel good." In *Drifting,* Robby says, "There was a war and the only thing I was scared of was that they will again start making positive films to raise the morale, and again there will be no place for my film." *Drifting* is Guttman's most autobiographical film. In the opening sequence, the diegetic and extradiegetic filmmakers (Robby and

Guttman) present this critique at the outset, when the protagonist addresses the camera in a monologue. Complaining about the lack of support his new movie has received from gay and straight establishment, Robby shifts in his monologue from third to first person, from talking about the hero of his forthcoming film to talking about himself:

> If the film dealt with a social problem, or if the hero at least had a political opinion: if he were a soldier, if he were a resident in a developing town, if he served on a naval destroyer, if he become religious, if he were a war widow. But if he must be a homosexual, then at least he should suffer; he shouldn't enjoy it. The state is burning; there's no time for self-searching. There's a war now. There's always a war. He left the army of his own will, without any reason. The viewers won't accept it. There are too many dead relatives. He's not sympathetic, not thoughtful; he scorns all those who want the best of him. He's not even a sensitive soul, a composed intellectual. Why should they [the viewers] identify with me? Why should they identify with him?[23]

According to Robby/Guttman, homosexuals do not have a right to representation, not only because they do not serve "national interests" but also, in the rare cases when they are represented, they must be constructed as sad, suffering people. Obviously, Guttman is not arguing for a "positive" image of gay men; in fact, he sharply critiques it in the monologue. Guttman is aiming for something completely different. In an interview, Foucault once said: "People can tolerate two homosexuals they see leaving together, but if the next day they're smiling, holding hands and tenderly embracing one another, they can't be forgiven. It is not the departure for pleasure that is intolerable, it is waking up happy."[24]

Bersani critiques this quote by Foucault for desexualizing homosexual desire:

> There may be nothing to say about those gays holding hands after a night of erotic play. Don't, Foucault warns us, read *their* tenderness as the exhausted aftermath of cocksucking that would "really" be a disguised devouring for the mother's breast, or a fucking that would "really" be heterosexual repossession of a lost phallic woman, or a being fucked that would "really" be obsessively controlled reenactment of the mother's castration by the father in the primal scene. No, those homosexuals gaily embracing as they

go to breakfast in Castro or somewhere off Christopher Street are blankly, superficially, threateningly happy. "There is," Foucault says, "no anxiety, there is no fantasy behind happiness," and with no fantasies to fantasize about, the silenced interpreter becomes the intolerant homophobe.[25]

What Bersani means is that it is sexual fantasies about gay sex behind the happiness of the gay couple that are threatening to the intolerant

Figure 17. Loss and alienation in the Tel Aviv gay scene. Robby (Jonathan Segal) in Amos Gutmann's *Drifting*. Courtesy of Miri Gutmann.

homophobe. The gay man's smile is in itself not troubling; troubling is the thing that it masks—passionate gay intercourse with its terrifying potential for dissolution of the "self." When Robby/Guttman argues that homosexual men, according to the straight mind, cannot be happy and enjoy life, it is because gay sex that would make gay men smile is intolerable in heterosexual culture, on account of its threatening appeal of loss of ego, of self-debasement. Homosexual people must suffer—they must not "get it" and certainly they must not enjoy it—because male-male sexual desire threatens the traumatic undoing of the psychic and national "self" on which heterosexuality is based.

In *Amazing Grace,* Yonatan advertises and celebrates the risk of loss of ego boundaries by having sex with the AIDS body of Thomas. In one episode, he imagines himself sick, cared for by Thomas's mother who lies him down on the bed in a posture that evokes the Christian imagery of the Pietà. He submits to the sentence of death that culturally defines his homosexual subjectivity, but by this self-sacrifice and subjugation he also evades it.

Bersani writes that "if the rectum is the grave in which the masculine ideal . . . of proud subjectivity is buried, then it should be celebrated for its very potential for death. . . . It may, finally, be in the gay man's rectum that he demolishes his own perhaps otherwise uncontrolled identification with the murderous judgment against him."[26] In the rectum, as in a grave, Yonatan puts to rest an identity which is before all else the mark of death. In the last image of the film, Yonatan is seen lying on an armchair in his backyard, a beam of light illuminating his face, and he smiles. Yonatan finds *jouissance* in the ecstatic suffering of self-annihilation, experiences grace in self-shattering, an amazing grace.

The Queer Voice: Time Off

Eytan Fox's *Time Off* challenges the construction of queer male subjectivity through sound rather than image. The film strives to unravel the stitches that suture the cinematic sound and image, and the way they produce an illusion of a coherent subjectivity, by articulating gay male sexuality through the disembodied voice. Describing a male gay relationship within military homosociality, the film uses the queer disembodied voice to resist and undermine fixity of sexual as well as national subjectivity and repression of homosexual desire.

Mary Ann Doane argues that the cinematic situation is structured by a series of spaces—the film diegesis, the screen and the auditorium—

Figure 18. Celebrating the risk of "self" loss. Thomas (Sharon Alexander, left) and Yonatan (Gal Hoyberger, right) in Amos Gutmann's *Amazing Grace*. Courtesy of Dagan Price.

organized hierarchically or hidden by each other. The heterogeneous material elements of a traditional narrative film—sound and image— are sutured through sound techniques (voice-over, voice-off and syn-chronization), along with invisible editing and narrative transparency, producing an illusion of a coherent homogeneous realistic space. According to Doane, this imaginary homogeneity exists not only in the observed space, but also in the space of the spectator: the viewer is "wrapped" in a sensory illusion of a "fantasmatic body" created by the audiovisual space and the spectator's own perception of the cinematic text, constituting the viewer's identification with the screen. In other words, the spectator identifies body to "body," reads the "body" of the film as analog to his/her own body. This process helps "sustain the narcissistic pleasure derived from the image of a certain unity, cohesion, and hence an identity grounded by the spectator's fantasmatic relation to his/her own body."[27] Sound perspectives and "techniques, which spatialize the voice and endow it with 'presence,' guarantee the singularity and stability of a point of audition, thus holding at bay the potential trauma of dispersal, dismemberment, difference."[28] Doane claims that the construction of the voice in classical film aims to reassure the spectator's unified subjectivity, which is forever indebted to and inseparable from the institution that creates it.

Following those arguments, Kaja Silverman claims that by masking the work of sound/image production, narrative cinema guarantees not only the coherence of any subjectivity, but also specifically that of male subjectivity. Narrative cinema denies its material heterogeneity in order to construct an imaginary unified and coherent male subjectivity and to lessen male anxieties of castration and fragmentation evoked by sexual difference. According to feminist film theory, in classical film those male fears represent the woman as lack. Silverman shows how this image of the woman is communicated not only through the representation of a woman's body as a fetishistic object of the male gaze, but also through the construction of the woman's voice. Examining classic Hollywood cinema of the forties, she argues that when women's voices are linked to their bodies through synchronization of sound and image, women are threatened with silence, that is, with the elimination of their subjectivity.

Further, women's voices are narratively taken away by men who speak for them. Their voice is held within the imaginary world of the film, but out of their control, spoken by male agency. For Silverman, the only way the woman's voice can avoid male agency and, in turn, escape the "semiotics [that] obliges the female voices to signify the female body, and the female body to signify lack"[29] is by being disembodied. In this way, the female voice "escapes the anatomical destiny to which classical cinema holds its female characters."[30]

These arguments could be relevant also to the representation of male homosexuality in popular imagery, as the gay man, more often then not, is projected as a "feminine," "castrated" person. The heterosexual male subject's fears of castration are located in both the front (the penis) and the back (the rectum) of his body. The anus provokes castration anxiety, because it indicates the anatomo-fantasmatic potential of the male body to resemble the "castrated" body of the female. This castration anxiety cannot be disavowed by the fantasy of the woman's body as castrated, for even if the straight male subject manages to avoid gay anal sex and only has heterosexual sex, his body still has the potential to be penetrated. In this system of anxieties, as D. A. Miller notes, the body of the male homosexual lessens male heterosexual's fears of castration:

> For even if his success in confining this sex (socially as well as psychically) to the castration attributed to it in the primal scene were far less problematic than its ever demonstrably the case, his anus would remain to raise, on his own male person, the very possibility (of being fucked and so forth) that, with all the force of binary opposition, he had projected onto *her* vagina. Accordingly, he requires another binarism to police the difference between man and woman as, by the back door, it reenters to make a difference within man. So it is that, with a frequency long outlasting the formative years, however particularly striking then, straight men unabashedly *need* gay men, whom they forcibly recruit (as the object of their blows or, in better circles, just their jokes) to enter into polarization that exorcises the "woman" in the man through assigning it to a class of man who may be considered no "man" at all. Only between the woman and the homosexual together may the normal male subject imagine himself covered front and back.[31]

This construction and function of the body of the male homosexual in heterosexuality's psychosexual dynamic may explain why gay men in popular cinema are often threatened with muteness. (Joseph L. Mankiewicz's 1959 film *Suddenly, Last Summer* is a good example or, in the context of Israeli cinema, Avi Nesher's 1978 *Sing Your Heart Out* in which the gay character barely speaks throughout the film.) In order to avoid the homophobic scenario that forces the gay man's voice to mark the gay man's body and the gay man's body to mark castration, *Time Off* articulates homosexual desire through the disembodied voice.

The film describes two days in the life of a paratroop unit about to join the war in Lebanon, focusing on the relationship between a young soldier, Yonatan Miller (Hanoch Re'im), who is becoming aware of his gay sexuality, and his platoon commander, Erez (Gil Frank). Erez deliberately makes life more difficult for Yonatan than all the other soldiers, either because he suspects Yonatan's homosexuality or because he himself is attracted to him. Although Erez flirts with Malli, the female unit clerk, his sexuality becomes suspicious: One of the soldiers says, "I think our lieutenant has an earring." The night preceding their departure for Lebanon, the soldiers are given an off-duty pass. Yonatan plans to visit his mother, who lives in Jerusalem, but only reaches her answering machine or gets a busy signal. He and three of his platoon mates go to a coffeehouse where they meet a group of American Jewish girls who invite them to their hotel. Since he is not terribly interested in this offer, he is not sorry when the taxi cannot take all. He prefers to walk through Jerusalem's Gan Ha'Atzmaut (Independence Park), a well-known meeting place for gay men. In the park, he spots Erez leaving with another man. Following them to the public bathroom, Yonatan sits in an adjacent stall and hears the voices of their passion as they have sex. When it is time to return to camp, Yonatan is late in reaching the platoon's meeting place, and Erez asks for an explanation. Unwilling to expose his commander's homosexual identity in front of his soldiers, Yonatan refuses. Erez orders him to do push-ups until he can come up with an explanation. Yonatan begins shouting and pulls from his pocket Erez's officer's identification card, which he had lost in the bathroom. Surprised at seeing his lost card, Erez stops the hazing, but tells Yonatan that he will not be getting weekend leave because of his outburst. After all the soldiers have boarded the bus taking them to Lebanon, Erez approaches Yonatan and wordlessly takes his officer's card from him.

The film emphasizes sound rather than sight in four key scenes. In the first, the soldiers are lying on the ground, their eyes closed, listening intently to the soothing voice of their commander Erez:

> No one dare open his eyes even halfway, is that clear? Everyone inhale, hold your breath and then slowly let it out. Inhale, hold it, very slowly let it out. Relax your whole body. Your toes, your fingers, your face, relax your whole body. You feel nothing. Only the sweat dripping down your neck. You love it—the smell of it. You're dying to take off your clothes, your smelly socks, your shirt, your shoes, your pants. . . . Warm water is flowing over your body. You look into the mirror. You see the water trickling from your head down to your face, your shoulders, your chest, your stomach. The mirror is covered with steam, you can't see a thing, no one dares

to open his eyes even halfway, everyone takes a breath and lets it out. Now you're under the blankets. The radio is playing weekend music. Dire Straits, Arik Einstein. Soon the phone calls will begin but you want one more minute of relaxation. Only one. Alone. Without anyone else.[32]

Erez's hypnotic voice constructs for the soldiers an auto-erotic narcissistic fantasy that also produces for Yonatan a homoerotic pleasure, as he moves his hand in the direction of his groin. At one point, through a light touch of their feet, Erez commands his soldiers to form rows, leaving Yonatan lying on the ground immersed in his fantasy. The platoon's call to attention, given in response to their commander's order, cruelly cuts off Yonatan's masturbatory fantasy, leaving him humiliated, embarrassed, and ridiculous before the other soldiers and his commanding officer. Later in the shower room, Yonatan will try to re-create his commander's autoerotic, homoerotic fantasy, but it is once again shattered by Erez's voice as he approaches the shower room with his portable radio (as described in his monologue). He himself arrives to act out the fantasy he created earlier.

The second key scene takes place in the bus when the soldiers, after a stormy political argument, ask Yonatan to play the guitar and sing "something for the heart." Yonatan sings "A Love Song for the Sea," a song that expresses yearning for maternal embrace, for a warm, protected homey space—similar imagery to what appeared before in Erez's monologue. Erez is the only one who refuses to identify with Yonatan's voice, sealing off his ears with the headphones of his Walkman.

The third key scene occurs in the toilet stall, as Yonatan listens to the passionate sounds of his commander. Yonatan sees only Erez's red paratrooper's boots behind the shoes of his partner, as they engage in anal sex, as well as their clasped hands over the dividing wall. As in the first scene, Erez's voice produces for Yonatan a homoerotic, autoerotic, narcissistic fantasy, marked by Yonatan's constant movement on the toilet seat. The light in the bathroom, extinguished immediately when the men come, and relit seconds later, marks the conclusion of Yonatan's fantasy and his awakening from it.

The fourth key scene, ending the film, takes place during the platoon's nighttime journey to Lebanon, after Erez has taken the "incriminating" officer's card from Yonatan. A long camera movement pans over the sleeping soldiers, as their heads rest on the shoulders of their

Figure 19. The "queer voice." Yonatan (Hanoch Re'im, left) in Eytan Fox's *Time Off*. Courtesy of Eytan Fox.

comrades. The camera moves across the faces of Yonatan and Erez, the only ones awake. Meanwhile the song "Love Song to the Sea" is heard on the radio in the background, this time sung by a female voice. Erez asks the driver to raise the volume and speaks to Yonatan without looking at him, "Do you hear the song, Miller?" and, while bending his head, adds, "Do you hear me, Yonatan?" The music, marked as Yonatan's homosexual voice, which in the second scene had been a meaningless sound for Erez to which he refused to listen and identify, becomes now the queer language through which he speaks. Discussing music as a language without meaning, Claude Lévi-Strauss argued that "the listener, who is first and foremost a subject with the gift of speech, should feel himself irresistibly compelled to make up the absent sense, just as someone who has lost a limb imagines that he still possesses it through the sensations present in the stump."[33] Indeed, Erez desires to complete the music and give it meaning. It becomes an instrument through which the two men, distanced by ranks and Zionist ideals of proud Sabra heterosexual masculinity, subvert the oppressive military phallic laws and express queer identification. Not only does Erez ask for the volume to be raised, but he also uses the song as his own voice and through it attempts to touch Yonathan. The song, then, is homosexualized twice:

once as Yonatan's queer voice and second as Erez appropriates it as his own lost homosexual voice.

In each of the four key scenes described above, the voice is disembodied. In the first scene, Yonatan closes his eyes listening to Erez's voice. He places the figure of Erez in space. But when his eyes are closed, he cannot clearly know Erez's exact position, in addition to the fact that Erez moves around for most of the time. In the second scene, Erez, seated in the front of the bus, hears Yonatan's voice singing with the other soldiers in the back of the bus, but he does not see Yonatan. In the third scene, Yonatan, seated in the bathroom stall adjacent to the one Erez is in, hears his commander's moans, but sees only his shoes and hands. In the fourth scene, Erez and Yonatan both hear a disembodied voice, singing a "Love Song to the Sea" on the radio. By using the disembodied voice (music and words) to articulate queer identification, the film puts into question not only the unity and coherence of subjectivity as such, assumed by synchronized image and sound, but also the imagined sexual fixity of the male military subjectivity.

Certain conditions make it possible for the film and the characters to derive pleasure from hearing the queer voice. Drawing on psychoanalytic theory, Doane argues that auditory pleasure lies in the difference "between the present experience and the memory of satisfaction: '[b]etween a (more or less inaccessible) memory and a very precise (and localizable) immediacy of perception is opened the gap where pleasure is produced.'"[34] Thus, memories of the primal auditory experience, of the hallucinatory satisfaction provided by the voice, define auditory pleasure. For the child, space, argues Doane, "is defined initially in terms of audible, not the visible: 'It is only in a second phase that the organization of visual space insures the perception of the object as *external.*'"[35] The first differences between voices are traced along the axis of the mother's and father's voices. Further, the voice has greater control of space than sight does. One can hear around corners and through walls. Hence, for a child, the voice is an instrument of demand even before language exists. It lends itself to a fantasy of power and mastery created by the expansion or rebuilding of the body. The voice also locates the forms of unity and separation between bodies. The mother's soothing voice is the first model of narcissistic, harmonious and unified auditory pleasure. However, this imaginary unity is still linked to the earliest experience of the voice, which is broken by the unpleasant feeling of difference and separation created by the interference of the father's voice. This voice acts with the mother's consent as an agent of separation and defines her voice as an irretrievably lost object of desire. The father's voice is not the narcissistic measure of harmony, but rather the voice of prohibition.

In *Time Off,* Yonatan's parents are absent. His mother's voice is only heard on the answering machine. The father is not mentioned at all. Yonatan's symbolic "parents" in the film are Erez and the platoon clerk Malli. In the first key scene, Erez's soothing voice, describing a desire for safe domestic space, produces a harmonious narcissistic pleasure represented, psychoanalytically, by the maternal voice. However, his voice is also the prohibiting voice of the father, slashing harmony and narcissistic enjoyment when he calls the platoon to attention and cuts off Yonatan's fantasy. Erez's voice embodies, then, both the mother's and the father's voices. By being the paternal agent of separation, Erez constitutes the mother's voice, that is his very own voice, as a lost object of desire that Yonatan will try to regain throughout the film.

Yonatan's relationship with Malli differs from that of his fellow soldiers. While the soldiers envy Erez for what they think is an intimate relationship with Malli, seeing her as an object of sexual desire, for Yonatan she represents a source of identification with femininity, lost maternity, desire for Erez. In the second scene, Yonatan's song is associated with motherhood not only through the song's lyrics, but also through Malli's entrance into the frame exactly when the following words of the song are heard: "Mother, light a flower of flame." After returning from the shower room, crawling under the clean sheets he brought from home, Yonatan calls Malli to say good-night. As she stands in the darkness unable to see who has called her, Malli cannot provide him with the imaginary unity of the maternal voice, which is in the "father's" province. By refusing to identify with Yonatan's "feminine" voice, Erez repudiates his queer voice as the "son", as well as his own voice of desire.

The third and fourth scenes mark a turnabout in the identification of the "father" with the homosexual desire of the "son", taking place when the lost voice of desire of the "mother" is restored to him. The turnabout is set in motion by two literally and figuratively lost objects of desire—an apple and Erez's officer's card—which are unintentionally abandoned by the characters and become representatives of lost queer identification and its mediated realization. In the third scene, before encountering Erez, Yonatan sits on a bench in the park opposite a man who is trying to seduce him. Smiling, Yonatan gazes away

from the man and amuses himself with an apple given to him by
Malli. Suddenly, he sees Erez walking toward him. He drops the apple
and hides behind a tree. Erez sits down on the bench just vacated by
Yonatan, picks up the apple and plays with it, just as Yonatan had. The
man sitting opposite him gets up and sits down next to him. Erez gets
up and walks away, followed by the man. The apple, then, becomes
an object mediating Erez's and Yonatan's homosexual identification.

In the following scene, Yonatan derives pleasure from the voice of
Erez having sex with another man in the park's public bathroom. The
"father"/Erez's queer voice of desire produces for Yonatan a harmonious
narcissistic homoerotic fantasy, which this time, contrary to the first
scene, is not cut brutally by the "father's" prohibiting voice, but
reaches satisfaction. Yonotan's knowledge of Erez's homosexuality
motivates him to use Erez's officer's card, which he lost in the public
bathroom, again, as a mediating object of queer identification between
them. In this case, the officer card represents not only military and
national identity, but also sexual identity. Yonatan's re-appropriation
of the card enables him to communicate, within the homosocial space,
queer identification with his gay commanding officer that resists the
military hetero-male order. Yonatan does not use his knowledge of Erez's
sexual identity to humiliate him, as Erez did to him in the first scene,
but rather uses it to express solidarity and understanding. The last scene
of the film represents a mutual identification between the two men when
Erez addresses Yonatan through the disembodied voice, the voice of
the song on the radio, marked by the film as the queer voice. In this
scene, the disembodied queer voice envelopes the bodies of Erez and
Yonatan, as well as embracing the bodies of the other dozing soldiers,
listening to the music, laying their heads on their comrades' shoulders.
Echoing in the bus, the disembodied queer voice homoeroticizes the
entire military space, challenging the fixity of male homosocial military identity.

Problems in the Representation
of Mizrahi Gay Men

While the Israeli new queer cinema addresses ques-
tions of homophobia and gay subjectivity, it retains a deafening silence
on issues of race and racism, especially when it concerns the interethnic
tension between Mizrahim and Ashkenazim. The new queer cinema
followed the Aguda's Ashkenazi middle-class sexual politics that left
Mizrahi homosexuals no alternative but to identify with a Eurocentric

gay identity that ignored the ethnic diversity of the Israeli gay community. Overly obsessed with the sexual "self," the Israeli gay mainstream culture abstracted the psyche from its racial formation, therefore refusing to acknowledge that not all the gays are Ashkenazim and that Ashkenazi gay sexuality itself is informed by ethnicity. The Aguda's use of the pink triangle to advertise its cultural activities challenged, on the one hand, the dominant national discourse by associating the homosexual Holocaust and the Jewish Holocaust, linking homophobia and anti-Semitism. On the other hand, it also submitted Mizrahi gays and lesbians to a Western narrative of homophobia, which excludes ethnicity in the formation of sexual identity. By emphasizing homophobic society as the enemy that *all* gays should fight against, Ashkenazi queer culture disavowed the racism that Mizrahi gays and lesbians confront in and outside the gay community.

Furthermore, in the narrative of the pink triangle, Israeli gay identity is constructed against an anti-Semitic enemy, a role assigned in the modern history of Jews to the Arabs, therefore leaving no legitimized cultural space for Mizrahi queers to express their Arab culture and heritage which was structurally eliminated from gay identity discourse. Ironically, the term "gay pride" adopted by the Aguda from the Euro-American "gay pride" is originally derived from American "black power" and "black pride" of the sixties. If Ashkenazi gay activism were more aware of the history of its own queer terminology it would recognize that race and ethnicity are structural elements within its sexual politics, while also acknowledging that people with a history of oppression can organize without ignoring different forms of identity. As Kobena Mercer and Isaac Julien have suggested, "Politics is about making connections—practically, with the forming of alliances between different social groups, and at a cognitive level with the recognition of diverse categories of race, class, gender, ethnicity, and sexuality in the articulation of power relations."[36] Israeli queer culture does not admit to the complexities that arise at the junctions of multiple identity categories, especially in regard to race and ethnicity. This reflects the fear of losing Ashkenazi hegemony and the authority of defining "gay identity," a term often masking the struggle for power over representation.

In his documentation of the Israeli gay community, Lee Walzer describes the denial by both gay Ashkenazim and Mizrahim whenever the issue of ethnic discrimination is raised: "denial that there ever was a problem and denial that such a problem exists today."[37] However, the rhetorical formulation that Walzer uses to discuss the subject indicates his very own disavowal of ethnic oppression. Beyond the fact that Walzer enforces Orientalist stereotypes and racist explanations for the "problem of the gap" between Mizrahim and Ashkenazim and avoids exploring the issue critically, his discussion is also character- ized by splitting levels of arguments, which structure the logic of denial in Freudian fetishism.[38] He writes, for example: "The prob- lems between Ashkenazim and Mizrahim are not primarily race- or color-motivated, *although* such prejudice also exists" or "Gaps in education and income levels between Mizrahim and Ashkenazim have narrowed, *although* they are still too wide."[39] Walzer's fetishis- tic disavowal can therefore be rendered thus: "I know that ethnic dis- crimination against Mizrahim exists in Israel, but in my narrative it does not exist." Through this disavowal, Walzer fetishizes the Ashkenazi gay identity as the norm.

Ethnic disavowal also characterizes the films of Guttman who, despite his subversive sexual politics, has nothing to say about the inter- sectionality of sex and ethnicity. While the social margins in his films are sexualized and form a critique of the homophobic dominant dis- course, they are rarely figured in terms of ethnic oppression and racism, despite the fact that some of his characters are Mizrahim. The ethnic identity and the social marginality of the Mizrahi heroes are exploited and manipulated to serve Guttman's radical vision of sexu- ality. He uses racist Orientalist types, stereotypes and images, whose racist quality is often masked by the claim that they are part of gay "camp" subculture or what has been called "gay sensibility," with its harmless joyful play of stereotypes.

Bar 51, for example, rehearses the colonial stereotype of the Oriental "feminine" boy in the figure of Aranjuez (Alon Aboutboul), a "sissy" Mizrahi gay man with orange hair, extravagant dress, and effeminate talk, working in a sleazy striptease bar as a dresser. His char- acter decorates the film's camp aesthetic and dramatizes the idea of the performativity of identity. Aranjuez is actually Israel Azulay who, with his sister Sara—known in the bar as Zara—left their home in the suburbs of Tel Aviv. However, the ethnic identity of Aranjuez as a Mizrahi gay man plays no role in the film. By erasing ethnicity from his sexual politics, Guttman assumes that all gays share the same experience of oppression. In other words, Guttman uses sexuality as a metaphorical substitution of ethnicity.

This kind of ahistorical analogy between sex and ethnicity has the effect of obscuring and concealing the specific form of oppression experienced by Mizrahi gay men. As bell hooks has argued, "to make synonymous experience of homophobic aggression with racial oppression deflects attention away from the particular dual dilemma that non-white gay people face, as individuals who confront both racism and homophobia."⁴⁰ Furthermore, by constructing such an analogy, Guttman implicitly posits "Ashkenaziness" as the norm.

The Israeli new queer cinema produces and enforces Ashkenazi gay normative identity through the repetition of a colonial fantasy that confines Mizrahi men to a rigid set of ethnic roles and identities. The exotic Oriental boy and the hypermasculine Mizrahi male are major images through which Mizrahi men become visible in the Ashkenazi urban gay subculture. This colonial fantasy attempts to fix the position of Mizrahi male subjectivity into a space that mirrors the object of Ashkenazi needs and desires. Fox's short film *Gotta Have Heart* (1997), is an attempt by the new queer cinema to ally with and to be part of the Ashkenazi middle-class consensus and the national ideology. The film describes the lives of two Ashkenazi gay men, Gur (Chak Barkman) and Nohav (Uri Omanoti), who share a dream to find a husband, get married, and live happily ever after (the Hebrew title of the film is *Husband with a Heart*). There is also the character of Mitzi (Osenat Hakim), a young woman who plans to have a child with Gur when they become thirty-five years of age. Contrary to Guttman's "alienating" imagery of (homo)sexuality and critique of the Zionist body Master Narrative, Fox presents a different vision of male homosexuality that conforms to the dominant national discourse. When Nohav says that he does not wish to join the army, Gur, a paratroop unit veteran, scolds him in the name of his civic duty. Gur hopes to get admitted to Bezalel Art Academy and to become an architect, while Nohav dreams to dance with his lover at the Eurovision Song Contest (a major camp cultural event for gay people in Israel.)

But everybody's object of desire is Marito (Sami Huri), a dark, muscular, hypervirile bisexual Mizrahi stud, the central dancer in folkdance evenings held at the settlement where they live. The Mizrahi male is objectified into "otherness" by the Ashkenazi gay gaze that inscribes on his body fears and fantasies of the "wild," "animalistic" nature of Oriental sexuality. This stereotypical convention of racial representation is especially manifest in the scene where Marito invites Gur to his apartment, waiting for him dressed only in his underwear, sitting on the bed—sensually eating a watermelon with his hands in a way that recalls racist imagery of blacks in slavery. Fear of aggressive sexuality shifts to desire as Marito calms his threatened lover while unbut-

Figure 20. Object of the Ashkenazi gay man's gaze. Marito (Sami Huri) as the Mizrahi stud in Eytan Fox's *Gotta Have Heart*. Courtesy of Eytan Fox.

toning his shirt: "[Sex] is my art. . . . Don't be afraid, boy." Such a representation of Oriental sexuality which governs the gaze of Ashkenazi gay culture not only continues the pattern of the Zionist colonial exploitation and objectification of the Mizrahi male body, but also leaves no space for the institution of Mizrahi gay identity, as well as blocking any attempt for queer Mizrahi-Ashkenazi social and political interaction. Surprisingly, in the anal sex between the two, Marito takes the passive position. This may be seen as a counter-image to the racist construction of the Mizrahi man as a hypermasculine stud. Immediately after the sex, however, Marito is seen in the shower, vigorously scrubbing his body with the soap, washing away the "filth" of gay sex. He is depicted as a man who feels uncomfortable with his sexuality, incapable of being emotionally attached to either gay or straight partner, in contrast to the Ashkenazi gay man who accepts his sexual identity. Marito is destined to be trapped in his troubled sexual body, while Gur and Nohav aspire to goals beyond sexuality, unattainable for the Mizrahi male subject. Thus, it seems neither surprising or important that we know nothing about Marito's life. He has no history or future plans; he functions only as a fantasized sexual object of the Ashkenazi homosexual man. (His fictive name—Marito—echoes romantic fantasies of the Latin lover, not his Jewish-Mizrahi origin, as opposed to the Hebrew names of Gur and Nohav.) After he understands that Marito is not "good husband material," Gur rejects his offer for a last dance and instead joins Nohav for a dance, fulfilling his Eurovision dream, as well as the film's "Eurovision" of an Ashkenazi gay identity.

Additional problems in the representation of Mizrahi gay men arise in Fox's television series *Florentin.* The show tells the story of Israelis in their twenties living in the south Tel Aviv neighborhood of Florentin, Israel's version of SoHo or Tribeca. The two main gay protagonists are Iggi (Uri Bannay), an effeminate, openly gay Mizrahi man, and Tomer (Avshalosm Polak), an Ashkenazi "straight-looking" closeted homosexual. By constructing the Mizrahi gay man as already "out," Fox can conveniently avoid addressing the specific experience of "coming out" for Mizrahi queers, therefore assuming a common narrative of homosexual identity formation, which is always Ashkenazi. While the show describes in detail Tomer's "coming out" drama and his complex relationships with his family, Iggy's family ties are rarely mentioned. Confessing to his family about his sexual orientation, Tomer destroys the illusionary harmony of the patriarchal, middle-class, nuclear family and finds comfort and support among his friends.

The assumption of this narrative is that everyone comes out the same way and that all families are the same. However, unlike the stereotypical Ashkenazi nuclear family, the extended Mizrahi family provides a necessary source of support against ethnic discrimination, which cannot be so easily replaced by other social systems. Economically,

Figure 21. The effeminate Mizrahi homosexual. Iggi (Uri Bannay) in Eytan Fox's *Florentin*. Courtesy of Eytan Fox.

Figure 22. Queer romance between the Mizrahi openly homesexual man (Uri Bannay, left) and the Ashkenazi "straight-looking," closeted homosexual (Avshalom Polak, right) in Eytan Fox's *Florentin*. Courtesy of Eytan Fox.

moving out of the parents' house after army service is not an easy task for many Mizrahim, especially if one is a provider of the entire family. (The rate of unemployment is especially high among Mizrahim in Israel). Further, the Ashkenazi narrative of "coming out" privileges gay identity as the most important task of any homosexual. It might also be true to argue that for Mizrahi homosexuals coming from a working-class background, gay identity is not always the prime target. There is a desire to do other things (get an education or a job, for example) and "coming out" is not paramount in the construction of Mizrahi identity. The queer urban culture, dominated by middle-class Ashkenazim, never addressed those issues of class in the construction of sexual identity. When a Mizrahi gay comes out, what does he come out into? Coming out into the Ashkenazi gay "scene" and culture is sometimes not an attractive option for Mizrahi queers.

Florentin enforces the notion that true identity may be revealed in sexuality. The secret hidden truth of sexuality must be confessed because sex is a natural basic element in human identity. Coming to terms with his queerness, Tomer becomes a more free, open, complete, in-touch-with-his-body person, as Iggi is, with whom he will couple at the end of the series. This essentialist notion of sex, as Mercer and Julien have argued, "is in fact based on the prevailing Western concept of sexuality which *already contains racism*":

> Historically, the European construction of sexuality coincides with the epoch of imperialism and the two inter-connect . . . the person of the savage was developed as the Other of civilization and one of the first 'proofs' of this otherness was the nakedness of the savage, the visibility of its sex. This led Europeans to assume that the savage possessed an open, frank and uninhabited 'sexuality'—unlike the sexuality of the European which was considered to be fettered by the weight of civilization.[41]

Florentin repeats this colonial concept of sexuality though the relationship between Tomer and Iggi. Returning from a post-military service trip to India, Tomer moves in with his old friend Toti and her gay roommate Iggi. Still silent about his sexuality, Tomer feels uncomfortable with Iggi's queer extravaganza, especially the sounds of lust that Iggi makes during sex, that he overhears through the walls. For his part, Iggi is indifferent to Tomer's criticism and even enjoys teasing his stuffy new friend. As the process of his "coming out" progresses, Tomer finds himself sexually attracted to Iggi, jealous of his "natural," "authentic" unmediated relation toward his body. This is dramatized in the scene in which Iggi belly dances to the music of the famed Egyptian singer Om Kolthom. Later, when he finds himself alone in the apartment, Tomer plays the music of Om Kolthom and bellydances, erotically touching his body. The "seductive," "exotic" Eastern music unbuttons the rational Western-Ashkenazi gay man, opening him to a different, unfamiliar realm of the senses that he had never previously experienced.

This Orientalist fantasy is extended to the sexualized body of the Mizrahi gay man who becomes an object of study and desire of the Ashkenazi homosexual subject. The identity of the Mizrahi queer man is reduced to his corporeality, to his "natural," thus uncivilized, sexuality, in a way that enables the Ashkenazi gay culture not only to control and regulate the representation of Mizrahi gayness, but also to construct an Eurocentric gay consciousness whose underlying assumption is the naturalness of sexuality. In other words, rather than not being part of Ashkenazi gay culture, the oppressed image of the Mizrahi gay man is implicated in Ashkenazi queer sexual politics and its claim for a liberation of the homosexual through sexuality. Thus, the Israeli gay community can no longer deny its own discursive oppression of Mizrahi homosexuals and must question the ethnocentric assumptions behind its sexual agenda.

Notes

INTRODUCTION

1. Ella Shohat, *Israeli Cinema: East/West and the Politics of Representation* (Austin: University of Texas Press, 1987).
2. Judith Butler, "Against Proper Objects," *Difference*, no. 6, 2–3, (1994): 21.
3. Leo Bersani, *Homos* (Cambridge, Mass.: Harvard University Press, 1995); Michael Warner, "Introduction," in *Fear of a Queer Planet: Queer Politics and Social Theory,* ed. Michael Warner (Minneapolis: University of Minnesota Press, 1993), vii–xxxi; David M. Halperin, *Saint Foucault: Towards a Gay Hagiography* (New York: Oxford University Press, 1995).
4. Judith Butler, *Bodies That Matter: On the Discursive Limits of "Sex"* (New York: Routledge, 1993), 113.
5. Arif Dirlik, "The Postcolonial Aura: Third World Criticism in the Age of Global Capitalism," in *Dangerous Liaisons: Gender, Nation and Postcolonial Perspectives,* eds. Anne McClintock, Aamir Mufti, and Ella Shohat (Minneapolis: University of Minnesota Press, 1997), 492–501; Anne McClintock, *Imperial Leather: Race, Gender, and Sexuality in the Colonial Contest* (New York: Routledge, 1995); Ella Shohat and Robert Stam, *Unthinking Eurocentrism: Multicuturalism and the Media* (London: Routledge, 1994); Aijaz Ahmad, *In Theory: Classes, Nations, Literatures* (London: Verso, 1992).
6. Edward W. Said, *Orientalism* (New York: Pantheon, 1978).
7. Homi K. Bhabha, *The Location of Culture* (London: Routledge, 1994).
8. Bhabha, "Of Mimicry and Man: The Ambivalence of Colonial Discourse," in *The Location of Culture,* 85.
9. See, for example, Kobena Mercer, *Welcome to the Jungle: New Positions on Black Cultural Studies* (New York: Routledge, 1994); Anne McClintock, *Imperial Leather;* Ann Laura Stoler, *Race and the Education of Desire: Foucault's "History of Sexuality" and the Colonial Order of Things* (Durham, N.C.: Duke University Press, 1977); *Talking Visions: Multicultural Feminism*

in a Transnational Age, ed. Ella Shohat (Cambridge, Mass.: MIT Press, 1998).

10. Paul Willemen, "Looking for the Male," *Framework* 15–17:16 (1981); Richard Dyer, "Don't Look Now: The Male Pin-Up," in *The Sexual Subject: A "Screen" Reader in Sexuality* (London: Routledge, 1992), 265–276; Steve Neale, "Masculinity as Spectacle," in *The Sexual Subject*, 277–290; Screening the Male: Exploring Masculinities in Hollywood Cinema, ed. Steven Choan and Ina Rea Hark (London: Routledge, 1993); Peter Lehman, *Running Scared: Masculinity and the Representation of the Male Body* (Philadelphia: Temple University Press, 1993); Paul Smith, *Clint Eastwood: A Cultural Production* (London: UCL Press, 1993); Dennis Bingham, *Acting Male: Masculinities in the Films of James Stewart, Jack Nicholson, and Clint Eastwood* (New Brunswick, N.J.: Rutgers University Press, 1994); Susan Jeffrods, *Hard Bodies: Hollywood Masculinity in the Reagan Era* (New Brunswick, N.J.: Rutgers University Press, 1994). See also *Boys: Masculinities in Contemporary Culture*, ed. Paul Smith (Boulder, Colo.: Westview Press, 1996); Gaylyn Studler, *This Mad Masquerade: Stardom and Masculinity in the Jazz Age* (New York: Columbia University Press, 1996); Steven Cohan, *Masked Men: Masculinity and the Movies of the Fifties* (Bloomington: Indiana University Press, 1997); Judith Halberstam, *Female Masculinity* (Durham, N.C.: Duke University Press, 1998); *Masculinity: Bodies, Movies, Culture*, ed. Peter Lehman (New York: Routledge, 2001).

11. Smith, *Clint Eastwood*, 157.

12. Leo Bersani, *The Freudian Body: Psychoanalsis and Art* (New York: Columbia University Press, 1986); Gilles Deleuze, *Masochism: Coldness and Cruelty* (New York: Zone Books, 1989); Gaylyn Studlar, *In the Realm of Pleasure: Von Sternberg, Dietrich, and the Masochistic Aesthetic* (New York: Columbia University Press, 1988); Kaja Silverman, *Male Subjectivity at the Margins* (New York: Routledge, 1992).

13. Lehman, *Running Scared*, 28.

14. Eve Kosofsky Sedgwick and Michael Moon, "Divinity: A Dossier, a Performance Piece, a Little Understood Emotion, " in Eve Kosofsky Sedgwick, *Tendencies*, (Durham, N.C.: Duke University Press, 1993), 246–247.

15. D. A. Miller, "Anal Rope," in *Inside/Out: Lesbian Theories, Gay Theories*, ed. Diana Fuss (New York: Routledge, 1991), 119–141; Lee Edelman, *Homographesis: Essays in Gay Literary and Cultural Theory* (New York: Routledge, 1994); Leo Bersani, "Is the Rectum a Grave?" in *AIDS: Cultural Analysis, Cultural Activism*, ed. Douglas Crimp (Cambridge, Mass.: MIT Press, 1988), 197–222.

16. Robert Stam, *Subversive Pleasures: Bakhtin, Cultural Criticism and Film* (Baltimore: The Johns Hopkins University Press, 1989), 13. See also Michael Gardiner, *The Dialogics of Critique: M. M. Bakhtin and the Theory of Ideology* (London: Routledge, 1992).

17. V. N. Volosinov, *Marxism and the Philosophy of Language*, trans. Ladislav Matejka and I. R. Titunik (Cambridge, Mass.: Harvard University Press, 1973), 22 (his italics).

18. M. M. Bakhtin, *Speech Genres and Other Late Essays*, trans. Vern W. McGee, ed. Caryl Emerson and Michael Holquist (Austin: University of Texas Press, 1986), 136.

19. Nathan Gross and Ya'acov Gross, *The Hebrew Film: The History of Cinema in Israel* [in Hebrew] (Jerusalem: privately published, 1991); Meir Schnitzer, *Israeli Cinema: Facts, Plots, Directors, Opinions* [in Hebrew] (Jerusalem:

Kinneret Publishing House, 1994); Hillel Tryster, *Israel Before Israel—Silent Cinema in the Holy Land* (Jerusalem: Steven Spielberg Jewish Film Archive, 1995); Amy Kronish, *World Cinema: Israel* (Madison-Teaneck: Fairleigh Dickinson University Press, 1996).

20. Igal Bursztyn, *Face as Battlefield* [in Hebrew] (Tel Aviv: Hakibbutz Hameuchad, 1990); Nurith Gertz, *Motion Fiction: Israeli Fiction in Film* [in Hebrew] (Tel Aviv: The Open University of Israel Press, 1993); Nitzan S. Ben-Shaul, *Mythical Expressions of Siege in Israeli Films* (Lewiston: Edwin Mellen Press, 1997); Ariel Scweitzer, *Le Cinema Israeli de la Modernité* (Paris, 1997); *Fictive Looks: On Israeli Cinema* [in Hebrew], ed. Nurith Gertz, Orly Lubin, and Judd Ne'eman (Tel Aviv: The Open University of Israel, 1998).

21. Nurith Gertz, "The 'Others' in '40s and '50s Israeli Films: Holocaust Survivors, Arabs, Women" [in Hebrew], in *Fictive Looks*, 381.

22. Kronish, *World Cinema: Israel*, 181.

23. Sander L. Gilman, *Difference and Pathology: Stereotypes of Sexuality, Race and Madness* (Ithaca, NY: Cornell University Press, 1985); Daniel Boyarin, *Unheroic Conduct: The Rise of Heterosexuality and the Invention of the Jewish Man* (Berkeley: University of California Press, 1997); David Biale, *Eros and the Jews: From Biblical Israel to Contemporary America* (New York: Basic Books, 1992).

24. On Mizrahi feminism, see, for example, Ella Shohat, "Mizrahi Feminism: The Politics of Gender, Race, and Multiculturalism," in *News from Within*, April 1996, 17–26; Henriet Dahan-Kalev, "Feminism Between Ashkenaziness and Mizrahiness," in *Sex, Gender and Politics*, ed. Dafena Izeraeli [in Hebrew] (Tel Aviv: Hakibbutz Hameuchad, 1999), 217–266.

CHAPTER ONE: THE ZIONIST BODY MASTER NARRATIVE

1. Michel Foucault [1978], *The History of Sexuality, Volume I: An Introduction*, trans. Robert Hurley (New York: Vintage Books, 1990).

2. Leo Bersani, *Homos* (Cambridge: Harvard University Press, 1995), 81.

3. Foucault, *The History of Sexuality*, 54.

4. Sander L. Gilman, *Freud, Race and Gender* (Princeton: Princeton University Press, 1993); Daniel Boyarin, *Unheroic Conduct: The Rise of Heterosexuality and the Invention of the Jewish Man* (Berkeley: University of California Press, 1997); Michael Gluzman, "Longing for Heterosexuality: Zionism and Sexuality in Herzl's *Altneuland*" [in Hebrew], in *Theory and Criticism— An Israeli Forum* 11 (winter, 1997): 145–163.

5. Cited in Gilman, *Freud, Race and Gender*, 31.

6. On analogies between Jewish men and homosexuals, see, for example, Gilman, *Freud, Race and Gender*, 162–163; Marjorie Garber [1992], *Vested Interests: Cross-Dressing and Cultural Anxiety* (New York: Routledge, 1997), 224–233.

7. Cited in Gilman, *Freud, Race and Gender*, 42.

8. Ibid., 42–43.

9. Ibid., 77.

10. Boyarin, *Unheroic Conduct*, 4–5.

11. Cited in Boyarin, *Unheroic Conduct*, 283–284.

12. Cited in Shmuel Almog, *Nationalism, Zionism, Antisemitism: Essays and Studies* [in Hebrew] (Jerusalem: Bialik Institute, 1992), 208.

13. Cited in George L. Mosse, *The Image of Man: The Creation of Modern Masculinity* (New York: Oxford University Press, 1996), 152.
14. Ibid., 152.
15. Cited in David Biale, *Eros and the Jews: From Biblical Israel to Contemporary America* (New York: Basic Books, 1992).
16. Sander L. Gilman, *Difference and Pathology: Stereotypes of Sexuality, Race and Madness* (Ithaca: Cornell University Press, 1985), 158. See also Gilman, *Freud, Race and Gender,* 105.
17. See, for example, Anita Shapira, *Land and Power: The Zionist Resort to Force 1881–1948,* trans. William Temper (Stanford: Stanford University Press, 1992); Biale, *Eros and the Jews*; Boyarin, *Unheroic Conduct,* 271–312.
18. Cited in Yossef Halahemi, "To See Their Land of Yearning" [in Hebrew], *Cinematheque* 63 (May–June, 1992): 32.
19. Ibid., 31–32.
20. Cited in Almog, *Nationalism, Zionism, Antisemitism,* 212.
21. Ibid., 208.
22. My arguments here are inspired by Slavoj Žižek's and Pascal Bonitzer's discussions on the relations between the evolution of the cinematic editing and Hitchcock's suspense. Slavoj Žižek, "The Hitchcockian Blot," in *Looking Awry: An Introduction to Jacques Lacan through Popular Culture* (Cambridge: MIT Press, 1991), 88–106. Pascal Bonitzer, "Hitchcockian Suspense," in *Everything You Always Wanted to Know about Lacan (But Were Afraid to Ask Hitchcock),* ed. Slavoj Žižek (London: Verso, 1992), 15–30.
23. Igal Bursztyn, *Face as Battlefield* [in Hebrew] (Tel Aviv: Hakibbutz Hameuchad, 1990), 44.
24. Slavoj Žižek, "Grimaces of the Real, or When the Phallus Appears," *October* 58 (1991): 57.
25. Sigmund Freud, "The Uncanny," trans. Alix Strachey, in *Sigmund Freud: Psychological Writings and Letters,* ed. Sander L. Gilman (New York: Continuum, 1995), 121.
26. Malden Dolar, "I Shall Be with You on Your Wedding-Night: Lacan and the Uncanny," *October* 58 (1991): 23.
27. On the relation between repetition compulsion, passivity and unpleasure in psychoanalysis, see this book, Chapter Two, note 19.
28. Homi K. Bhabha, *The Location of Culture* (London: Routledge, 1994), 1.
29. Judith Butler, *Bodies That Matter: On the Discursive Limits of "Sex"* (New York: Routledge, 1993), 3.
30. Ibid.
31. Freud, "The Uncanny," 146.
32. Žižek, "Grimaces of the Real, or When the Phallus Appears," 55.
33. Ibid., 56.
34. Kaja Silverman, "Fassbinder and Lacan: A Reconsideration of the Gaze, Look and the Image," *Camera Obscura* 19 (1989): 71–73.
35. By race and racism, I am not referring to the representation of the Jewish people as "race" as in the fin-de-siècle European anti-Semitic discourse, but rather to the racial discourse of the Zionist domination.
36. One cannot simply associate Zionism with European colonialism. The Zionist movement and Israel, allied to Western colonial interests, exercised colonialist discourse and politics toward Eastern land and populations. At the same time, as Ella Shohat argues, "Zionism can not be simplistically equated with colonialism or imperialism. Unlike colonialism, Zionism con-

stituted a response to millennial oppression and, in the counterdistinction to a classical paradigm, in this case metropolis and colony were located in the self-same place." Moreover, Eretz Yisrael/Palestine had always been the symbolic place for the Jewish people, and Israel itself, as an emerging nation, has similarities with Third World nations. "Master Narrative/ Counter Readings: The Politics of Israeli Cinema," in *Resisting Images: Essays on Cinema and History,* ed. Robert Sklar and Charles Musser (Philadelphia: Temple University Press, 1990), 256. For further discussion, see also Emmanuel Sivan, *Arab Political Myths* [in Hebrew] (Tel Aviv: Am Oved Publishers, 1997), 202–209; Joseph Massad, "The 'Post-Colonial' Colony: Time, Space, and Bodies in Palestine/Israel," in *The Pre-Occupation of Postcolonial Studies,* ed. Fawiza Afzal-Khan and Kapana Seshadri-Crooks (Durham: Duke University Press, 2000), 311–346.

37. Shohat, "Master Narrative/Counter Readings," 270.
38. Biale, *Eros and the Jews,* 183.
39. Cited in Rachel Elboim-Dror, *Yesterday's Tomorrow, Volume A: The Zionist Utopia* [in Hebrew] (Jerusalem: Yad Izhak Ben-Zvi, 1993), 135.
40. Ibid., 168.
41. Theodor Herzl [1896], *The State of the Jews* [in Hebrew] (Jerusalem: Kesht-Tarbot, 1996), 27.
42. Boyarin, *Unheroic Conduct,* 302.
43. Ibid., 309 (my italics).
44. Foucault, *The History of Sexuality,* 143.
45. Ibid., 138.
46. Ibid., 137 (my italilcs).
47. Ann Laura Stoler, *Race and the Education of Desire: Foucault's 'History of Sexuality' and the Colonial Order of Things* (Durham: Duke University Press, 1995).
48. Cited in Rachel Elboim-Dror, *Yesterday's Tomorrow, Volume B: Selection from Zionist Utopias* [in Hebrew] (Jerusalem: Yad Izhak Ben-Zvi, 1993), 203.
49. Ibid., 197.
50. Ibid., 263.
51. Ella Shohat, *Israeli Cinema: East/West and the Politics of Representation* (Austin: University of Texas Press, 1987), 42.
52. Shohat has discussed the construction of the Arabs as anti-Semitic gentiles in *Israeli Cinema* 50.
53. Cited in Nissim Levy, *The History of Medicine in the Holy Land: 1799–1948* [in Hebrew] (Haifa: Hakibbutz Hameuchad, 1998), 46.
54. Ibid., 480–481.
55. Edward W. Said, "Invention, Memory and Place," *Critical Inquiry* 26, no. 2 (winter 2000): 187.
56. See Levy, *The History of Medicine in the Holy Land,* 486.
57. Cited in Amos Elon, *Herzl* (New York: Holt, Rinehart and Winston, 1975), 289.
58. Sander L. Gilman, *The Jew's Body* (New York: Routledge, 1991), 169–193.
59. Cited in Gilman, *The Jew's Body,* 179.
60. The construction of the Ashkenazi "whiteness" cannot be set apart from economic and political processes and agendas that took place during and after World War II, intensified with the establishment of the State of Israel in 1948. As Caren Kaplan has shown, the construction of Jewish immigrants' whiteness in North America expressed not only the desire to escape anti-Semitism,

but also articulated an attempt to improve their economical status. US social policy and national politics contributed to the whitening of Jews of European origin by sponsoring and favoring European ethnic groups over other ethnic groups such as African Americans. The American support of the Zionist Movement and of the State of Israel produced the notion that Jews in America and in Israel were part of the Western world, protected from the Arab enemy. The effect of this growing support also included the elision of Sephardi Jews from both American and Zionist discourses of the "modern" Middle East. The production of Zionist Ashkenazi whiteness can be seen as a Jewish triumph over discrimination and anti-Semitism in Europe, but it also expresses a change from a marginal social and economic class to a new national status, based upon the discrimination and exploitation of Arabs and Arab-Jews. Caren Kaplan, "'Beyond the Pale': Rearticulating US Jewish Whiteness," in *Talking Visions: Multicultural Feminism in a Transnational Age,* ed. Ella Shohat (Cambridge: MIT Press, 1998), 451–484.

61. Richard Dyer, *White* (London: Routledge, 1997), 14.
62. Ibid., 39.
63. See Moki Tzor, *Kehilateno: The Philosophy, Exertions and Desires of the Pioneers* [in Hebrew] (Jerusalem: Yad Izhak Ben-Zvi, 1988), 10.
64. On representations of the male body in Eisenstein's cinema, see Thomas Waugh, *Hard to Imagine: Gay Male Eroticism in Photography and Film from Their Beginnings to Stonewall* (New York: Columbia University Press, 1996), 124–125, 132–137.
65. Klaus Theweleit, *Male Fantasies: Women, Floods, Bodies, History, Vol. 1,* trans. Stephen Conway (Minneapolis: University of Minnesota Press, 1987).
66. Ella Shohat and Robert Stam, *Unthinking Eurocentrism: Multiculturalism and the Media* (London: Routledge, 1994), 140.
67. Dyer, *White,* 162.
68. Ibid., 207–208.
69. Benedict Anderson [1983], *Imagined Communities: Reflection on the Origin and Spread of Nationalism* (London: Verso, 1991), 11–12.
70. See Hanan Hever, "The Living Is Alive and the Dead Is Dead" [in Hebrew], *Siman Keriah* 19 (1986): 188–195.
71. Christian Metz, *The Imaginary Signifier: Psychoanalysis and the Cinema,* trans. Celia Britton, Annwyl Williams, Ben Brewster, and Alfred Guzzetti (Bloomington: Indiana University Press, 1982), 277.
72. Ibid., 276.
73. See Biale, *Eros and the Jews,* 192–196.

CHAPTER 2: CANNON FODDER

1. My conversations with Judd Ne'eman, as well as his writings on Israeli cinema, informed some of my observations about the relationship between death and the male body in Israeli cinema.
2. Anita Shapira, *Land and Power: The Zionist Resort to Force, 1881–1948,* trans. William Templer (Stanford: Stanford University Press, 1992), 318.
3. George L. Mosse, *Fallen Soldiers: Reshaping the Memory of the World Wars* (New York: Oxford University Press, 1990), 32.
4. Ella Shohat, *Israeli Cinema: East/West and the Politics of Representation* (Austin: University of Texas Press, 1987), 59.

NOTES TO PAGES 50–53 **179**

5. Mosse, *Fallen Soldiers,* 78.
6. Benedict Anderson, *Imagined Communities: Reflections on the Origin and Spread of Nationalism* (London: Verso, 1991), 36.
7. Ibid., 9.
8. For a comparison of the novel and the film, see Nurith Gertz, *Motion Fiction: Israeli Fiction in Film* [in Hebrew] (Tel Aviv: The Open University of Israel Press, 1993), 63–94.
9. Mosse, *Fallen Soldiers,* 72–73.
10. Ibid., 27.
11. Klaus Theweleit, *Male Fantasies, Volume 1,* trans. Stephen Conway (Minneapolis: University of Minnesota Press, 1987), 231.
12. Ibid., 244.
13. Theweleit, *Male Fantasies, Volume 2,* 160.
14. Ibid.,147.
15. Ella Shohat was the first to identify the subversive dimension of those films that demystified the mythical sabra identity. However, she argues that eventually the films do not challenge the national consensus, because they "tend to couch their discourse in psychological terms, focalizing the effects of the Israeli political situation and militarization through the Sabra protagonists." (Shohat, *Israeli Cinema,* 222). Shohat ignores the gender subversion of those films that is intertwined with national and political concerns.
16. Judd Ne'eman, "The Empty Tomb in the Postmodern Pyramid: Israeli Cinema in the 1980s and 1990s," in *Documenting Israel: Proceedings of a Conference Held at Harvard University on May 10–12, 1993,* ed. Charles Berlin (Cambridge: Harvard College Library, 1995), 120.
17. Ibid., 121.
18. "Dominant fiction" and "historical trauma" are two theoretical concepts Kaja Silverman uses to describe the consequences of World War II for male subjectivity in classical Hollywood cinema. "Dominant fiction" is "the ideological system through which the normative subject lives its imaginary relation to the symbolic order." "Historical trauma" is "any historical event, whether socially engineered or of natural occurrence, which brings a large group of male subjects into . . . intimate relation with lack that they are at least for the moment unable to sustain an imaginary relation with the phallus, and so withdraw their belief from the dominant fiction." Kaja Silverman, *Male Subjectivity at the Margins* (New York: Routledge, 1992), 54–55.
19. According to Carol Clover, the psychoanalysts Jean Laplanche and J. B. Pontalis argue that repetition compulsion (what they call "*Wiederhoungszwang*") has its roots in displeasure: "[W]here there is '*Wiederhoungszwang*' there is historical suffering—suffering that has been more or less sexualized as 'erotogenic masochism' ['feminine' masochism]." Carol J. Clover, *Men, Women and Chain Saws: Gender in the Modern Horror Film* (Princeton: Princeton University Press, 1992), 213. Kaja Silverman in her analysis of Freud's *fort/da* game argues that the male subject who reenacts his relation to an event in the past does not renegotiate his position from a passive to an active one. The compulsive nature of the repetitive force runs directly counter to the notion of mastery, and thus, this repetition—whether voluntary or not —is passive. Silverman claims that Freud links repetition compulsion to the death drive that seeks to reduce the organism once again to nothingness and thus challenges the organization of the self. Kaja Silverman,

"Masochism and Subjectivity," *Framework* 12 (1980): 2–9. See also Silverman, *Male Subjectivity at the Margins*, 54–65.

20. Nurith Gertz and Mihal Feridman emphasize the destruction of the male body and images of male homoeroticism in those films, but prefer to interpret such representations as reinforcing the national ideals rather than, as I suggest, subverting them. Nurith Gertz, *Motion Fiction*; Mihal Feridman, "Between Silence and Abjection: The Cinematic Medium and the Israeli War Widow," in *Fictive Looks: On Israeli Cinema*, ed. Nurith Gertz, Orly Lubin, and Judd Néeman (Tel Aviv: Open University Press, 1998), 33–43.

21. Sigmund Freud [1924], "The Economic Problems of Masochism," in *The Standard Edition of the Complete Psychological Works of Sigmund Freud*, trans. James Strachey (London: Hogarth Press, 1986), 162.

22. Silverman, *Male Subjectivity at the Margins*, 189.

23. For a full discussion on "feminine masochism" via an analysis of Freud's "A Child Is Being Beaten," see *Male Subjectivity at the Margins* 201–210.

24. Theodor Reik, *Masochism in Sex and Society*, trans. Margaret H. Beigel and Gertrud M. Kurth (New York: Grove Press, 1962), 243.

25. Ibid., 216.

26. For this view of masochism in Freud's theory, see Gaylyn Studlar, *In the Realm of Pleasure: Von Sternberg, Dietrich, and the Masochistic Aesthetic* (New York: Columbia University Press, 1988), 10–13.

27. Gilles Deleuze, *Masochism: Coldness and Cruelty* (New York: Zone Books, 1989), 13.

28. Ibid., 66.

29. Ibid., 65–66.

30. Silverman, *Male Subjectivity at the Margins*, 211.

31. Deleuze, *Masochism*, 31–32.

32. Reik, *Masochism in Sex and Society*, 145, 163.

33. Paul Smith, *Clint Eastwood: A Cultural Production* (Place: UCL Press, 1993), 166.

34. For detailed discussion on the fears and pleasures surrounding the representation of the male penis in cinema, see Peter Lehman, *Running Scared: Masculinity and the Representation of the Male Body* (Philadelphia: Temple University Press, 1993). Among his many observations, Lehman argues that the exposure of the male penis is powerfully regulated by patriarchal culture that seeks to keep the penis out of sight in order to perpetuate the mystique of the penis-phallus. While in *Paratroopers* the male penis is shown and critically discussed, the film nevertheless displaces heterosexual male anxieties of the failed penis onto the stigmatized body of the queer male, thus reconfirming the national heteromasculinity. Different national cinemas have varied attitudes toward the representation of the male penis. For example, Lee Parpart makes an interesting case regarding Canadian cinema, arguing that the visualization of male genitals does not provoke anxieties in this national cinema, because Canadian nationalism is not heavily invested in phallic masculinity. Lee Parpart, "The Nation and the Nude: Colonial Masculinity and the Spectacle of the Male Body in Recent Canadian Cinema(s)," in *Masculinity: Bodies, Movies, Culture*, ed. Peter Lehman (New York: Routledge, 2001), 167–192.

35. Mihal Feridman suggests that Yochi's will represents a special version of the Jewish tradition of the *yebom* (marrying one's brother's widow). Friedman, "Between Silence and Abjection," 35.

36. Judith Butler, "Melancholy Gender/Refused Identification," in *Constructing Masculinity,* eds. Maurice Berger, Brian Wallis, and Simon Watson (New York: Routledge, 1995), 29.
37. Ibid., 31.
38. Silverman, *Male Subjectivity at the Margins,* 63.
39. Friedman, "Between Silence and Abjection," 33.
40. Leo Bersani [1987], "Is the Rectum a Grave?" in *AIDS: Cultural Analysis, Cultural Activism,* ed. Douglas Crimp (Cambridge: MIT Press, 1988), 212.
41. Theweleit, *Male Fantasiesm, Volume 2,* 319.
42. The film *The Vulture* (Yaki Yosha, 1981) also presents a masochistic relationship between two male warriors that is structured by anal anxiety. Boaz (Shraga Harpaz) blames himself for the loss of his buddy Menahem in the Yom Kippur War. He tries to escape the troubling past, but the stories of the wounded soldiers he hears on the radio and his connection with Menahem's parents, who wish to immortalize their son's memory, compel him to repeat the painful experience. As in *Repeat Dive,* Boaz disavows his friend's death by fetishizing the memory of the dead (he produces a memorial photo album of Menahem) and by getting romantically involve with Menahem's girlfriend. Feeling guilty, he is not able to perform sexually. In the film, his friend's death is structurally linked to his failed heterosexuality. Unable to have sex with Menahem's girlfriend, he tells her, "I know it is not my fault that he is dead and I'm alive, but he is dead and you are here in my house. I feel like a grave digger." The woman's body, like his friend's buried dead body, is marked as death and as a grave. Penetrating the female body, similarly to penetrating his dead friend's body, evokes castration anxiety in the heterosexual male subject.
43. D. A. Miller, "Anal *Rope,*" in *Inside/Out: Lesbian Theories, Gay Theories,* ed. Diana Fuss (New York: Routledge, 1991), 132.
44. Judith Butler, *Bodies That Matter: On the Discursive Limits of "Sex"* (New York: Routledge, 1993), 3.
45. Ibid., 112.
46. My analysis here echos Judith Halberstam's observations regarding the horror film. Judith Halberstam, *Skin Shows: Gothic Horror and the Technology of Monsters* (Durham: Duke University Press, 1995).
47. Kaja Silverman, *The Subject of Semiotics* (New York: Oxford University Press, 1993), 195.
48. Michel Foucault, *Discipline and Punish,* trans. Alan Sheridan (New York: Vintage Books, 1979), 26.
49. Unlike Freud—who argues that the sadist has a weak superego and a strong ego and that the masochist has overwhelming superego that turns against the ego—Deleuze suggests that the masochistic ego is only apparently crushed by the superego. The weakness of the masochistic ego is a strategy by which the masochist manipulates his torturer into the ideal role assigned to him/her. Deleuze argues that if the masochist is lacking anything it would be a superego and not an ego. "*The sadist,*" he claims, "*has no other ego than that of his victims.*" As a pure superego, he cruelly recovers his sexuality only when he diverts his power outward. (Deleuze, *Masochism,* 124).
50. Mary Douglas [1966], *Purity and Danger: An Analysis of the Concepts of Pollution and Taboo* (London: Ark Paperback, 1984), 113.
51. Deleuze, *Masochism,* 89.
52. For a different masochistic reading of the film and the novel on which the

film was based, see Yosefa Loshitzky, "The Bride of the Dead: Phallocentrism and War in Kaniuk and Gutman's *Himmo, King of Jerusalem*," *Literature/Film Quarterly* 21: 3 (1993): 110–132.

53. Studlar, *In the Realm of Pleasure*.
54. On Christian masochism, see Silverman, *Male Subjectivity at the Margins*, 195–201.
55. Diana Fuss, *Identification Papers* (New York: Routledge, 1995), 83–84.
56. Ibid., 84.

CHAPTER THREE: THE INVENTION OF MIZRAHI MASCULINITY

1. Cited in Tom Segev, *1949—The First Israelis*, trans. Neal Weinstein (New York: Henry Holt and Company, 1986), 157.
2. Cited in Ella Shohat, "Sephardim in Israel: Zionism from the Standpoint of Its Jewish Victims," in *Dangerous Liaisons: Gender, Nation and Postcolonial Perspectives*, eds. Anne McClintock, Aamir Mufti, and Ella Shohat (Minneapolis: University of Minnesota Press, 1997), 42.
3. Shohat, "Sephardim in Israel," 40–41.
4. On the use of practices of homogenization and differentiation in relation to Mizrahim, see *Mizrahim in Israel: A Critical Observation into Israel's Ethnicity*, eds. Hannan Hever, Yehouda Shenhav, Pnina Motzafi-Haller [in Hebrew] (Jerusalem: Van Leer Jerusalem Institute and Hakibbutz Hameuchad, 2002), 294–299.
5. Shohat, "Sephardim in Israel." 47.
6. Frantz Fanon, *Black Skin, White Masks*, trans. Charles Lam Markmann (New York: Grove Press, 1967), 165.
7. Cited in Shohat, "Sephardim in Israel," 42.
8. Cited in Moshe Lissak, *The Mass Immigration in the Fifties: The Failure of the Melting Pot Policy* [in Hebrew] (Jerusalem: Bialik Institute, 1999), 59.
9. Ibid., 64.
10. More on the Israeli quasi-eugenic selection policy, see Shohat, "Sephardim in Israel," 50; Lissak, *The Mass Immigration in the Fifties*, 64.
11. Cited in Shohat, "Sephardim in Israel," 50
12. Cited in Lissak, *The Mass Immigration in the Fifties*, 63.
13. Ibid., 62.
14. Fanon, *Black Skin, White Masks*, 225.
15. Cited in Segev, *1949—The First Israelis*, 170.
16. Ibid., 159–160.
17. Cited in Segev, *1949—The First Israelis*, 169–170.
18. Ibid., 170.
19. Ibid., 186–187.
20. In the fifties, both immigrants from Europe and from Arab countries were sprayed with DDT. Nevertheless, for Mizrahim the "disinfecting" process was perceived as more humiliating than for the Ashkenazim, because of the further discrimination they encountered in Israel.
21. On the stereotype of the Mizrahi as an Arab hater, see Shohat, *Israeli Cinema*, 123.
22. Cited in Segev, *1949—The First Israelis*, 187.
23. This longing for a new masculinity characterizes decolonizing societies, as elucidated in the writings of anti-colonialist theorists, such as Aime Cesaire and Frantz Fanon. Fanon wrote that "decolonization brings a nat-

ural rhythm into existence, introduced by new men, and with it a new language and new humanity. Decolonization is the veritable creation of a new man." Frantz Fanon, *The Wretched of the Earth,* trans.Constance Farrington (New York: Grove Press, 1963), 36. Discussing Fanon's "new man," Françoise Verges argues that "colonialism prevented colonized masculinity from becoming modern by branding it with the mark of the pre-modern. Decolonized masculinity would be heroic and modern." Françoise Verges, "Chains of Madness, Chains of Colonialism: Fanon and Freedom," in *The Fact of Blackness: Frantz Fanon and Visual Representation,* ed. Alan Read (Seattle: Bay Press, 1996), 61.

24. On the Israeli Black Panthers, see Shohat, "Sephardim in Israel," 63; and *The Black Panthers* [in Hebrew] (Jerusalem: Muserara Photography School, 1999).

25. Richard Majors, "Cool Pose: The Proud Signature of Black Survival," *Changing Men: Issues in Gender, Sex and Politics,* no.17 (winter 1986).

26. Cited in *The Black Panthers* (no page number).

27. Sami Shalom Chetrit, *The Ashkenazi Revolution Is Dead: Reflections on Israel from a Dark Angle* [in Hebrew] (Tel Aviv: Kedem Publishing, 1999), 57.

28. bell hooks, *Yearning: Race, Gender, and Cultural Politics* (Boston: South End Press, 1990), 58.

29. My reading here is inspired by Kobena Mercer's and bell hooks' works on racial and gender politics. bell hooks, "Representing the Black Male Body," in *Art on My Mind: Visual Politics* (New York: The New Press, 1995), 202–212; bell hooks, "Reconstructing Black Masculinity," in *Black Looks: Race and Representation* (Boston: South End Press, 1992), 87–114; Kobena Mercer, *Welcome to the Jungle: New Positions in Black Cultural Studies* (New York: Routledge, 1994).

30. Shohat, *Israeli Cinema,* 135. For different critical views on the Bourekas film, see also Judd Ne'eman, "Zero Degree in Film" [in Hebrew] *Kolnoa* 5 (1979): 20–23; Nurith Gertz, *Motion Fiction: Israeli Fiction in Film* [in Hebrew] (Tel Aviv: Open University of Israel Press, 1993), 27–32; Nitzan Ben-Shaul, *Mythical Expressions of the Siege in Israeli Films* (Lewiston: The Edwin Mellen Press, 1997), 100–112.

31. Michael Warner, "Introduction," in *Fear of a Queer Planet: Queer Politics and Social Theory,* ed. Michael Warner (Minneapolis: University of Minnesota Press), xxi.

32. Bhabha, *The Location of Culture,* p. 86

33. This process, in which the military and biethnic marriage were used to oppress the Mizrahi Black Panthers, also characterizes the official political discourse. In 1971, David Landor, the head of the press agency at the Israeli Prime Minister's Office, said: "The so-called Black Panthers are not black in any sense, neither in the pigment of their skin nor their political and economical status in Israel. . . . In fact, they are members of the same subgroup of humans as the Ashkenazi Jews. They can intermarry. . . . There is a current joke in Israel that the Ashkenazic-Sephardic issue will be solved in bed [*sic*]. In the long run, that is true, *although* it is an oversimplification. It will also be solved in school and in the army." Cited in David Schoebrun, Robert and Lucy Szekely, *The New Israelis* (New York: Atheneum, 1973, 159–160, my italics). Lander's anxieties of ethnic differences and the Black Panthers' protest are disavowed through heterosexual sex and heteronormative institutions of the education and the army. His ethnic

disavowal takes a form of racial fetishism. Threatened to lose his "white" skin color—that is, his white cultural authority—he essentializes differences of skin pigments and subordinates, through interethnic marriage, the Mizrahim to one Ashkenazi "white" ethnic group. However, this fantasy produces for him anther anxiety, that of too much ethnic sameness; thus he must disavow his own fantasy ("*although* it is an oversimplification"). Landor's colonial fantasy can be render thus: "'it is true' that all Jews have the same ("white") skin/culture, '*although*' some Jews do not have the same ("white") skin/culture. This racial fetishism enables Ashkenazi discourse to regulate and police Mizrahi identity. On racial fetishism, see Homi K. Bhabha's essay, "The Other Question: Stereotype, Discrimination and the Discourse of Colonialism," in *The Location of Culture*, 66–84.

34. Ella Shohat, "Columbus, Palestine and Arab-Jews: Toward a Relational Approach to Community Identity," in *Cultural Readings of Imperialism: Edward Said and the Gravity of History*, ed. Keith Ansell-Pearson, Benita Parry, and Judith Squires (New York: St. Martin's Press, 1997), 88–105.

35. In the official Zionist discourse, Mizrahi men are often imagined as embodying an earlier, immature and infantile stage of sexual development. Carl Frankenstein, a respected professor at the Hebrew University of Jerusalem, in 1951 compared the "primitive mentality" of Mizrahim to children, retarded and mentally disturbed people (cited in Segev, *1949—The First Israelis*, 157). The trope of the infantalized Mizrahi male was circulated in and reinforced in the modern Israeli imagery by films such as *Charlie and a Half* (Boaz Davidson, 1974), in which an adult Mizrahi man behaves naughtily with a child half his age and *Hasamba: The Undercover Kids* (Yoel Zilberg, 1971), in which a gang of Sabra kids defeats the notorious, yet infantile, Mizrahi male criminal. In *Paratroopers* the Mizrahi man is named "Yenoka" which means "baby" in Hebrew. This is reminiscent of Fanon's words that, for the colonialist mind, "the Negro is just a child" (Fanon, *Black Skin, White Masks*, 27), as well as what Octave Mannoni called the "Prospero complex," the "inborn" dependency of the black man on white leadership. According to this colonial trope of infantilization, as Ella Shohat and Robert Stam have observed, "the Third World toddler, even when the product of thousand years of civilization, is not yet in control of its body/psyche, and therefore needs the guiding hand of more 'adult' and 'advanced societies, gently pulling it into modern times." Ella Shohat and Robert Stam, *Unthinking Eurocentrism: Multiculturalism and the Media* (London: Routledge, 1994), 140.

36. Richard Dyer, *White* (London: Routledge, 1997), 25–26.

37. Shohat, *Israeli Cinema*, 174.

38. Fanon, *Black Skin, White Masks*, 63.

39. W.E.B. Du Bois, *The Souls of Black Folk* (New York: Dover, 1994), 2.

40. Edelman, "The Part of the (W)hole," 42–75; Hazel V. Carby, *Race Men: The W.E.B. Du Bois Lectures* (Cambridge: Harvard University Press, 1998).

41. Ella Shohat, *Israeli Cinema: East/West and the Politics of Representation* (Austin: University of Texas Press, 1987), 270–271.

42. The representation of the Mizrahi man as a homophobe appears also in the film *Paratroopers*. As I have described in Chapter Two, Wiseman's feminized Ashkenazi white body is represented against Yenoka's Mizrahi muscular and dark body. (In German, the name "Wiseman," *Weiss Mann*, literally means "white man"). Yenoka's sexual and homophobic violence

toward Wiseman, especially in the shower sequence, fixes the racist stereotype of the Mizrahi man as violent and deviant. This image of the Mizrahi male as a homophobe enables the film to displace the homosexual anxieties of Yair, Wiseman's Ashkenazi sadistic commander. Yair's heterosexual masculinity is formed through disavowed identification and figurative anal repudiation of Wiseman's queer body. The film disavows the Ashkenazi commander's anal anxieties and projects them onto the "pathological sexuality" of the Mizrahi man. In the course of the film, Yenoka and his friend abuse Wiseman by holding him strongly, while forcibly shoving food into his mouth. Similarly to the Freudian association between orality and pervasive male homosexuality, the film demonizes the mouth as a site of homophobic violence. Yair's anal fears are displaced, then, to this oral sodomitical scene where Yenoka is the sadistic molester and Wiseman is the innocent victim of figurative homosexual rape. By imagining the Oriental man as homophobic, heterocentric Ashkenazi culture disavows its own repressed homosexuality that threatens to undo from within the sexual order on which its national authority is based.

43. Homi Bhabha discusses the politics of metonyms in colonial discourse: "What radically differentiates the exercise of colonial power is the unsuitability of enlightenment assumption of collectivity and the eye that beholds it. For Jeremy Bentham (as Michel Perrot points out), the small group is representative of the whole society—the part is *already* the whole. Colonial authority requires modes of discrimination [cultural, racial, administrative . . .] that disallow a stable unitary assumption of collectivity. The 'part' [which must be the colonialist foreign body] must be representative of the 'whole' [conquered country], but the right of representation is based on its racial difference." Homi Bhabha, *The Location of Culture* (London: Routledge, 1994), 111. See also Lee Edelman, "The Part of the (W)hole: Baldwin, Homophobia and Fantasmatics of 'Race,' " in *Homographesis: Essays in Gay Literary and Cultural Theory* (New York: Routledge, 1994), 42–78.
44. Edelman, *Homographesis*, 208.
45. Fanon, *Black Skin, White Masks,* 194.
46. Revach has also directed and starred in dramas such as *Little Man* (1978), *On the Fringe* (1987) and *A Bit of Luck* (1992). My discussion refers only to his Bourekas comedies.
47. Mikhail Bakhtin, *Rableais and His World,* trans Helene Iswolsky (Bloomington: Indiana University Press, 1984), 364.
48. Shohat was first to discuss aspects of Bakthinian carnivalesque in the Bourekas film (Shohat, *Israeli Cinema,* 131). I am adding to her argument Bakhtin's concept of the grotesque body and its specific manifestation in Ze'ev Revach's films.
49. Bakhtin, *Rableais and His World,* 317.
50. Shohat, *Israeli Cinema,* 135–136.
51. Anne McClintock, *Imperial Leather: Race, Gender, and Sexuality in the Colonial Context* (New York: Routledge, 1995), 68.
52. Michael Warner, "Homo-Narcissism; or Heterosexuality," in *Engendering Men: The Question of Male Feminist Criticism,* ed. Joseph A. Boone and Michael Cadden (New York: Routledge, 1990), 191.
53. Ibid., 202.

CHAPTER FOUR: HOMOLAND

1. Meir Khanna, quoted in Inbal Perlson, "Joined Beautifully at the Margins" [in Hebrew], *Mitzad Shnni* (May 1998): 24.
2. Arab men married to Jewish women improve not only their socio-economic condition but that of their offspring'. Interracial families insist that their children be raised and recognized as Jewish to secure them privileges denied to Arab Israeli citizens and certainly to Palestinians. At the same time, these families are forced to deny their Arab identity. Perlson, "Joined Beautifully at the Margins," 24–25.
3. Homi K. Bhabha, "Signs Taken for Wonders: Questions of Ambivalence and Authority under a Tree outside Delhi, May 1817," in *The Location of Culture* (London: Routledge, 1994), 114.
4. For an analysis of the ways that these changes are reflected in Israeli films of the eighties, see Ella Shohat, *Israeli Cinema: East/West and the Politics of Representation* (Austin: University of Texas Press, 1989), 237–74; and Judd Ne'eman, "The Empty Tomb in the Postmodern Pyramid: Israeli Cinema in the 1980s and 1990s," in *Documenting Israel: Proceedings of a Conference Held at Harvard University on May 10–12, 1993,* ed. Charles Berlin (Cambridge: Harvard College Library, 1995), 117–151.
5. On heterosexual interracial sexual relations in Israeli cinema, see Yosefa Loshitzky, "From Orientalist Discourses to Woman's Melodrama: Oz and Wolman's *My Michael,*" *Edebiyat* 5 (1994): 99–123; Loshitzky, "Forbidden Love in Israeli Cinema" [in Hebrew], *Theory and Criticism: An Israeli Forum,* no. 18 (2001): 207–214.
6. Robert J. C. Young, "Hybridity and Diaspora," in *Colonial Desire: Hybridity in Theory, Culture, and Race* (London: Routledge, 1995), 25.
7. Ibid., p. 26 (my emphasis).
8. Young argues that hybridity and homosexuality both signify degeneration, but although he claims that "at one point, hybridity and homosexuality did coincide" (26), he fails to show how or at which point. For this kind of historical work, see Siobhan B. Somerville, *Queering the Color Line: Race and the Invention of Homosexuality in American Culture* (Durham, NC: Duke University Press, 2000).
9. Zionist filmmakers such as Helmar Lerski, Nathan Axelrod, and Baruch Agadati were inspired by Sergei Eisenstein's use of montage as well as by his representation of the male body. In Zionist films, as in Eisenstein's, Zionist male bodies are forever striving upward, shot against the Promised Land's horizon: visual signifiers for the pioneers' aspirations and aesthetic refinement.
10. Edward W. Said, *Orientalism* (New York: Pantheon, 1978), 309.
11. Joseph A. Boone, "Vacation Cruises; or, The Homoerotics of Orientalism," *PMLA* 110 (1995): 92.
12. Lee Edelman, "Seeing Things: Representation, the Scene of Surveillance, and the Spectacle of Gay Male Sex," in *Homographesis: Essays in Gay Literary and Cultural Theory* (New York: Routledge, 1994), 185.
13. Edelman, p. 185.
14. Lola Young, *Fear of the Dark: "Race," Gender, and Sexuality in the Cinema* (London: Routledge, 1996), 103.
15. Gayatri Chakravorty Spivak, "Can the Subaltern Speak?" in *Colonial Discourse and Post-colonial Theory: A Reader,* eds. Patrick Williams and Laura Chrisman (New York: Columbia University Press, 1994), 97.

16. Ella Shohat, "Gender and the Culture of Empire: Toward a Feminist Ethnography of the Cinema," *Quarterly Review of Film and Video* 13, nos. 1–2 (1991): 63.

17. Homi K. Bhabha, "Of Mimicry and Man," in *Location of Culture,* 86.

18. Homi K. Bhabha, "The Other Question: Stereotype, Discrimination, and the Discourse of Colonialism," in *Location of Culture,* 81.

19. Leo Bersani, "Is the Rectum a Grave?" in *AIDS: Cultural Analysis, Cultural Activism,* ed. Douglas Crimp (Cambridge: MIT Press, 1988), 215.

20. Bersani, "Is the Rectum a Grave?" 222.

21. In *Homos*, Bersani acknowledges that antiredemptive sexuality is sometimes effected by the exploitative practice of Western colonialism. He writes: "It is easy to see [Gide's] *The Immoralist* as yet another example of sexual imperialism—both gay and straight—practiced by European travelers to colonized African countries. And I don't mean that there was anything radical in the failure of these travelers to think of the Africans from whom they bought cheap and, to their minds, exotic sex as people with whom they might establish a relation. On the contrary: the superficiality of their contacts reflected a more or less conscious conviction of the inherent inferiority of these sexual partners. The natives were insignificant, to be used for the travelers' momentary pleasures. French visitors to Tunisia complemented their country's economic colonization with generally untroubled sexual colonization. Gide was certainly not immune to colonizing impulses (as he himself recognized), and yet those very impulses were perhaps the precondition for a potential revolutionary eroticism. By abandoning himself to the appearances of sexual colonialism Gide was able to free himself from the European version of relationships that supported the colonialism." (*Homos* [Cambridge: Harvard University Press, 1995], 122–23). Bersani's last sentence may also be relevant to Guttman's sexual politics, although this argument in no way dismisses the racist and colonialist elements in *Drifting.*

22. For an Orientalist critique of Arab and Palestinian representations in Israeli cinema, see Shohat, *Israeli Cinema.*

23. Said, *Orientalism,* 167, 190, 188.

24. The homosexualization of the Arab enemy appears in many Israeli cultural discourses, for example, that of the Israeli military. In the military imagination, the male fighting soldier is not only associated with phallic masculinity but opposed to images of otherness, such as male homosexuality, which is figured as an "inferior" and "degenerate" form of maleness. The curse used by Israeli male soldiers, "Go find a redheaded male Arab to 'shake' [fuck] you," produces the image of the Arab man as the ultimate other: a homosexual and a national "other," redheaded as a sign of biological alterity and given to violating normative masculinity through anal penetration. See Danny Kaplan, *David, Jonathan, and Other Soldiers: Identity, Masculinity, and Sexuality in Combat Units in the Israeli Army* [in Hebrew] (Tel Aviv: Hakibbutz Hameuchad, 1999), 159–160.

25. The film never-the-less gives some agency to the Palestinian, who refuses to take Robby's money in exchange for anal sex.

26. Jehoeda Sofer, "Testimonies from the Holy Land: Israeli and Palestinian Men," in *Sexuality and Eroticism among Males in Moslem Societies,* eds. Arno Schmitt and Jehoeda Sofer (Binghamton: Harrington Park, 1992), 114.

27. Ibid., 109.

28. Stephen O. Murray, "The Will Not to Know: Islamic Accommodations of

Male Homosexuality," in *Islamic Homosexualities: Culture, History, and Literature,* eds. Stephen O. Murray and Will Roscoe (New York: New York University Press, 1997), 21.

29. Jim Wafer, "Muhammad and Male Homosexuality," in Murray and Roscoe, *Islamic Homosexualities,* 91.
30. Wafer, p. 93.
31. Sofer, "Testimonies from the Holy Land," 118.
32. Palestinian society in Israel is heterogeneous, diverse, and constantly changing. Socio-religiously, it consists of a Muslim majority and Christian and Druze minorities. Some groups have different attitudes toward homosexuality that are conditioned not only by religious, but by political, social, and cultural contexts. A discussion of the multiple secular, religious, and other approaches toward (interracial) sexual relations between males in Palestinian society is beyond the scope of this study. Here I offer only one possible cultural perspective, the dominant one on homosexuality among religious Muslim Palestinian men.
33. For testimonials of gay Palestinians who have suffered discrimination by the Aguda, see Walzer, *Between Sodom and Eden,* 233–237.

CHAPTER FIVE: THE NEW QUEERS

1. Lee Walzer, *Between Sodom and Eden: A Gay Journey through Today's Changing Israel* (New York: Columbia University Press, 2000).
2. Leo Bersani, "Is the Rectum a Grave?" in *AIDS: Cultural Analysis, Cultural Activism,* ed. Douglas Crimp (Cambridge: MIT Press), 215.
3. Ibid., 215.
4. Ibid.
5. Ibid., 217.
6. Ibid.
7. Ibid. Bersani developed this notion in *The Freudian Body: Psychoanalysis and Art* (New York: Columbia University Press, 1986). There he argues that sexuality is masochistic and that "masochism serves life" rather than death because it allows "the human organism [to] survive . . . the gap between the period of shattering stimuli and the development of resistant or defensive ego structures" (39).
8. Bersani, "Is the Rectum a Grave?" 221.
9. Ibid., 222.
10. Yair Qedar, "From a Victim to a Victimizer" [in Hebrew], *Davar* (1993): 24.
11. Kaja Silverman, *Male Subjectivity at the Margins* (New York: Routledge, 1992), 362.
12. Brett Farmer, *Spectacular Passions: Cinema, Fantasy, Gay Male Spectatorship* (Durham: Duke University Press, 2000), 202.
13. Bersani, "Is the Rectum a Grave?" 208.
14. Ibid., 209.
15. Ibid., 208–209.
16. Ibid., 222.
17. Ibid., 209 (my emphasis).
18. Ibid., 221.
19. Jeff Nunokawa, "'All the Sad Young Men': AIDS and the Work of Mourning," in *Inside/Out: Lesbian Theories, Gay Theories,* ed. Diana Fuss (London: Routledge, 1991), 312.
20. Ibid., 319.

21. Walzer, *Between Sodom and Eden*, 40–41.
22. From *Amazing Grace [Hesed mufla]* (1992).
23. From *Drifting [Nagua]* (1983).
24. Cited in Leo Bersani, *Homos* (Cambridge: Harvard University Press, 1995), 77.
25. Ibid., 78–79.
26. Bersani, "Is the Rectum a Grave?" 222.
27. Mary Ann Doane, "The Voice in the Cinema: The Articulation of Body and Space," in *Film Theory and Criticism: Introductory Readings,* ed. Leo Braudy and Marshall Cohen (New York: Oxford University Press, 1999), 371.
28. Ibid., 371–372.
29. Kaja Silverman, *The Acoustic Mirror: The Female Voice in Psychoanalysis and Cinema* (Bloomington: Indiana University Press, 1988), 168.
30. Ibid., 130.
31. D. A. Miller, "Anal *Rope*," in *Inside/Out: Lesbian Theories, Gay Theories,* ed. Diana Fuss (London: Routledge, 1991), 135.
32. From *Time Off [After]* (1990).
33. Claude Lévi-Strauss, *The Naked Men,* trans. J. Cape (New York: Harper and Row, 1981), 647.
34. Doane, "The Voice in the Cinema," 370.
35. Ibid.
36. Kobena Mercer and Isaac Julien, "Race, Sexual Politics and Black Masculinity: A Dossier," in *Male Order: Unwrapping Masculinity,* ed. Rowena Chapman and Jonathan Rutherford (London: Lawrence and Wishart, 1988), 97. My reading of the representation of Mizrahi queerness is indebted in many aspects by Mercer's and Julien's arguments in this essay.
37. Walzer, *Between Sodom and Eden*, 48.
38. For example, Walzer reproduces the Orientalist imagery of Mizrahim as primitives, backwards and conservatives, contrary to the Zionist "modern" and "enlightened" society: "They came, in the main, from tradition-minded backgrounds to a revolutionary society," and "Some of them arrived illiterate in any language" (Walzer, *Between Sodom and Eden*). (ibid).
39. Ibid., 49 (my italics).
40. bell hooks, *Talking Back: Thinking Feminist, Thinking Black* (Boston: South End Press, 1989), 125.
41. Mercer and Julien, "Race, Sexual Politics and Black Masculinity," 106–107.

Filmography

Films mentioned in the text [Hebrew title], director, release date.

Adama, Helmer Lerski, 1947

Amazing Grace [*Hesed mufla*], Amos Gutmann, 1992

Avodah, Helmer Lerski, 1935

Bar 51, Amos Gutmann, 1985

Batito [*Hamuvtal battito*], Ze'ev Revach, 1987

Beyond the Walls [*Mi'achorei hasoragim*], Uri Barabash, 1986

A Bit of Luck [*Tipat mazal*], Ze'ev Revach, 1992

Casablan, Menachem Golan, 1973

Charlie and a Half [*Charlie ve'cehtzi*], Boaz Davidson, 1974

Clouds Over Israel [*Sinaia*], Ilan Eldad, 1962

Collective Adventure [*Harepateka kolectivit*], Alex Baris/Nigel
   Wingate, 1939

Day after Day [*Yom yom*], Amos Gitai, 1998

Double Buskilla [*Pa'ahmaim buskilla*], Ze'ev Revach, 1998

Drifting [*Nagua*], Amos Gutmann, 1983

Every Bastard a King [*Kol mamzer melech*], Uri Zohar, 1968

The First Film of Palestine, Murray Rosenberg, 1911

Florentin, Eythan Fox, 1997

Gotta Have Heart [*Bahal bahal lev*], Eythan Fox, 1997

Hamsin, Dan Wachsman, 1982

Hasmaba, The Undercover Kids [*Hasamba ve'narey hahefker*], Yoel
   Zilberg, 1971

He Walked through the Fields [*Hu halach ba'sadot*], Yoseph Millo, 1967
Hide and Seek [*Machbo'im*], Dan Wolman, 1980
Himmo, King of Jerusalem [*Himmo, Melech Yeruashalayim*], Amos Gutmann, 1987
Kaddim Wind: Moroccan Chronicle [*Ru'ach Kaddim: chronika marokait*], David Benchetrit, 2002
Ladies Hairdresser [*Sapar nashim*], Ze'ev Revach, 1984
Light Out of Nowhere [*Or min hahefker*], Nissim Dayan, 1973
Little Man [*Shraga hakatan*], Ze'ev Revach, 1978
Lookout [*Nekodat tazpoit*], Dina Zvi-Riklis, 1990
The Lover [*Hameahev*], Michal Bat-Adam, 1986
My Father's House [*Beit avi*], Herbert Kline, 1947
My Michael [*Michael sheli*], Dan Wolman, 1975
Nadia, Amnon Rubinstein, 1986
Oded the Wanderer [*Oded hanoded*], Natan Axelrod, 1933
On a Narrow Bridge [*Gesher tzar m'eod*], Nissim Dayan, 1985
One of Us [*Echad mi shelanu*], Uri Barabash, 1989
Only Today [*Rak hayom*], Ze'ev Revach, 1976
On the Fringe [*Buba*], Ze'ev Revach, 1987
Orphans of the Storm, D. W. Griffith, 1922
Over the Ruins [*Me'al hachuravot*], Natan Axelrod, 1938
Paratroopers [*Masa alunkot*], Judd Ne'eman, 1977
Pillar of Fire [*Amud ha'Esh*], Larry Frish, 1959
Rebels Against the Light [*Mordei Ha'Or*], Alexander Ramati, 1964
Repeat Dive [*Tzlila chozeret*], Shimon Dotan, 1982
Repeat Premiers [*Permiyerot chozerot*], Amos Gutmann, 1977
Ricochets [*Shtei etzba'ot mi'Tzidon*], Eli Cohen, 1986
Sabra [*Tzabar-chalutzim*], Alexander Ford, 1933
A Safe Place [*Makom batoach*], Amos Gutmann, 1977
Samir, David Ben-Chetrit, 1997
Sing Your Heart Out [*Halahaka*], Avi Nesher, 1978
Soldier of the Night [*Chayal halayla*], Dan Wolman, 1984
Suddenly, Last Summer, Joseph L. Mankiewicz , 1959
They Were Ten [*Hem hayu asarach*], Baruch Dienar, 1960
This Is the Land [*Zot hi ha'aretz*], Baruch Agadati, 1935
Time Off [*After*], Eythan Fox, 1990
The Vulture [*Ha'ayit*], Yaki Yosha, 1981
What a Gang! [*Chavura she'ka'zot*], Ze'ev Havatzelet, 1962
Wrong Number [*Ta'ut bamispar*], Ze'ev Revach, 1979

Index

Abergel, Reuven, 93
absorption, process of, 93.
activism, gay, 142, 150. *See also*
   Aguda
Aduma (Lerski), 22, 23, 25–31, 43
aesthetic, decadent, 146
African Americans, "double-
   consciousness" of, 107. *See also*
   Black Panthers, Mirahzi
Agadati, Baruch, 22, 42
Aguda, 134, 136, 150; demands of,
   146; establishment of, 142; pink triangle of, 164; sexual politics of,
   143, 163–164
Ahmad, Aijaz, 6
AIDS, 146, 149; disavowal of, 151;
   queer history of, 150
Amazing Grace (Guttman), 144, 146,
   148, 149, 150, 154, *155*
ambivalence: in colonial discourse, 7;
   in Zionist movement, 36
anal sex: in film, 159; in military
   films, 67; in phallocentric culture,
   135–136; and power relations, 139;
   as resistance to Israeli domination,
   122; in violent domination, 110
Anderson, Benedict, 45, 50
anti-Semitism: in gentile virility, 36;
   origins of, 19; and Zionist Ashkenazi "whiteness," 178n. 60
anti-sodomy law, 142
anus: castration anxiety provoked by,
   157; as grave, 67; male, 10; in Zionist discourse, 123

Arab culture, homosexuality in,
   139–140
Arab-Jews, 33; Ben-Gurion on, 87–88;
   exploitation of, 86; importation of,
   84; in racial discourse, 88, 90;
   Zionist exploitation of, 38–39. *See*
   also Mizrahim; Sephardim
Arabs: demonization of, 118; diseased
   body stereotype of, 38; erotization
   of, 126; homosexualization of,
   187n. 24; images of, 32; perceived
   sexuality of, 46; rebellion of, 49;
   Zionist exploitation of, 38–39
army, Israeli, gay male eroticism in,
   143. *See also* military films; soldiers
asceticism, 46, 146
Ashkenazi, 1, 4; colonial fantasy of,
   87; ethnic borders of, 103; families
   of, 168; gay identity of, 143, 165;
   heterosexuality of, 99; Mizrahi men
   viewed by, 86–87, 91; racist discourse of, 88; "whiteness" of, 34,
   39–40
Ashkenazi-Israeli biopower discourse, Mizrahim in, 90
The Ashkenazi Revolution Is Dead
   (Shalom-Chetrit), 96
Avodah (labor party), 119–120
Avodah (Lerski), 22, 24, 42, 43, 122
Axelrod, Nathan, 22, 23, 42

Bakhtin, Mikhail, 10–11, 12
baptism, as spiritual birth, 41, 42

Holocaust, 49, 150, 151
holy war, erotic meaning of, 140
homeland, in Zionist film, 29–30
homoeroticism, 5; cultural anxiety over, 121; and heterosexual miscegenation, 127; male, 180n. 20; in military film, 63, 73, 83; and miscegenation, 126, 131–132; threat of, 64
homo-narcissism, 117
homophobia: from Arab hatred to, 108–112; in Guttman's films, 150; and hybridity, 121; and intolerance, 153; Israeli, 137; of Mizrahi men, 111; and nationalist ideology, 133; racism and, 166; and threat of gay sex, 153; Western narrative of, 164; Zionist, 5
homosexuality: abjection of, 70; biracial, 132, *133;* construction of rape in, 96; cultural anxiety about, 121; as death-bearing practice, 149; Freud's demonization of, 82; in Guttman's films, 144; in heterocentric view, 110; homophobic repudiation of, 112; and hybridity, 120, 186n. 8; Islamic discourses of, 139; in Israeli cinema, 13; in Israeli cultural discourse, 14; as narcissism, 117; in popular imagery, 156; prohibition on, 65; repressed, 109; threatening appeal of, 154; Western notions of, 141; Zionist fear of, 89
homosociality: military, 66, 154; multi-ethnic male, 111
hooks, bell, 97, 166
Hora dance, 43
"human dust," Mizrahim described as, 88
hybridization: heterosexuality in, 120; and homosexuality, 186n. 8; Jewish Israeli fear of, 119
hygiene: and Zionist body's boundaries, 43; and Zionist manhood, 47
hypermasculinity, anxiety about, 91
hypersexuality: masculinity and, 137; myth about, 87

identification: heterosexual, 5; homosexual, 163; male masochistic, 80; with masculinity, 9, 147; as queer in Israeli cinema, 13
identity: assumptions of, 117; colonial, 6–7; Eurovision of Ashkenazi gay, 168; gay, 170; heterosexual, 70–71; historical construction of,

13; imagined national, 50; Israeli male heterosexual, 2; Jewish, 118; male heterosexual, 149; Mizrahi gay, 167; of Mizrahi heroes, 165; Mizrahi heterosexual male, 114–115; mythical Sabra, 179n. 15; performativity of, 165; and sexuality, 170; shattering national, 136; of the strong, 96; and the uncanny, 26; "white," 8
ideology: dominant, 103; of erotic liberation, 46; nationalist, 133, 134; Zionist, 13, 103, 126–127
image regime, 39
imagery: of diseased land of East, 37; homoerotic, 73; liquid, 131; of muscles, 43; oceanic, 127; phallic, 42
images: of diaspora Jew, 19; of doomed gay man, 150; of gay lifestyle, 143; of gays and lesbians, 142; in Guttman's films, 165; of Jewish-Arab conflict, 25; Jewish male femme, 14; male Mizrah macho, 91; of manliness, 12; of penetration, 68; phallic, 42; of sexual powerlessness, 146; of the uncanny, 27
imperialism, sexual, 187n. 21
impotence, racial engulfment and, 125, 126
inferiority complex, of Mizrahi man, 102
In His Own Hands (Shamir), 41
interracial sex, 11; encouraged, 102–103; and Israeli occupation, 126–127; and Israeli-Palestinian conflict, 121; between men, 140, 141; in Palestinian society, 188n. 32
Intifada, 53, 120
Islam, 43
Islam Nations, Jews of, 84
Israel, Palestinian society in, 188n. 32. *See also* Tel Aviv
Israel Defense Force (IDF), 49, 51
Israeli culture: Arab anal threat in, 137; death in, 150
Israeli gay community, 121; Palestinians in, 141; sexual agenda of, 171
Israeli Independence War (1954), 84
Israeli-Palestinian conflict: homoerotic desire and, 128; homosexualization of, 139; and interracial sexual unions, 121, 141; Intifada in, 53, 120; and Mizrahi masculinity, 108; and political films, 91. *See also* Jewish-Arab conflict

woman, 67; as lack, 156
women: oppression of, 146; as threat
to Jewish nation, 119; unavailability
of, 140. *See also* mothers
work, in Zionist films, 22
Wrong Number (Revach), 112

Yafe, Hillel, 37
Yemenite-Jewish male, in racist dis-
course, 90
Yom Kippur War (1973), 52, 119
Young, Lola, 127
Young, Robert, 120
youth, in myth, 50

Zionism: biopolitics of, 39; colonial
discourse of, 34; and colonialism,
176n. 36; of European Jewish diaspora, 85; masculine national ideology of, 23; queerness in, 5; racism
in, 33, 34; sexuality regulated by,
46; vision in, 21

Zionist, "white" body of, 44
Zionist conquest, narrative of, 126
Zionist culture, phallic masculinity
of, 146
Zionist discourse, Mizrahi men in,
184n. 35
Zionist ideology, 127; male Ashke-
nazi Sabra in, 13; racial
Manichaean dichotomies of,
126–127
Zionist male, heterosexual subjectiv-
ity of, 125
Zionist masculine order, desire in,
30
Zionist movement: American support
of, 178n. 60; films used by, 20;
Mizrahim exploited by, 86
Zionist national gendering project,
28, 89
Žižek, Slavoj, 25, 30
Zohar, Uri, 48
Zvi-Riklis, Dina, 118

About the Author

Raz Yosef holds a Ph.D. in cinema studies from New York University. He currently teaches in the Department of Film and Television at Tel Aviv University, Israel.